LOVE IN FOCUS

1

Yoko Nogiri

CONTENTS

film 1
Hello, Springtime of Life
003

film 2
Welcome to the Photography Club
053

film 3
The Secret Amemura-kun
087

film 4
The First Photo Shoot
115

Bonus Short
148

FILM 1

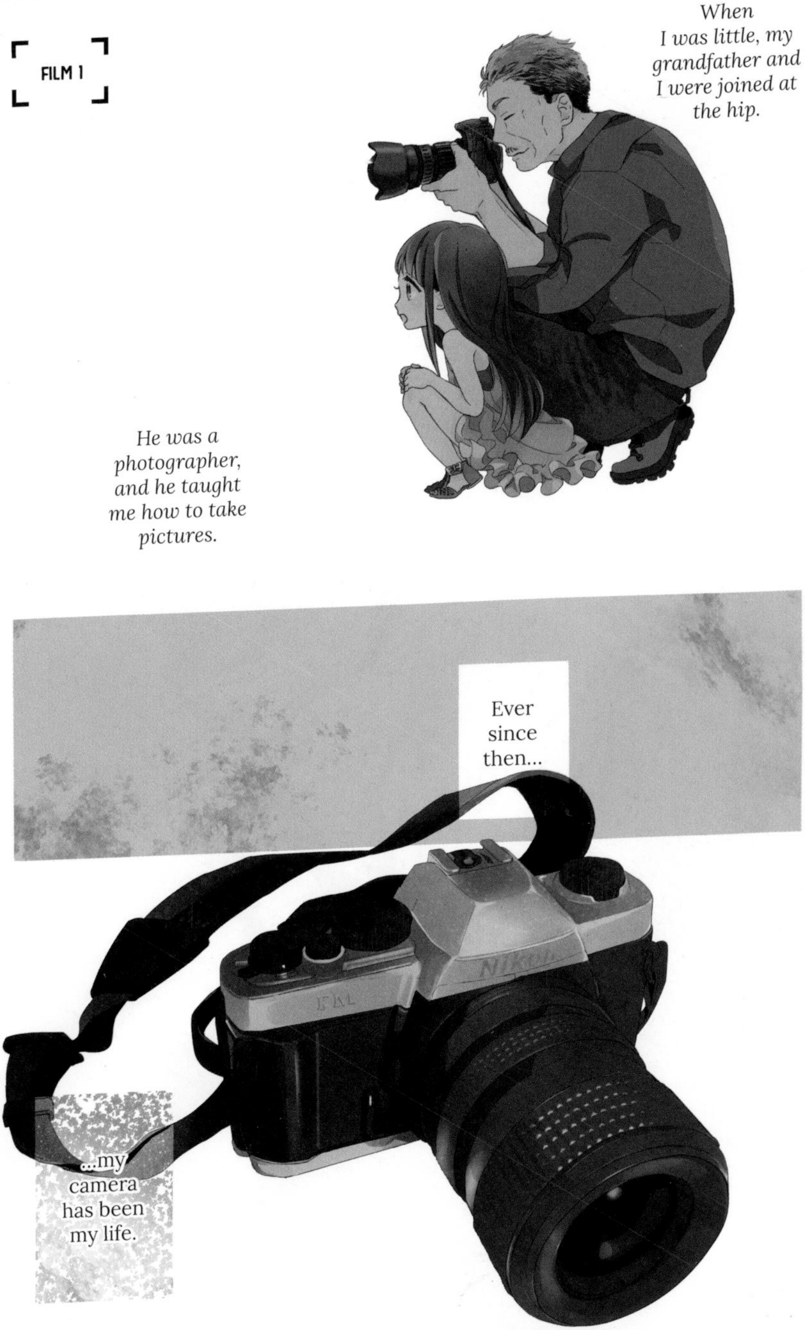
When I was little, my grandfather and I were joined at the hip.
He was a photographer, and he taught me how to take pictures.
Ever since then...
...my camera has been my life.
Nikon
FM

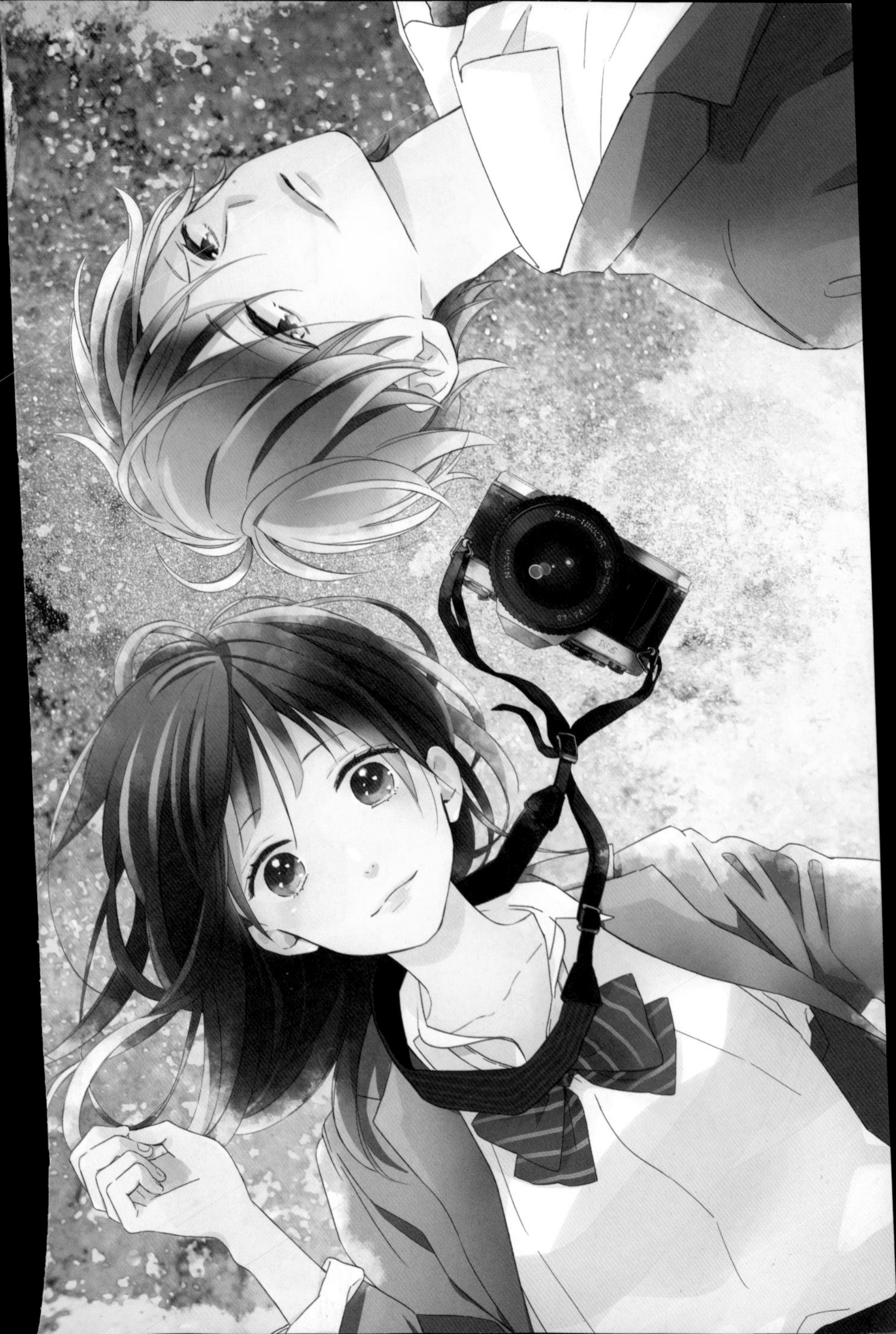

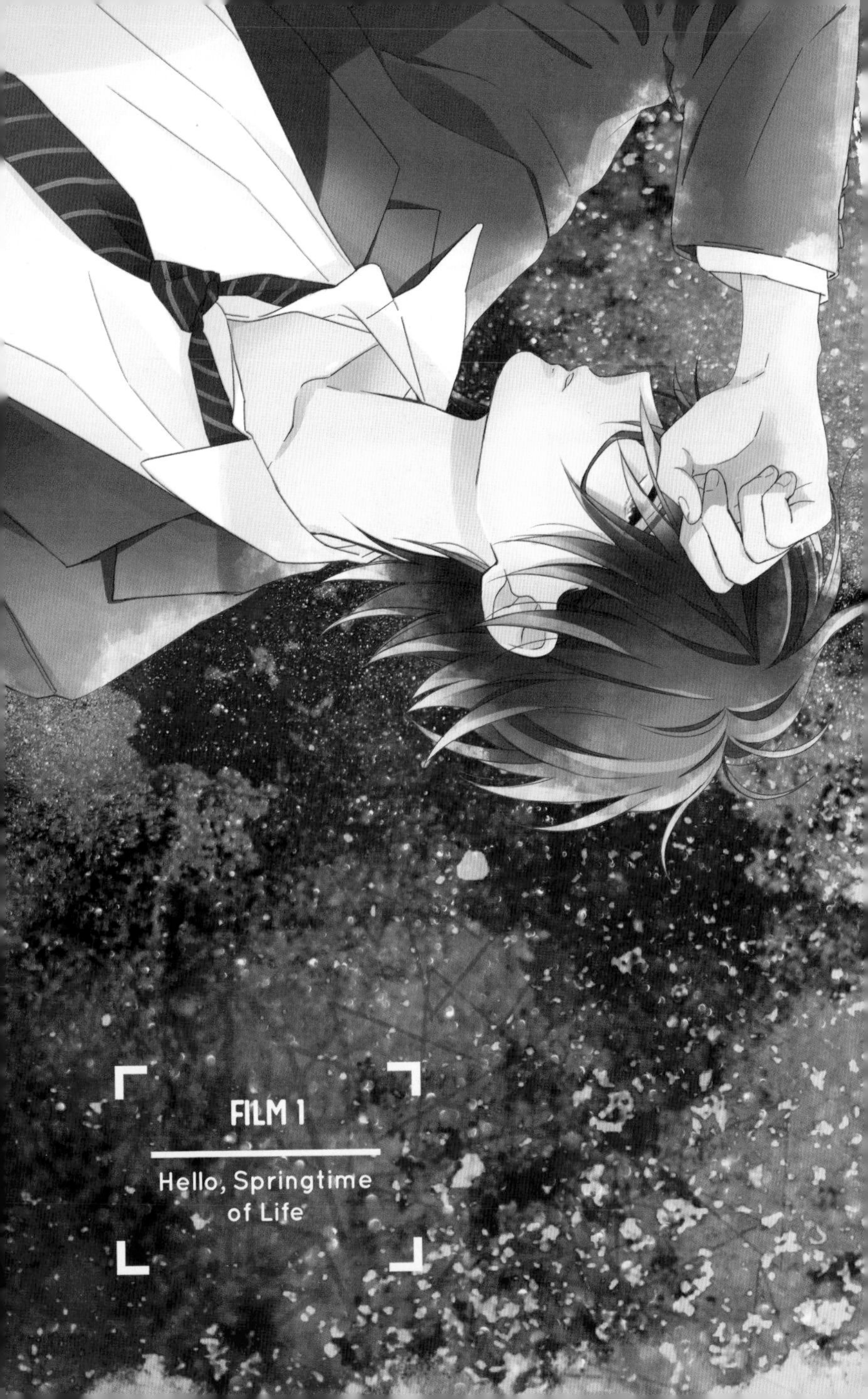
FILM 1
Hello, Springtime of Life

LOVE IN FOCUS

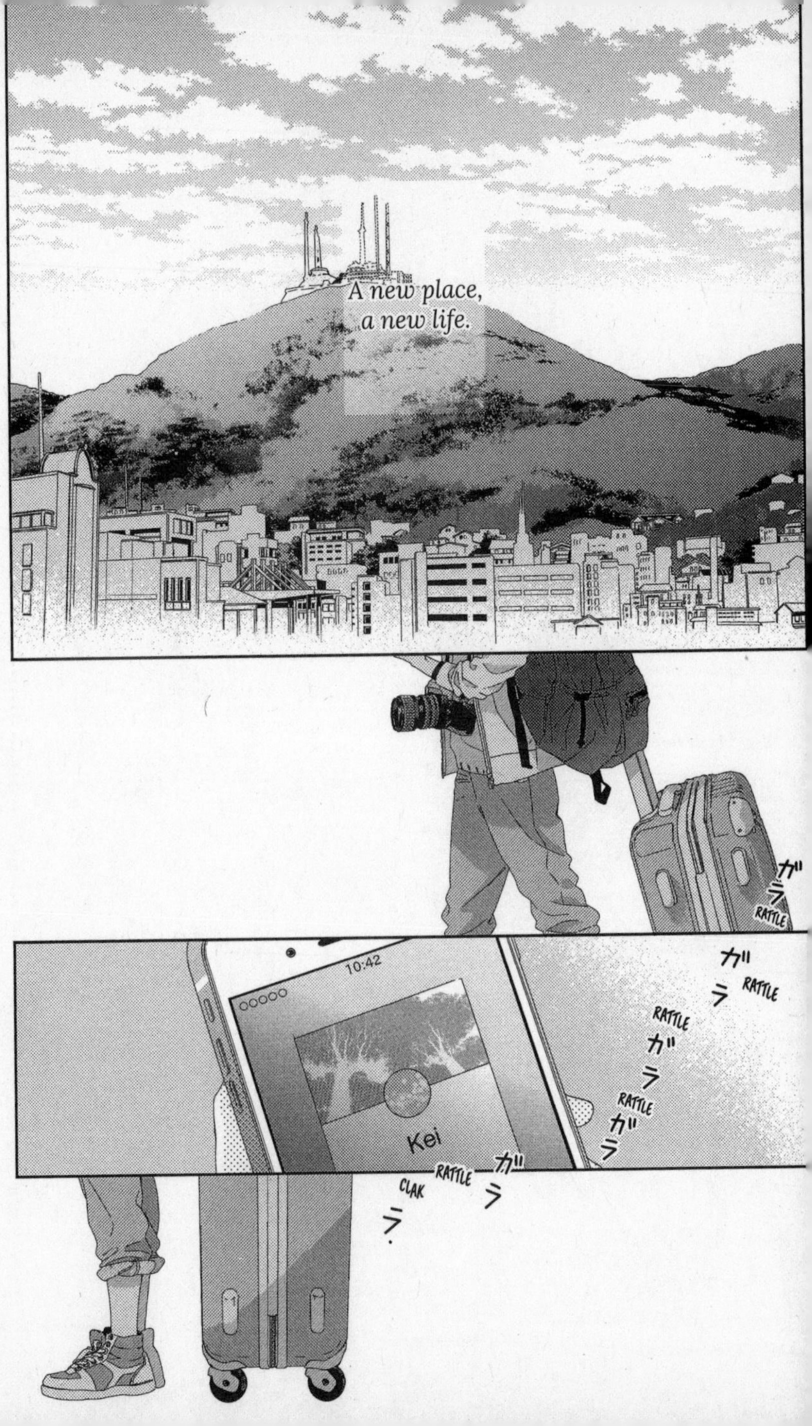
A new place,
a new life.
ガラ
RATTLE
10:42
Kei
ガラ
RATTLE
RATTLE
ガラ
RATTLE
ガラ
RATTLE
ガラ
CLAK
ラ.

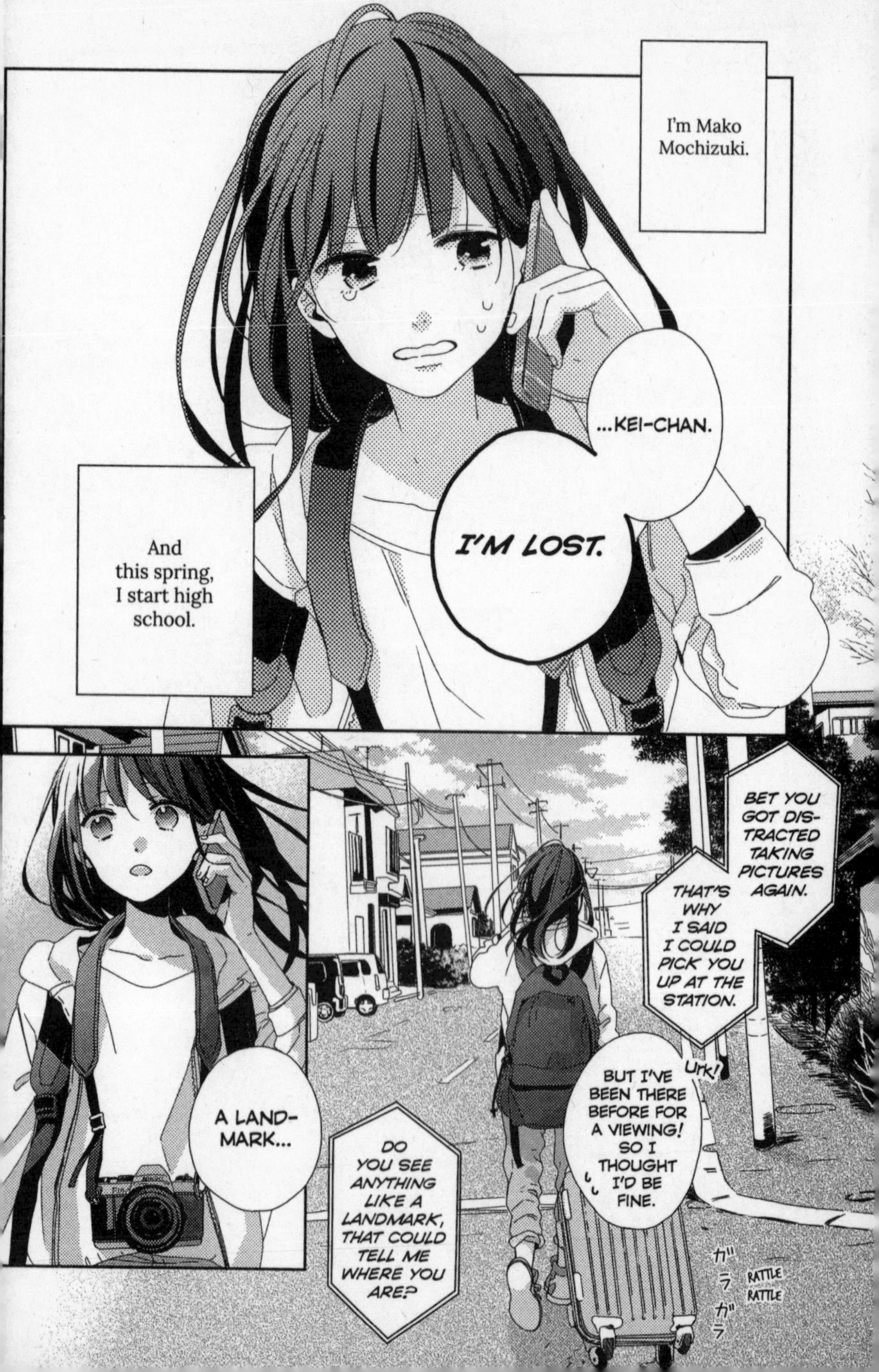
I'm Mako Mochizuki.
...KEI-CHAN.
I'M LOST.
And this spring, I start high school.
BET YOU GOT DISTRACTED TAKING PICTURES AGAIN.
THAT'S WHY I SAID I COULD PICK YOU UP AT THE STATION.
Urk!
BUT I'VE BEEN THERE BEFORE FOR A VIEWING! SO I THOUGHT I'D BE FINE.
DO YOU SEE ANYTHING LIKE A LANDMARK, THAT COULD TELL ME WHERE YOU ARE?
ガラガラ
RATTLE RATTLE
A LANDMARK...

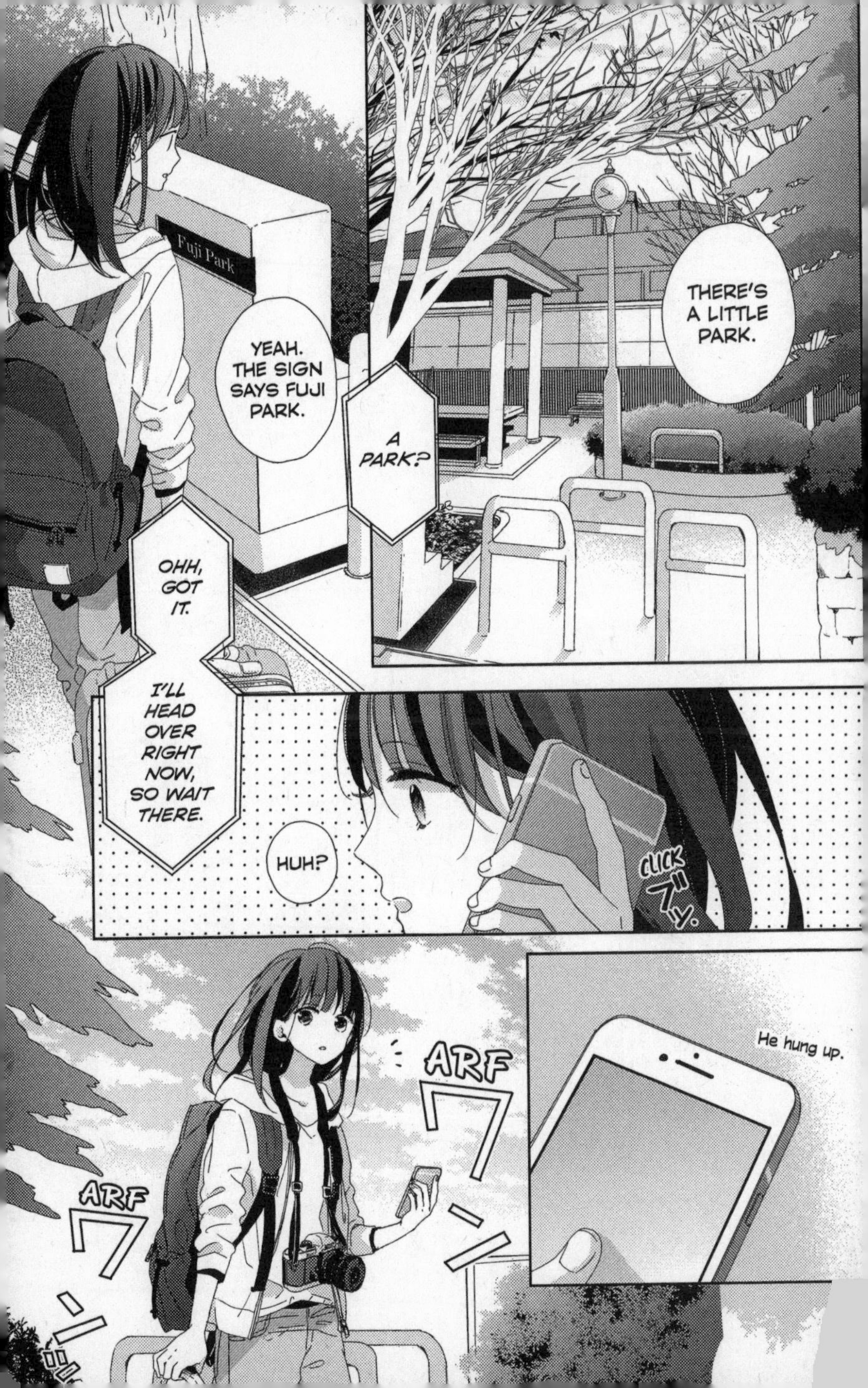
THERE'S A LITTLE PARK.
A PARK?
Fuji Park
YEAH. THE SIGN SAYS FUJI PARK.
OHH, GOT IT.
I'LL HEAD OVER RIGHT NOW, SO WAIT THERE.
CLICK
HUH?
He hung up.
ARF
ARF

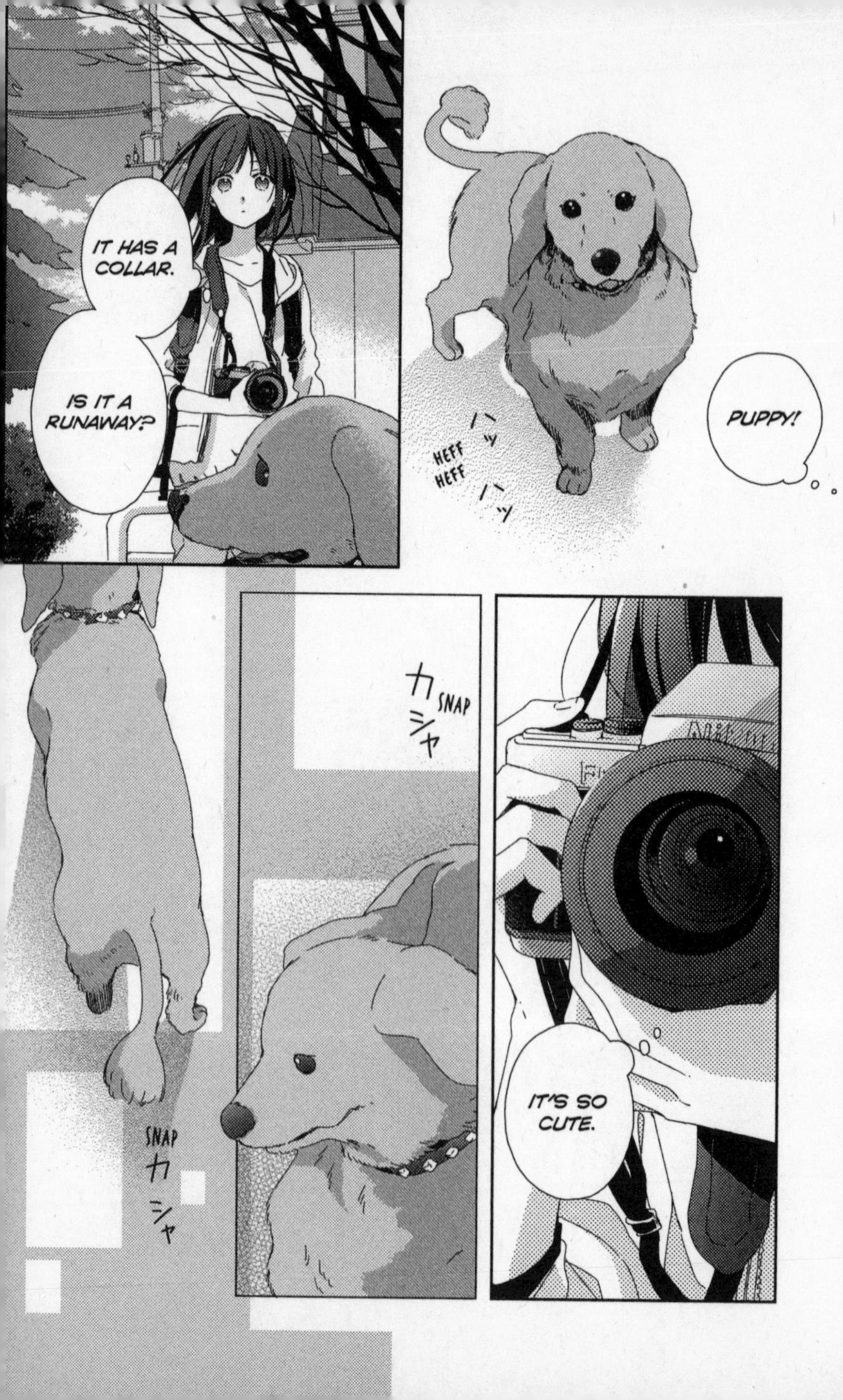
PUPPY!
ハッ ハッ
HEFF HEFF
IT HAS A COLLAR.
IS IT A RUNAWAY?
IT'S SO CUTE.
カシャ
SNAP
SNAP
カシャ

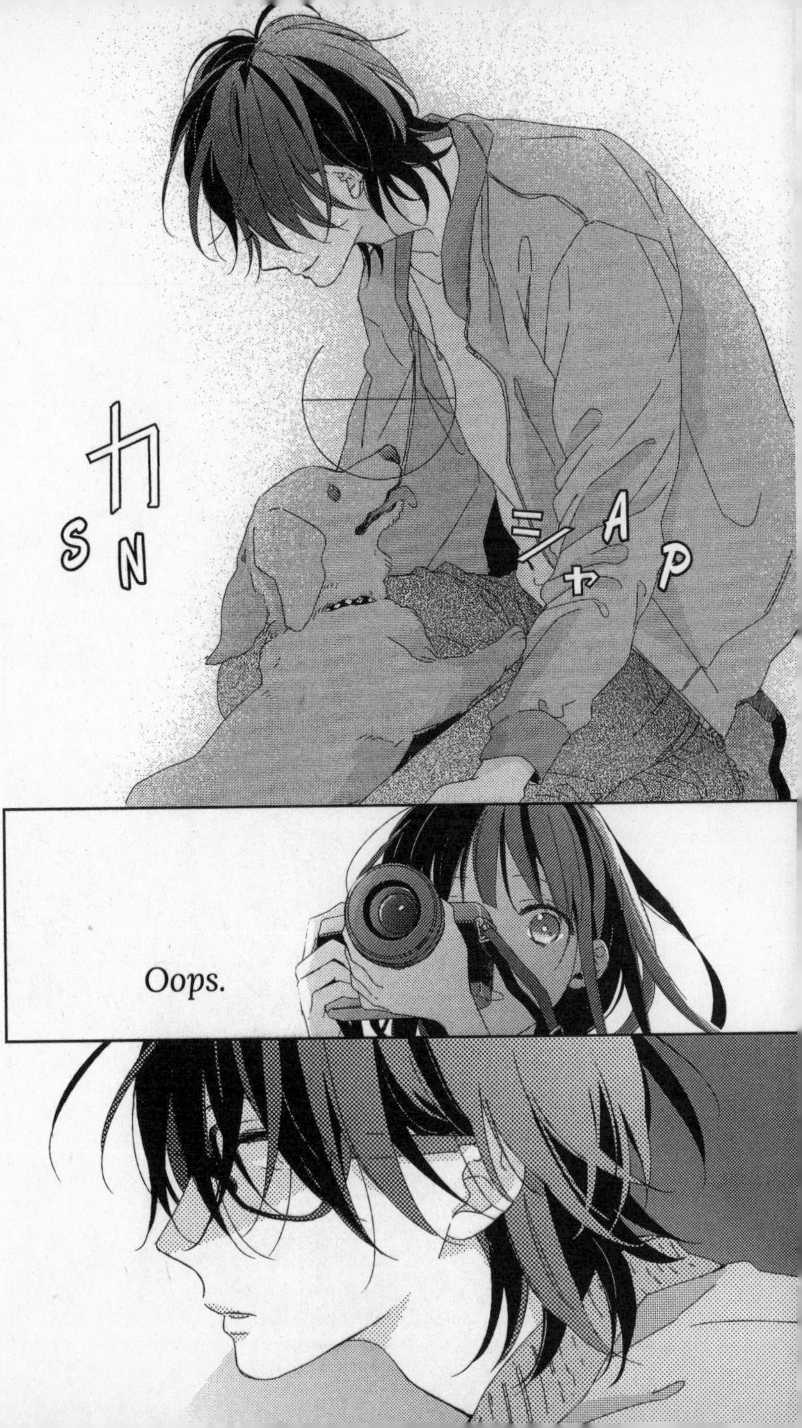
カシャ
SNAP
Oops.

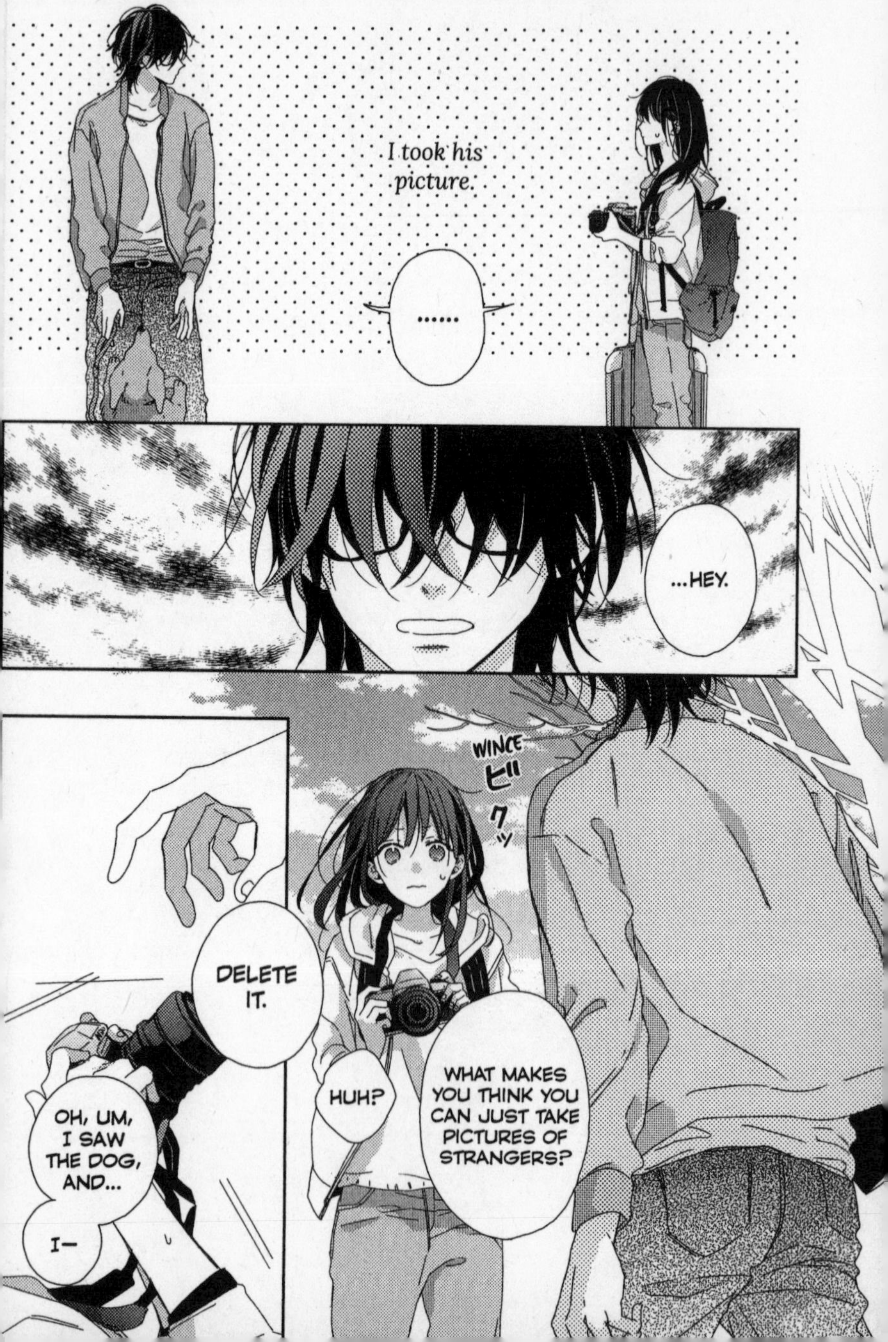

I took his picture.
......
...HEY.
WINCE
ビクッ
DELETE IT.
HUH?
WHAT MAKES YOU THINK YOU CAN JUST TAKE PICTURES OF STRANGERS?
OH, UM, I SAW THE DOG, AND...
I—

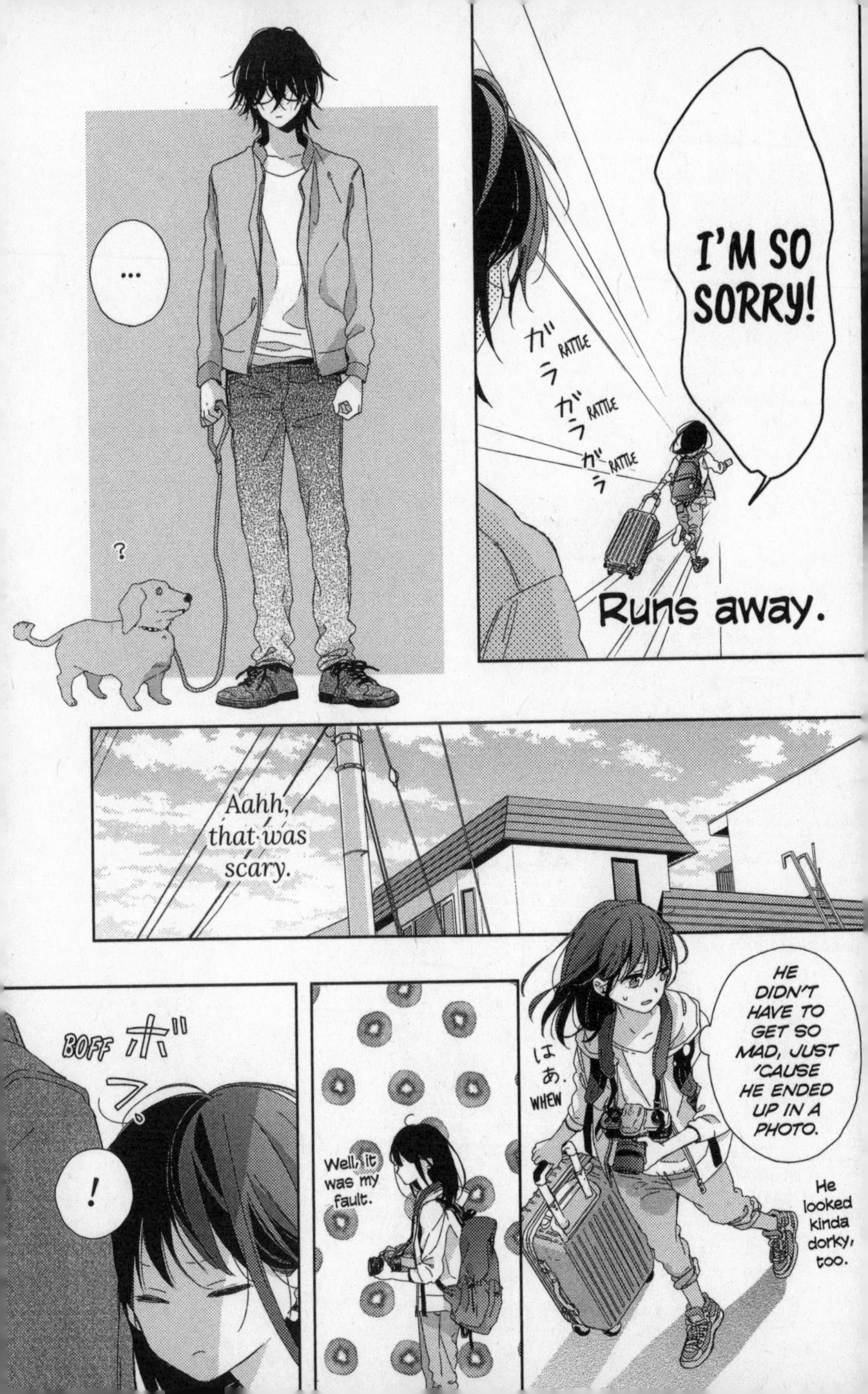
I'M SO SORRY!
ガラ RATTLE
ガラ RATTLE
ガラ RATTLE
Runs away.
...
?
Aahh, that was scary.
HE DIDN'T HAVE TO GET SO MAD, JUST 'CAUSE HE ENDED UP IN A PHOTO.
はあ. WHEW
He looked kinda dorky, too.
Well, it was my fault.
BOFF ボ
!

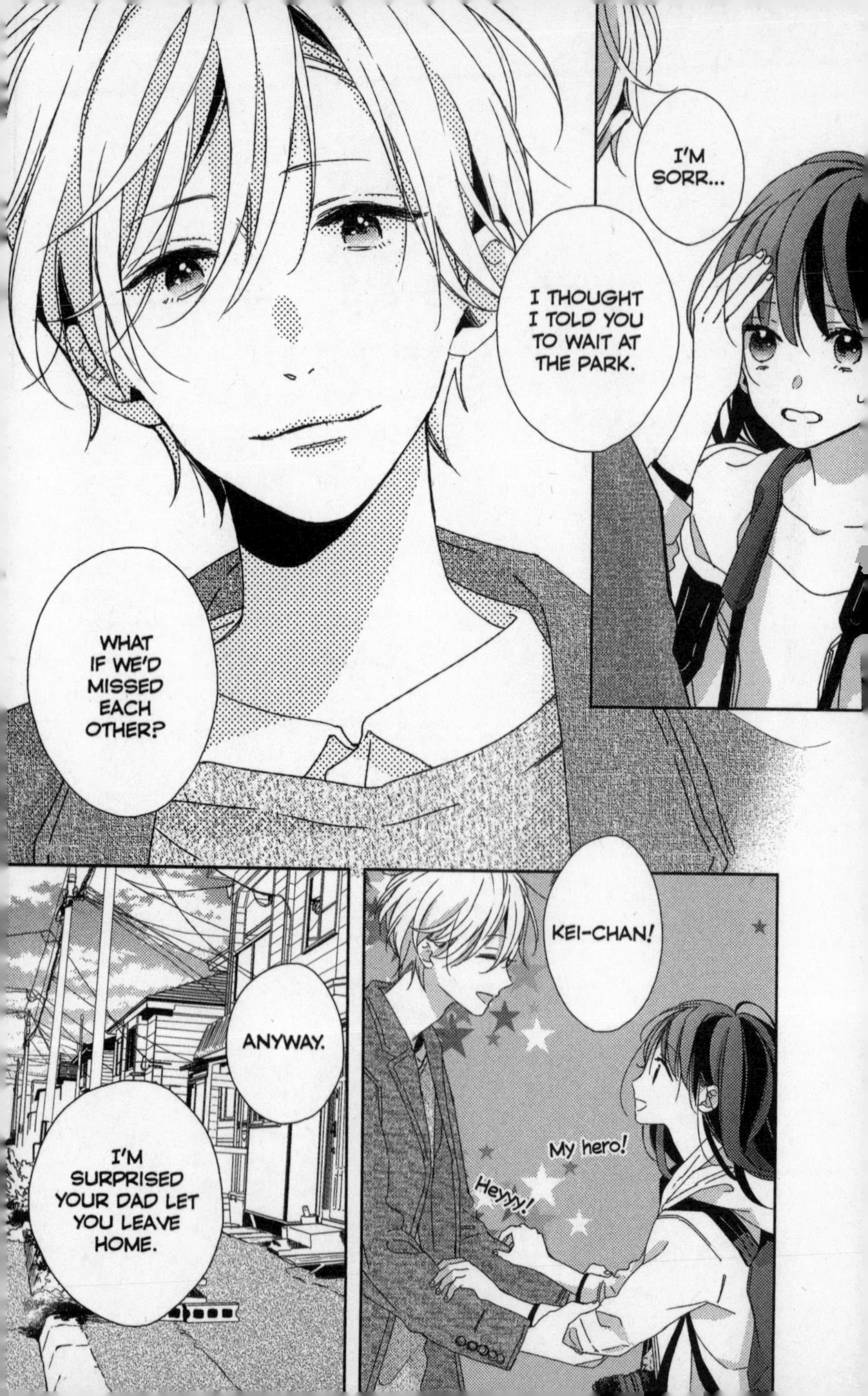
I'M SORR...
I THOUGHT I TOLD YOU TO WAIT AT THE PARK.
WHAT IF WE'D MISSED EACH OTHER?
KEI-CHAN!
My hero!
Heyyy!
ANYWAY.
I'M SURPRISED YOUR DAD LET YOU LEAVE HOME.

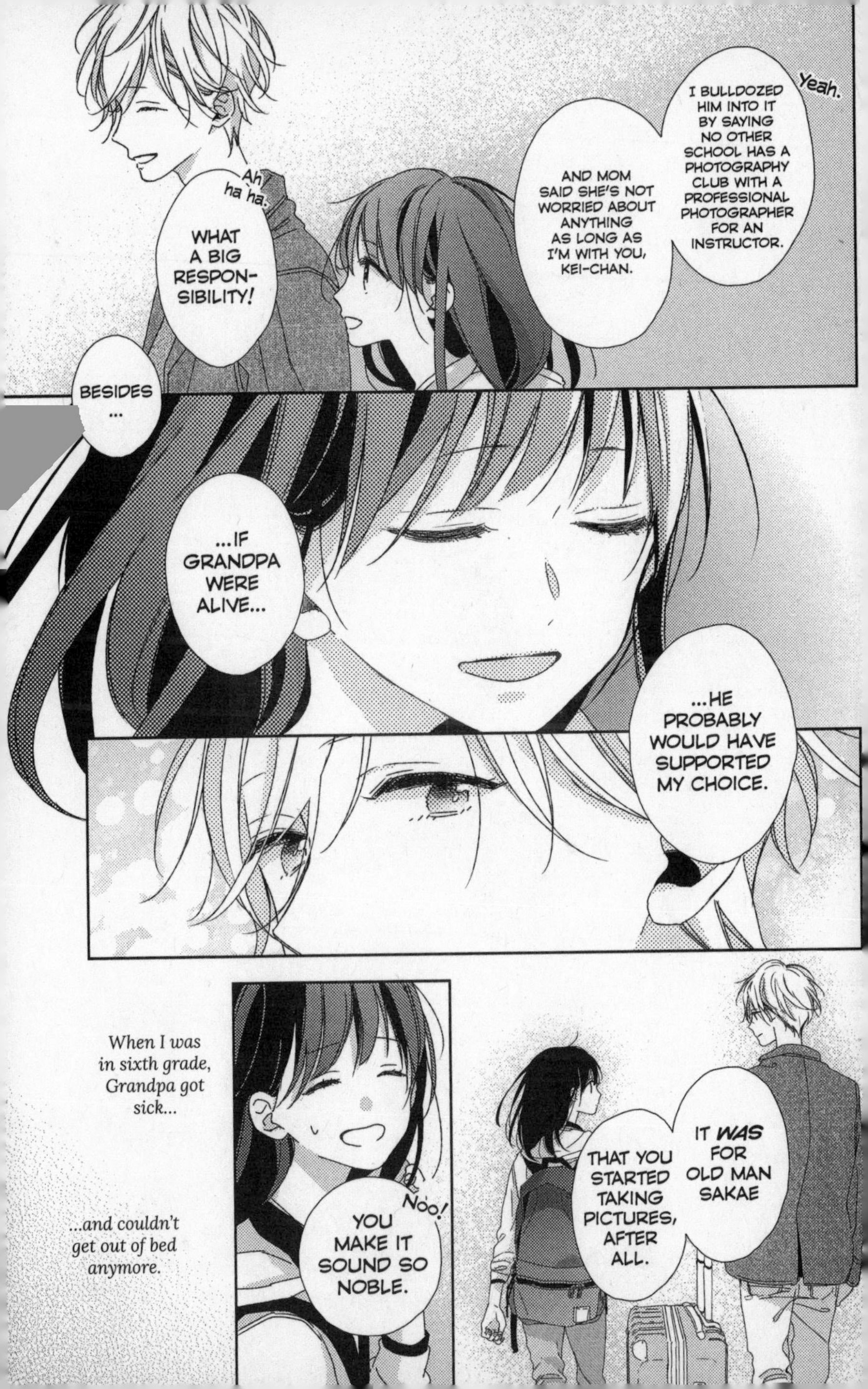
Yeah.
I BULLDOZED HIM INTO IT BY SAYING NO OTHER SCHOOL HAS A PHOTOGRAPHY CLUB WITH A PROFESSIONAL PHOTOGRAPHER FOR AN INSTRUCTOR.
AND MOM SAID SHE'S NOT WORRIED ABOUT ANYTHING AS LONG AS I'M WITH YOU, KEI-CHAN.
Ah ha ha.
WHAT A BIG RESPON-SIBILITY!
BESIDES...
...IF GRANDPA WERE ALIVE...
...HE PROBABLY WOULD HAVE SUPPORTED MY CHOICE.
IT *WAS* FOR OLD MAN SAKAE
THAT YOU STARTED TAKING PICTURES, AFTER ALL.
Nooo!
YOU MAKE IT SOUND SO NOBLE.
When I was in sixth grade, Grandpa got sick...
...and couldn't get out of bed anymore.

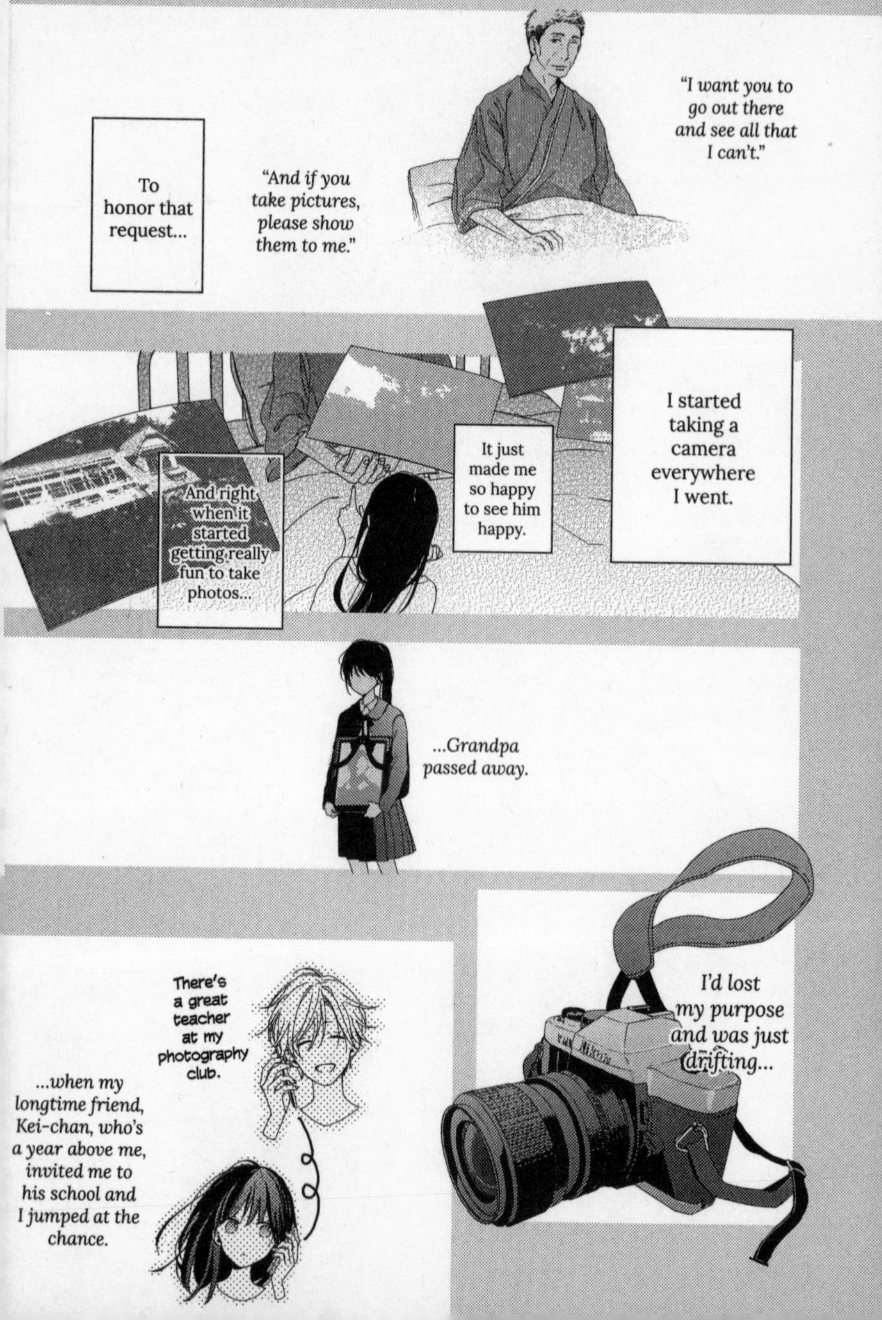
"I want you to go out there and see all that I can't."
"And if you take pictures, please show them to me."
To honor that request...
I started taking a camera everywhere I went.
It just made me so happy to see him happy.
And right when it started getting really fun to take photos...
...Grandpa passed away.
I'd lost my purpose and was just drifting...
There's a great teacher at my photography club.
...when my longtime friend, Kei-chan, who's a year above me, invited me to his school and I jumped at the chance.

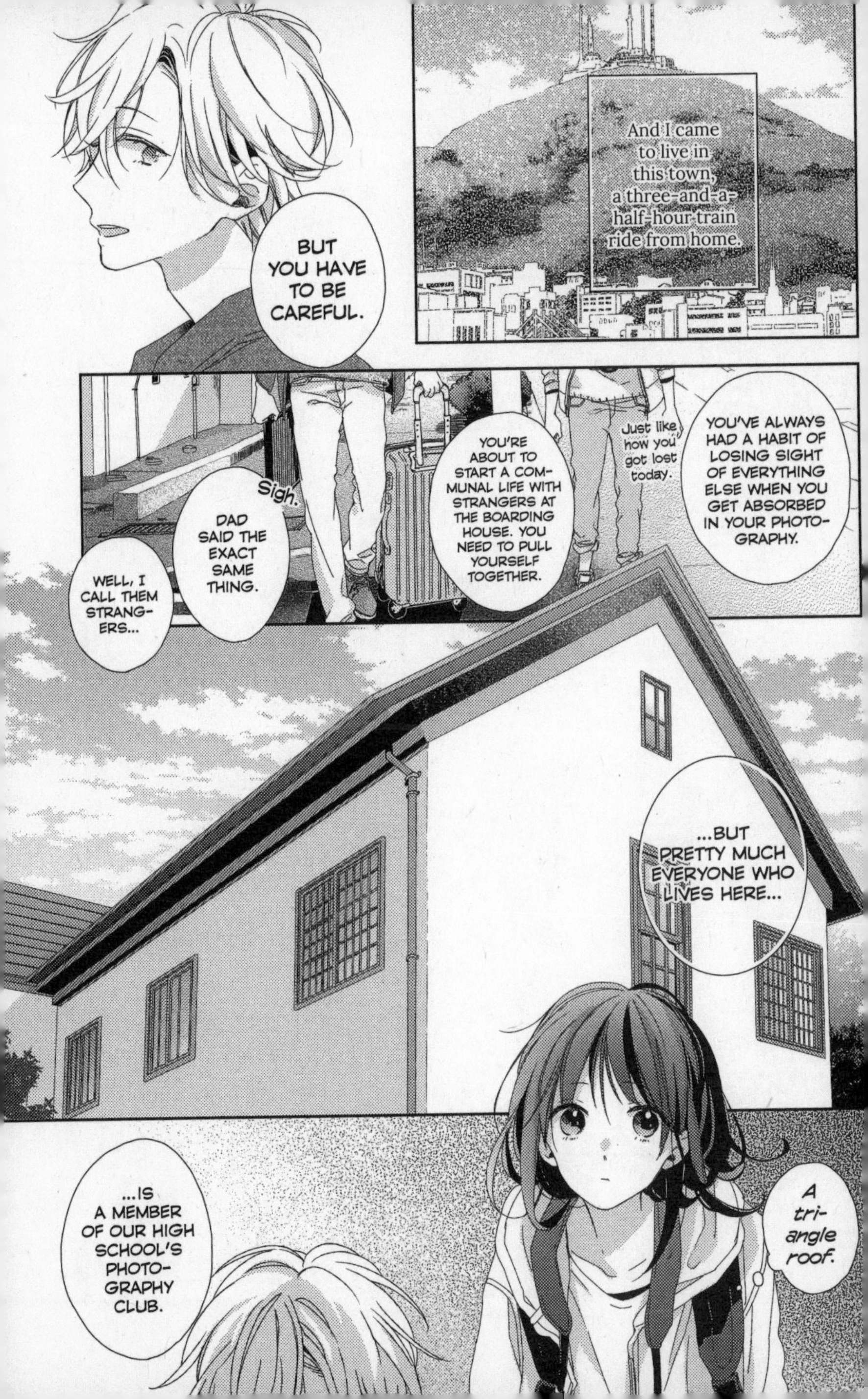
And I came to live in this town, a three-and-a-half-hour train ride from home.
BUT YOU HAVE TO BE CAREFUL.
YOU'VE ALWAYS HAD A HABIT OF LOSING SIGHT OF EVERYTHING ELSE WHEN YOU GET ABSORBED IN YOUR PHOTOGRAPHY.
Just like how you got lost today.
YOU'RE ABOUT TO START A COMMUNAL LIFE WITH STRANGERS AT THE BOARDING HOUSE. YOU NEED TO PULL YOURSELF TOGETHER.
Sigh.
DAD SAID THE EXACT SAME THING.
WELL, I CALL THEM STRANGERS...
...BUT PRETTY MUCH EVERYONE WHO LIVES HERE...
A tri-angle roof.
...IS A MEMBER OF OUR HIGH SCHOOL'S PHOTOGRAPHY CLUB.

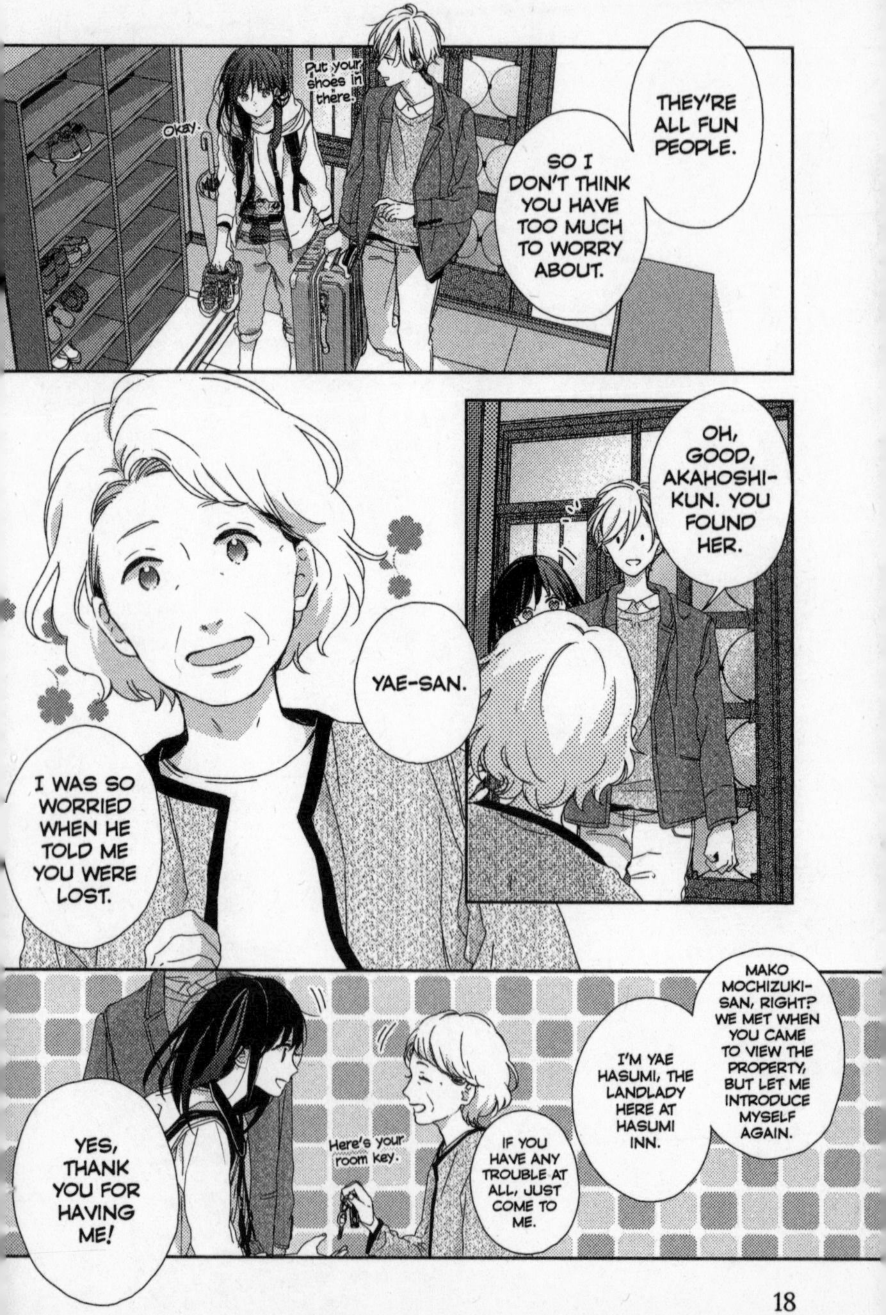
THEY'RE ALL FUN PEOPLE.
SO I DON'T THINK YOU HAVE TOO MUCH TO WORRY ABOUT.
Put your shoes in there.
Okay.
OH, GOOD, AKAHOSHI-KUN. YOU FOUND HER.
YAE-SAN.
I WAS SO WORRIED WHEN HE TOLD ME YOU WERE LOST.
MAKO MOCHIZUKI-SAN, RIGHT? WE MET WHEN YOU CAME TO VIEW THE PROPERTY, BUT LET ME INTRODUCE MYSELF AGAIN.
I'M YAE HASUMI, THE LANDLADY HERE AT HASUMI INN.
IF YOU HAVE ANY TROUBLE AT ALL, JUST COME TO ME.
Here's your room key.
YES, THANK YOU FOR HAVING ME!

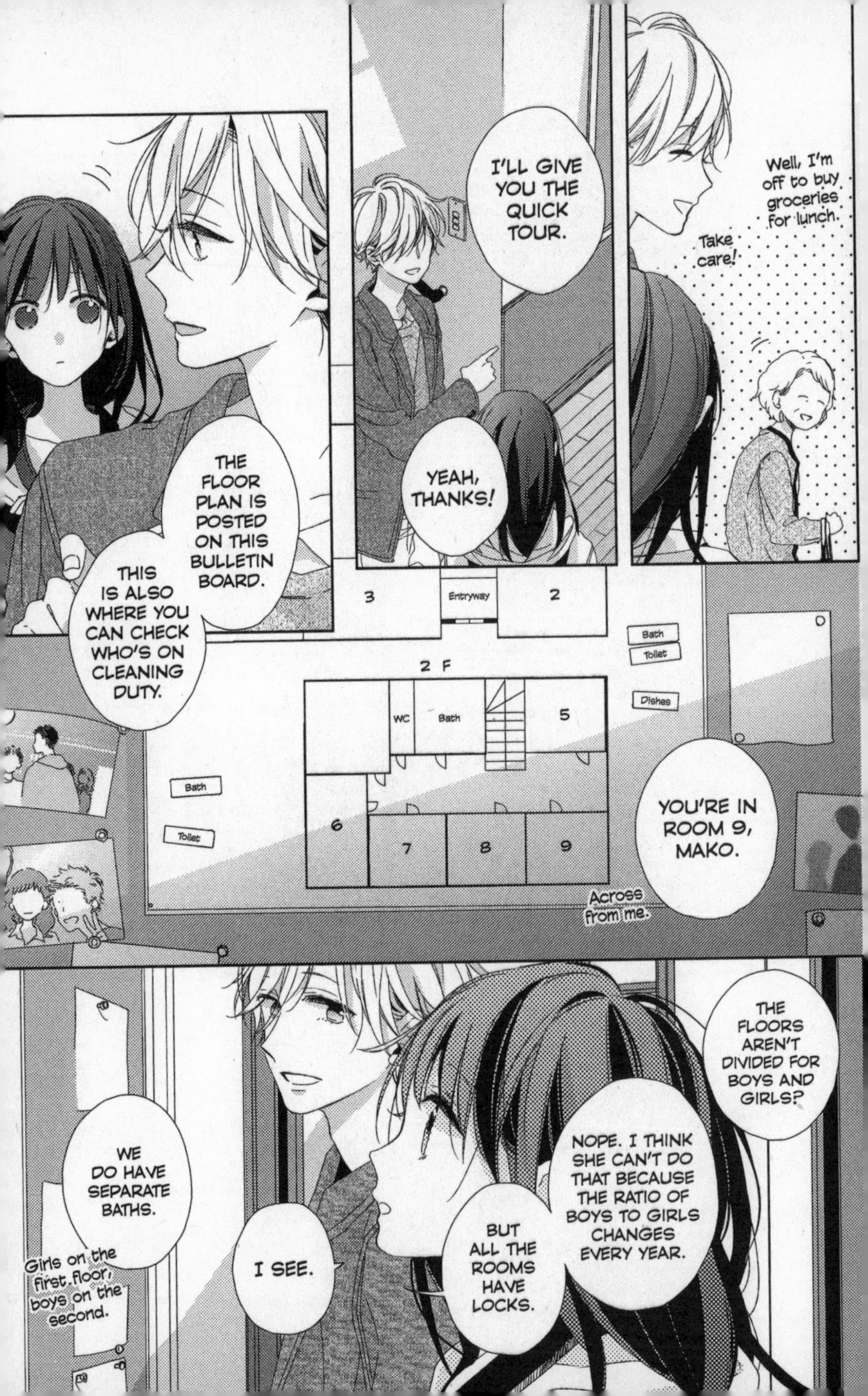
Well, I'm off to buy groceries for lunch.
Take care!
I'LL GIVE YOU THE QUICK TOUR.
YEAH, THANKS!
THE FLOOR PLAN IS POSTED ON THIS BULLETIN BOARD.
THIS IS ALSO WHERE YOU CAN CHECK WHO'S ON CLEANING DUTY.
Bath
Toilet
Dishes
2
Entryway
3
2 F
5
Bath
WC
6
7
8
9
Bath
Toilet
YOU'RE IN ROOM 9, MAKO.
Across from me.
THE FLOORS AREN'T DIVIDED FOR BOYS AND GIRLS?
NOPE. I THINK SHE CAN'T DO THAT BECAUSE THE RATIO OF BOYS TO GIRLS CHANGES EVERY YEAR.
BUT ALL THE ROOMS HAVE LOCKS.
I SEE.
WE DO HAVE SEPARATE BATHS.
Girls on the first floor, boys on the second.

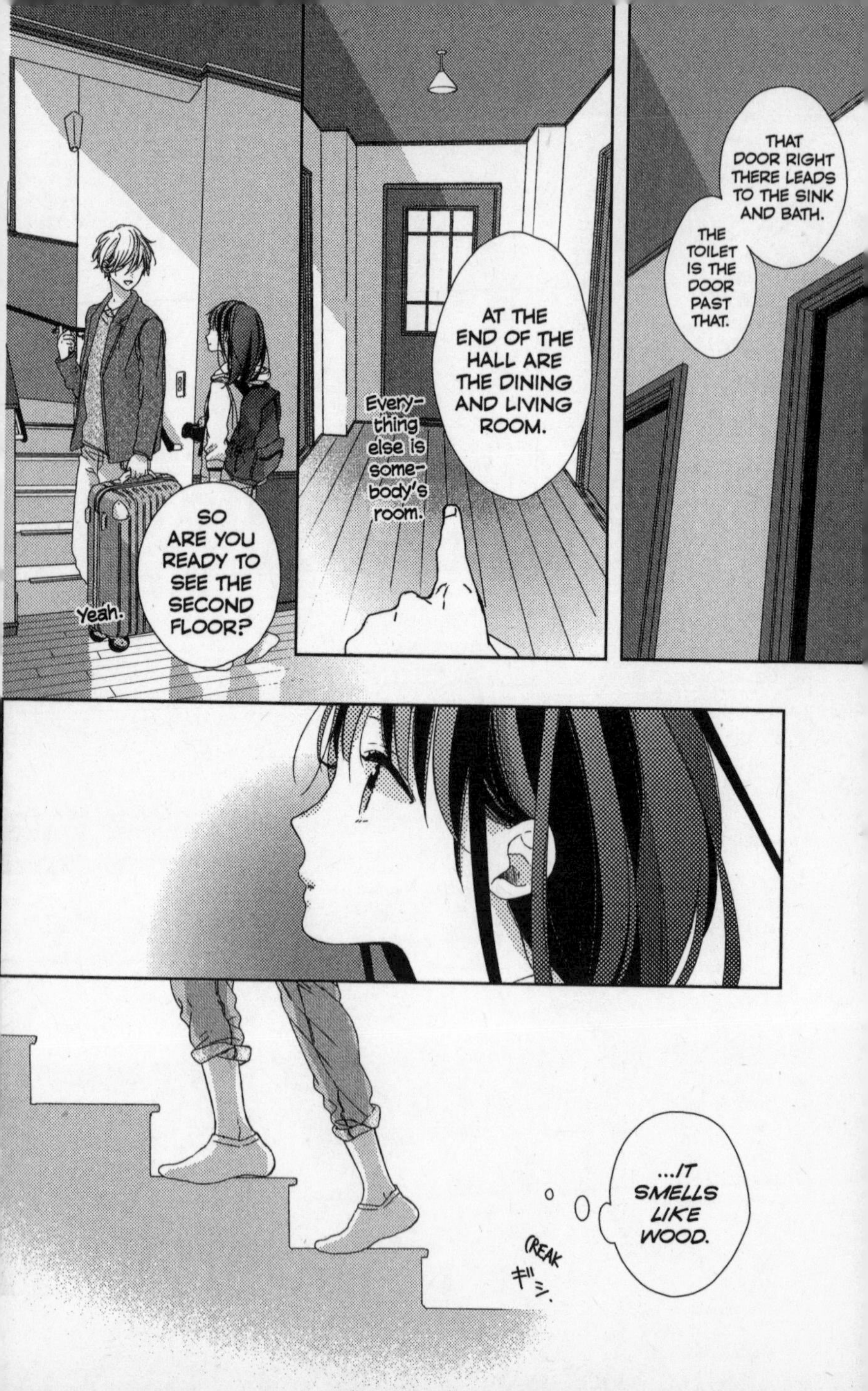
THAT DOOR RIGHT THERE LEADS TO THE SINK AND BATH.
THE TOILET IS THE DOOR PAST THAT.
AT THE END OF THE HALL ARE THE DINING AND LIVING ROOM.
Every-thing else is some-body's room.
SO ARE YOU READY TO SEE THE SECOND FLOOR?
Yeah.
...IT SMELLS LIKE WOOD.
CREAK
ギシ.

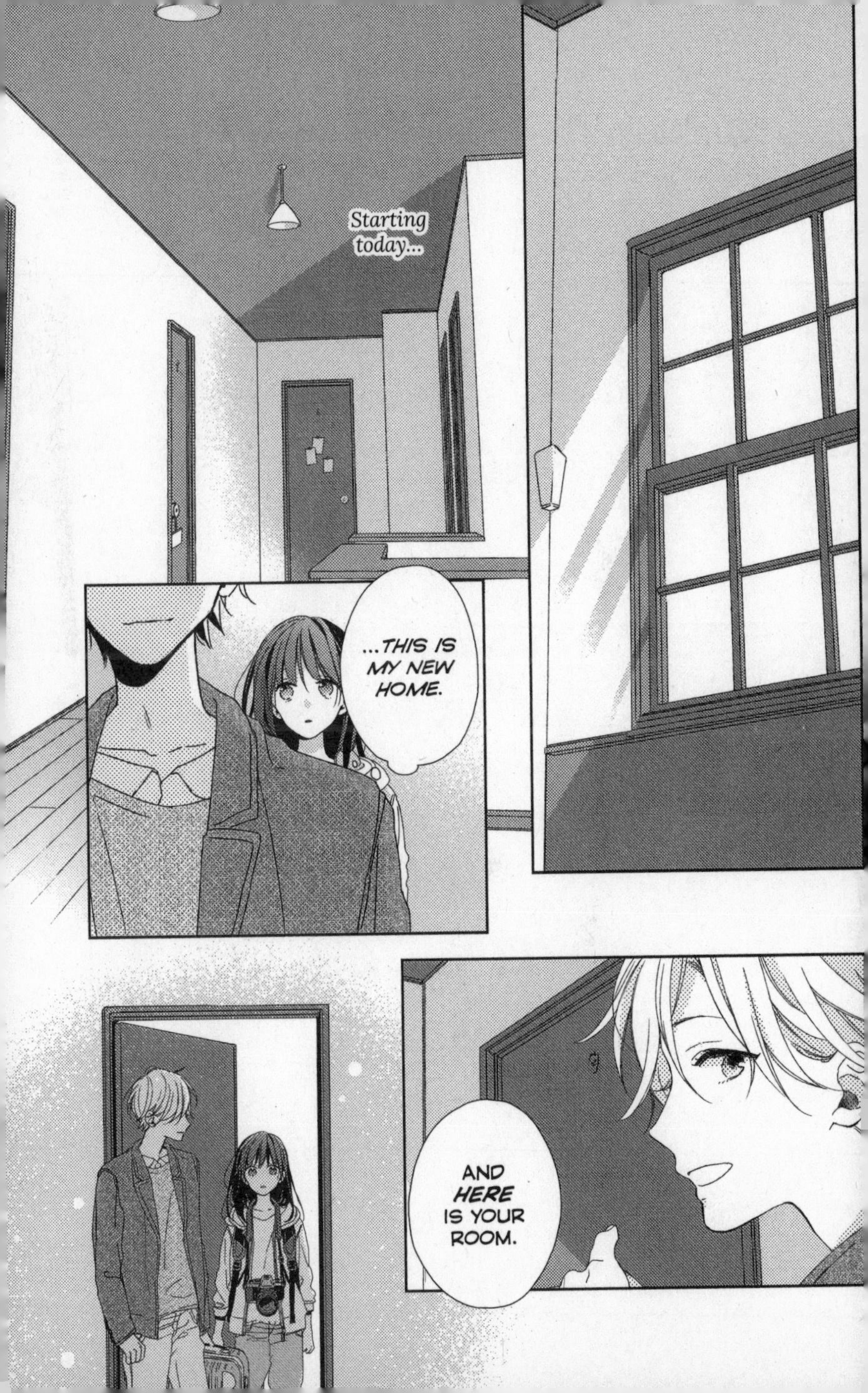
Starting today...
...THIS IS MY NEW HOME.
AND *HERE* IS YOUR ROOM.

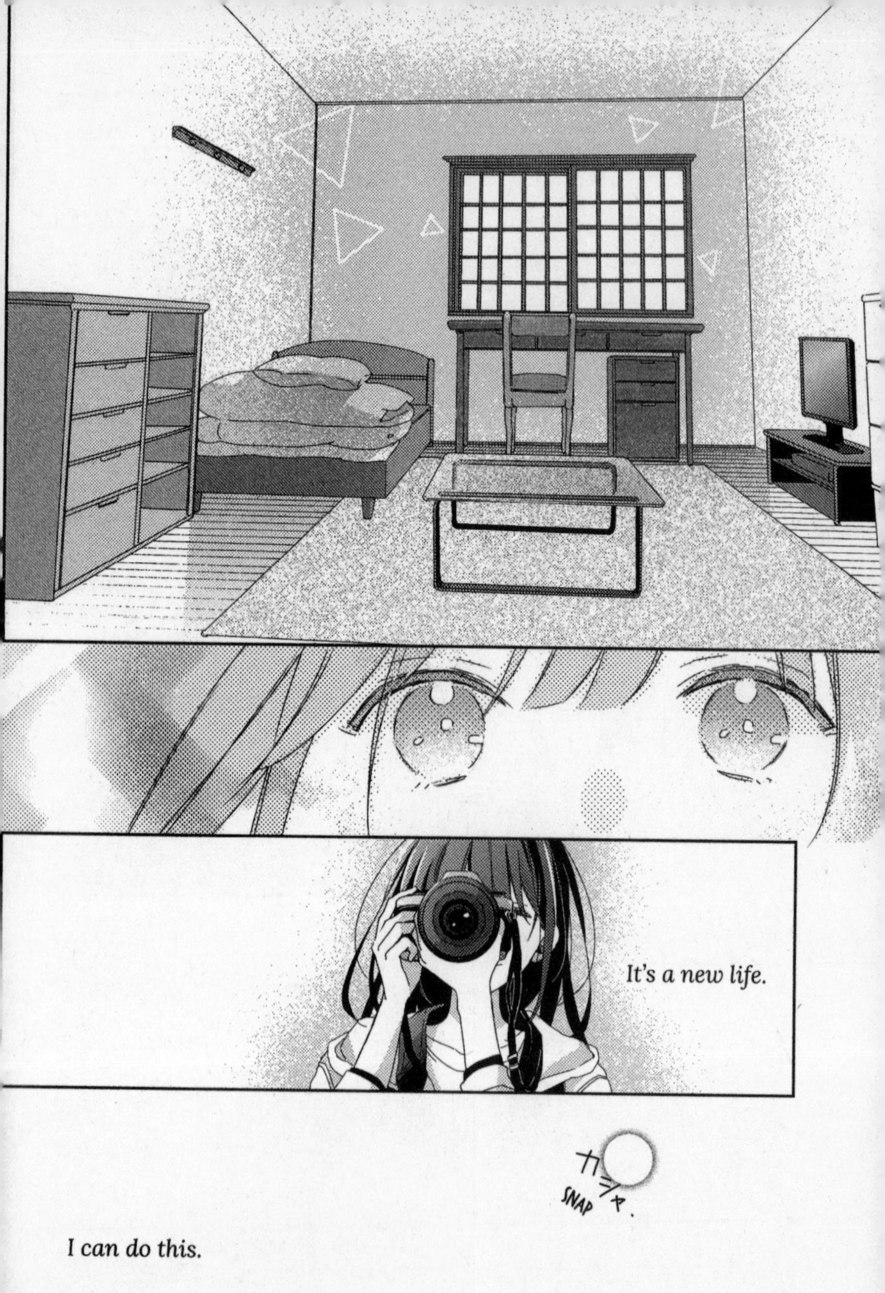
It's a new life.
カシャ
SNAP
I can do this.

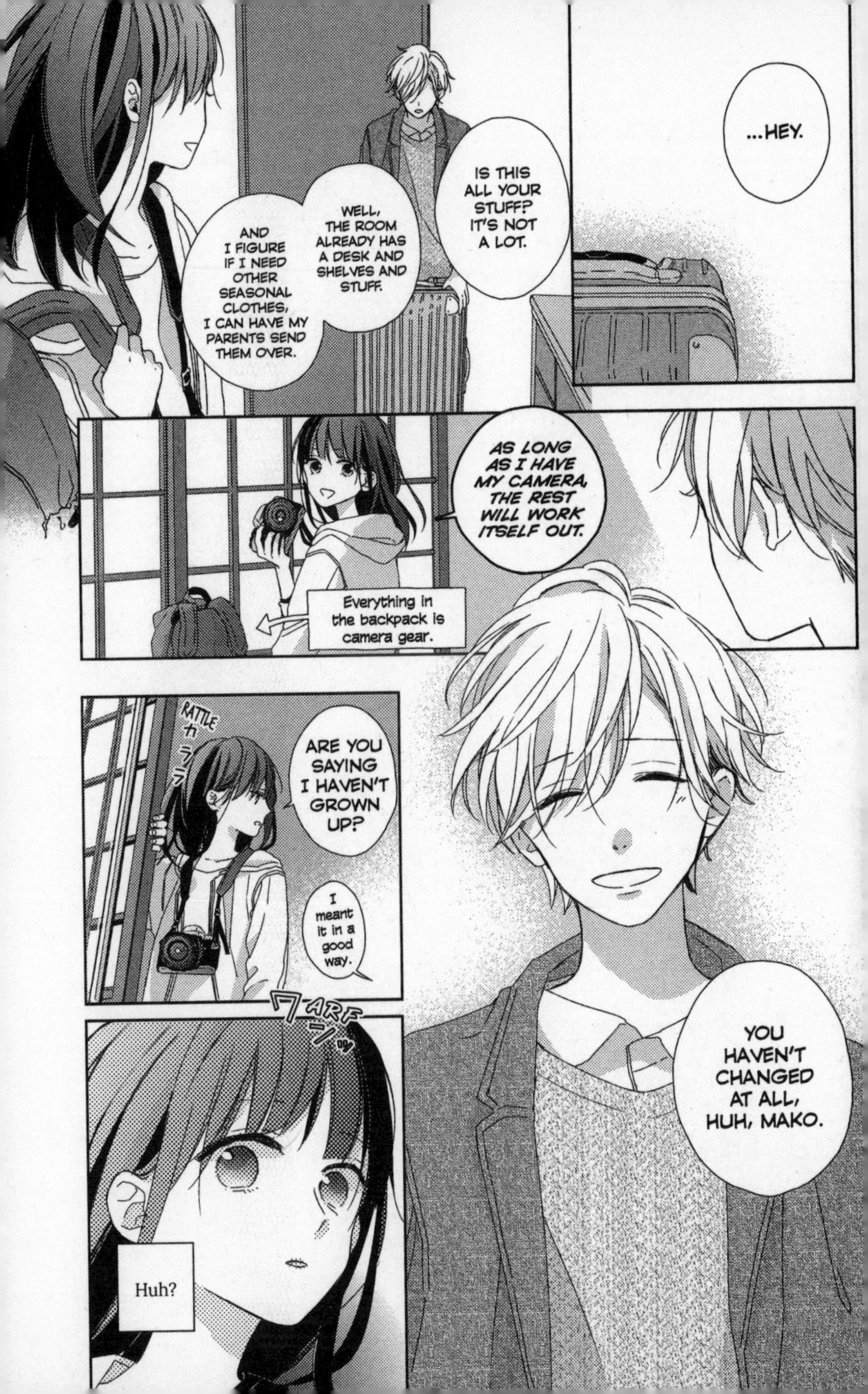
...HEY.
IS THIS ALL YOUR STUFF? IT'S NOT A LOT.
WELL, THE ROOM ALREADY HAS A DESK AND SHELVES AND STUFF.
AND I FIGURE IF I NEED OTHER SEASONAL CLOTHES, I CAN HAVE MY PARENTS SEND THEM OVER.
AS LONG AS I HAVE MY CAMERA, THE REST WILL WORK ITSELF OUT.
Everything in the backpack is camera gear.
YOU HAVEN'T CHANGED AT ALL, HUH, MAKO.
RATTLE
ARE YOU SAYING I HAVEN'T GROWN UP?
I meant it in a good way.
ARF
Huh?

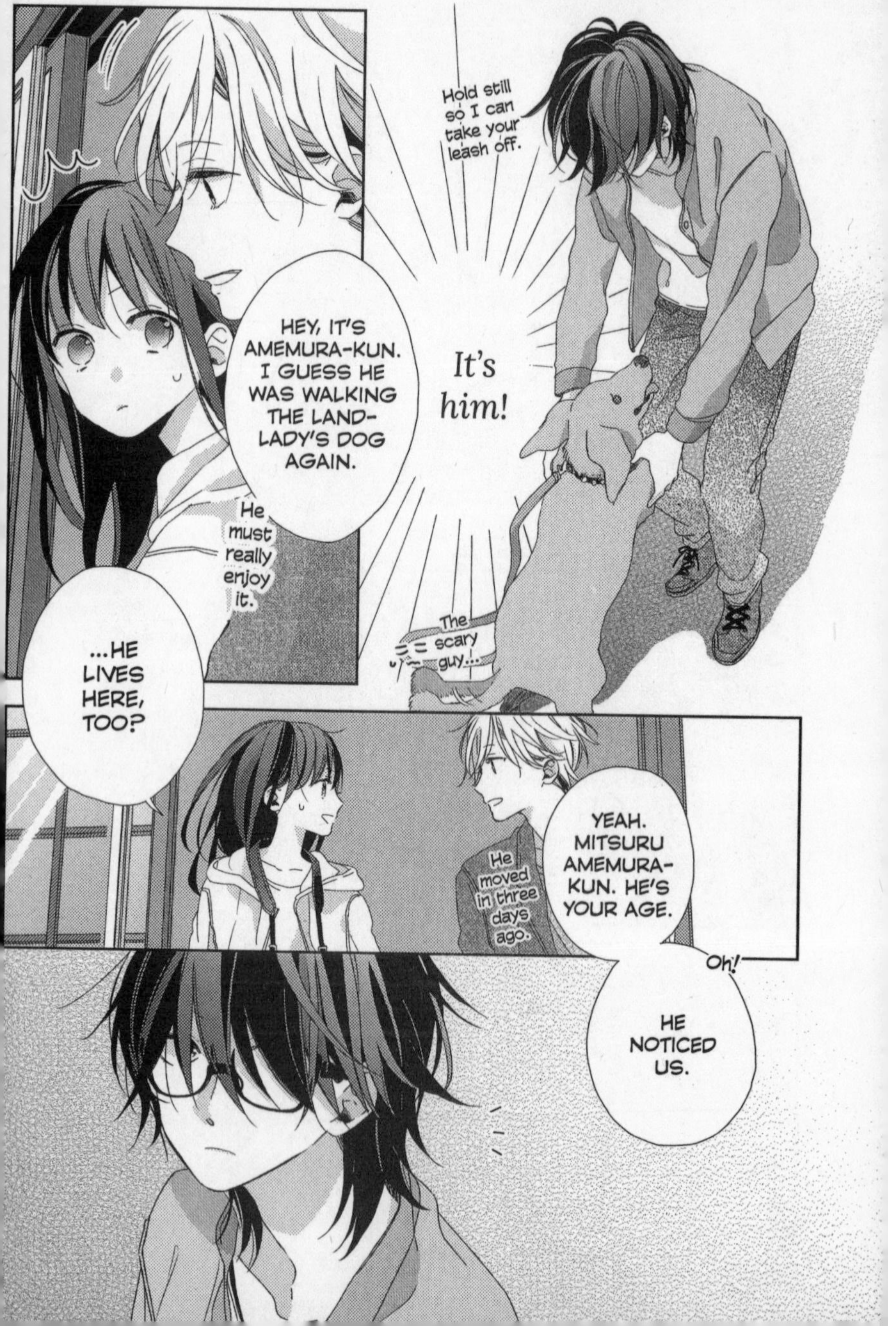
Hold still so I can take your leash off.
It's him!
HEY, IT'S AMEMURA-KUN. I GUESS HE WAS WALKING THE LAND-LADY'S DOG AGAIN.
He must really enjoy it.
The scary guy...
...HE LIVES HERE, TOO?
YEAH. MITSURU AMEMURA-KUN. HE'S YOUR AGE.
He moved in three days ago.
Oh!
HE NOTICED US.

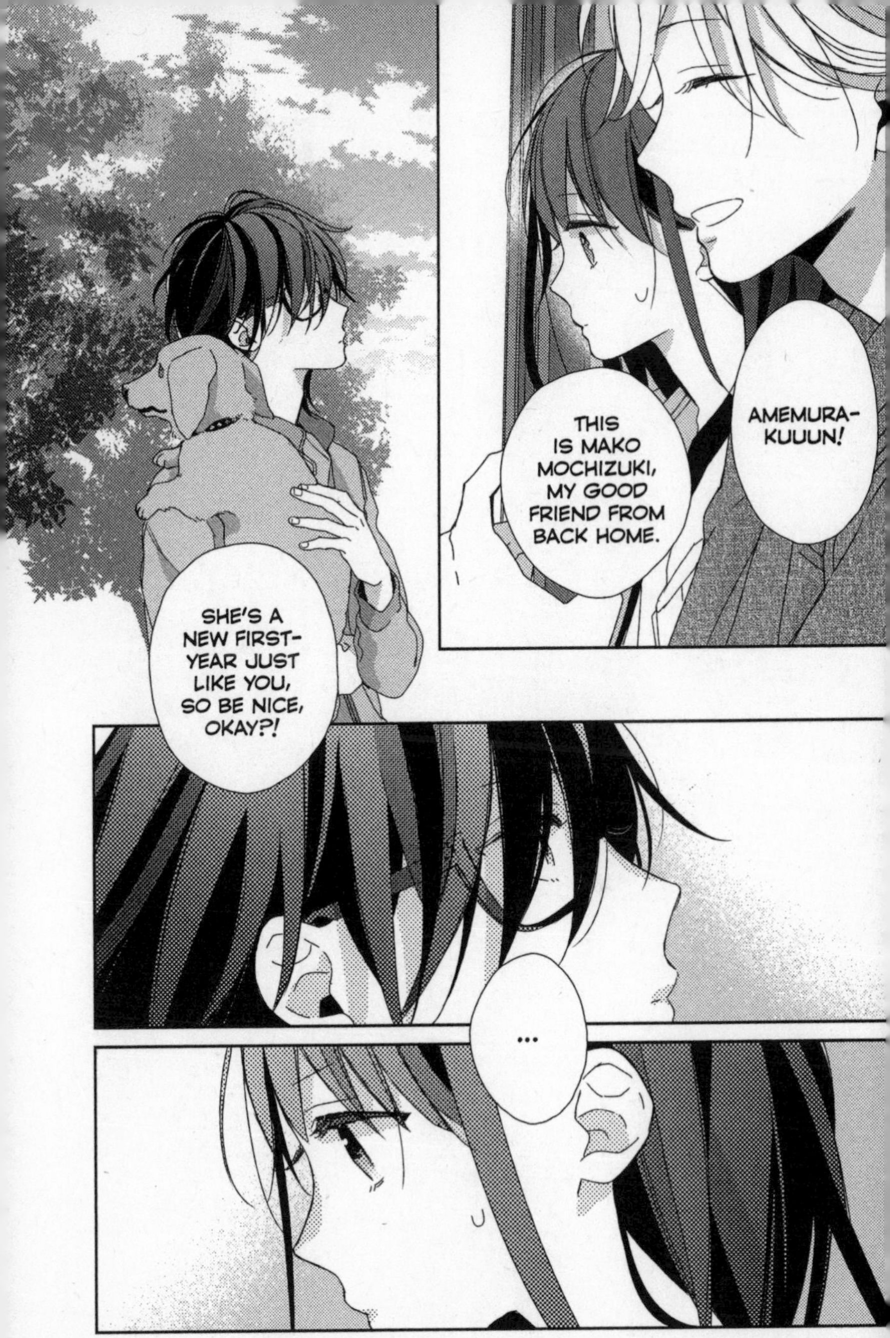
AMEMURA-KUUUN!
THIS IS MAKO MOCHIZUKI, MY GOOD FRIEND FROM BACK HOME.
SHE'S A NEW FIRST-YEAR JUST LIKE YOU, SO BE NICE, OKAY?!
...

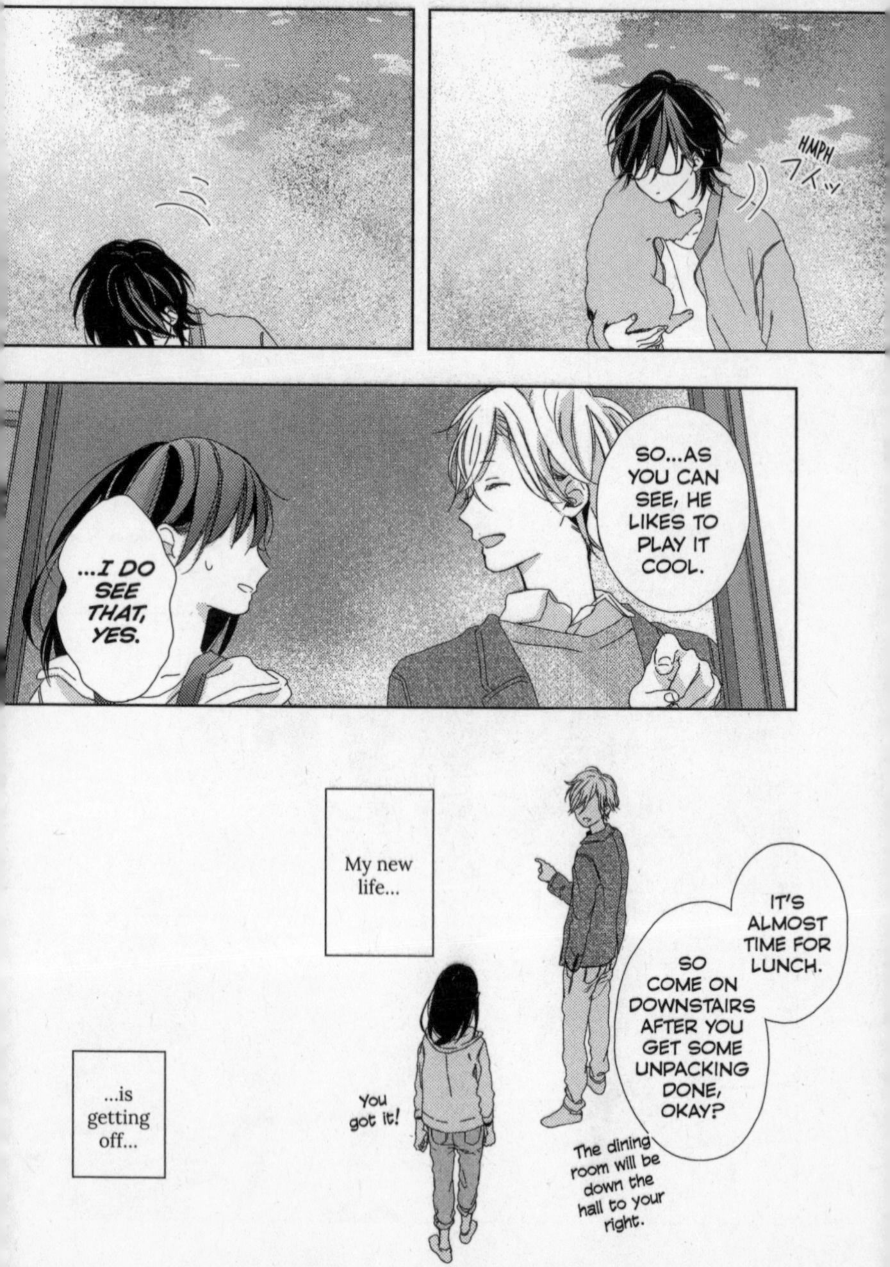
HMPH
へスッ
SO...AS YOU CAN SEE, HE LIKES TO PLAY IT COOL.
...I DO SEE THAT, YES.
IT'S ALMOST TIME FOR LUNCH.
SO COME ON DOWNSTAIRS AFTER YOU GET SOME UNPACKING DONE, OKAY?
The dining room will be down the hall to your right.
My new life...
You got it!
...is getting off...

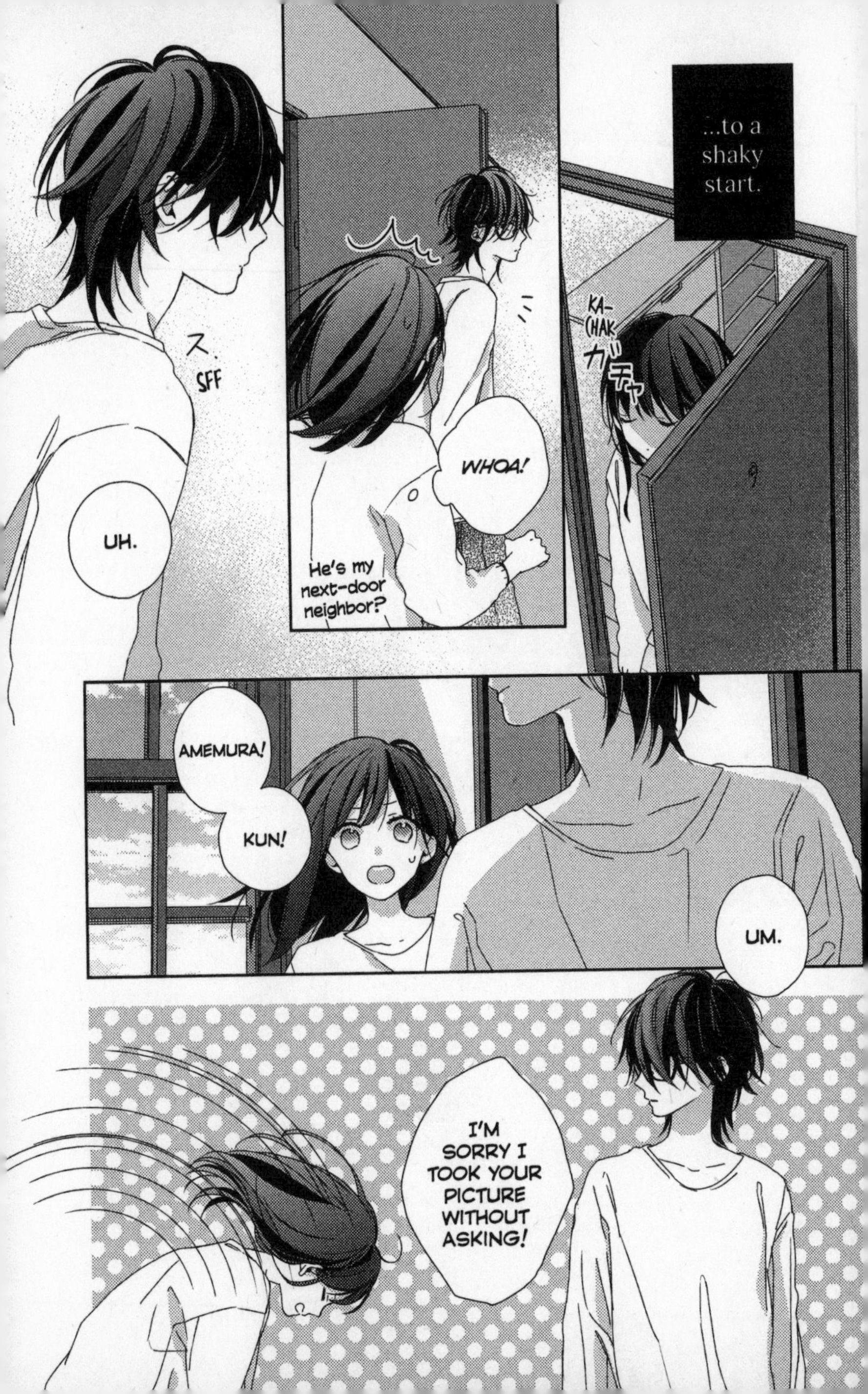
...to a shaky start.
KA-CHAK
ガチャ
WHOA!
He's my next-door neighbor?
ス
SFF
UH.
AMEMURA!
KUN!
UM.
I'M SORRY I TOOK YOUR PICTURE WITHOUT ASKING!

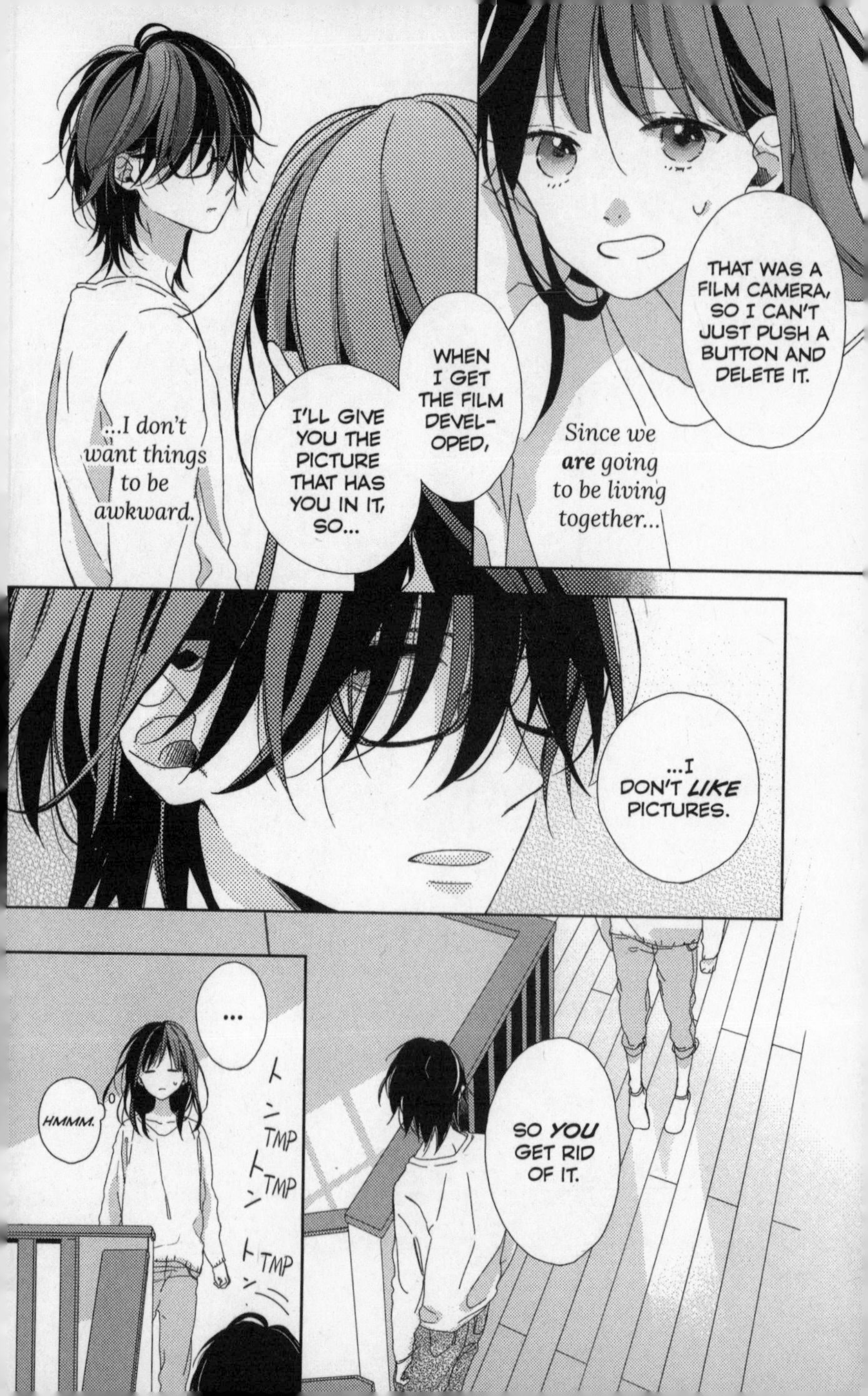
THAT WAS A FILM CAMERA, SO I CAN'T JUST PUSH A BUTTON AND DELETE IT.
Since we **are** going to be living together...
WHEN I GET THE FILM DEVEL-OPED,
I'LL GIVE YOU THE PICTURE THAT HAS YOU IN IT, SO...
...I don't want things to be awkward.
...I DON'T *LIKE* PICTURES.
SO *YOU* GET RID OF IT.
...
HMMM.
TMP
TMP
TMP

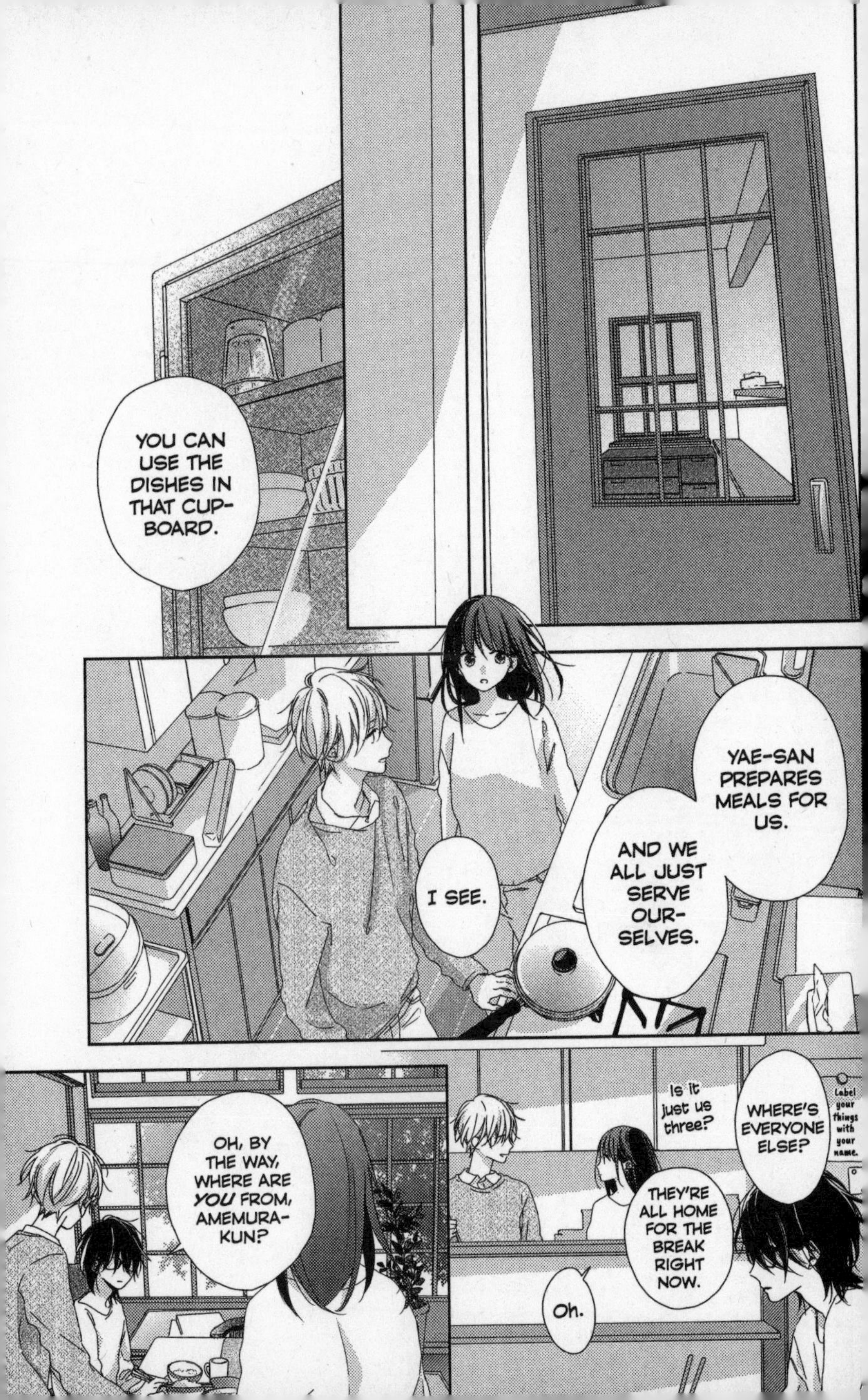

YOU CAN USE THE DISHES IN THAT CUPBOARD.
YAE-SAN PREPARES MEALS FOR US.
AND WE ALL JUST SERVE OURSELVES.
I SEE.
Label your things with your name.
WHERE'S EVERYONE ELSE?
Is it just us three?
THEY'RE ALL HOME FOR THE BREAK RIGHT NOW.
Oh.
OH, BY THE WAY, WHERE ARE *YOU* FROM, AMEMURA-KUN?

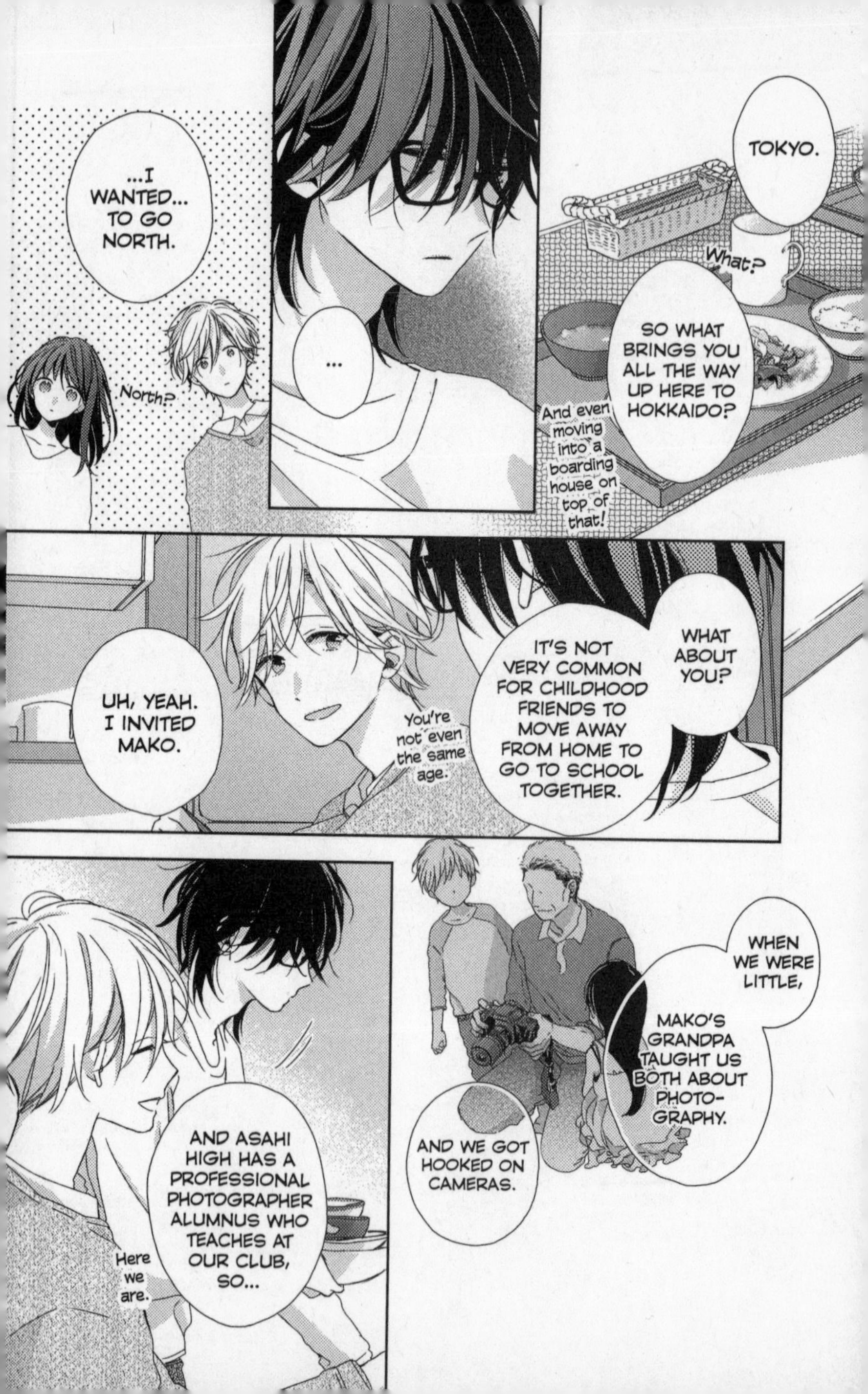
TOKYO.
What?
SO WHAT BRINGS YOU ALL THE WAY UP HERE TO HOKKAIDO?
And even moving into a boarding house on top of that!
...
...I WANTED... TO GO NORTH.
North?
WHAT ABOUT YOU?
IT'S NOT VERY COMMON FOR CHILDHOOD FRIENDS TO MOVE AWAY FROM HOME TO GO TO SCHOOL TOGETHER.
You're not even the same age.
UH, YEAH. I INVITED MAKO.
WHEN WE WERE LITTLE,
MAKO'S GRANDPA TAUGHT US BOTH ABOUT PHOTO-GRAPHY.
AND WE GOT HOOKED ON CAMERAS.
AND ASAHI HIGH HAS A PROFESSIONAL PHOTOGRAPHER ALUMNUS WHO TEACHES AT OUR CLUB, SO...
Here we are.

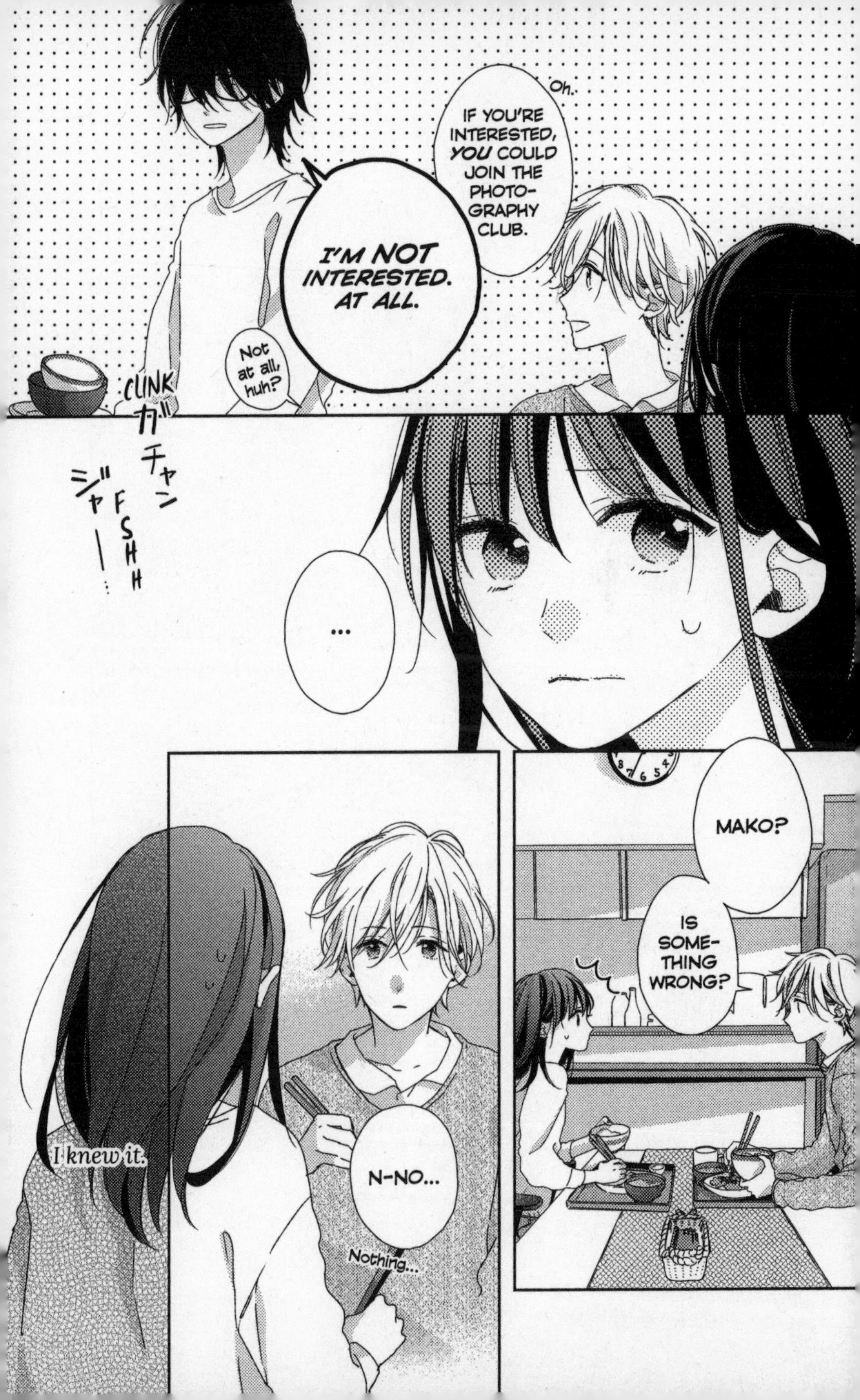

Oh.
IF YOU'RE INTERESTED, *YOU* COULD JOIN THE PHOTOGRAPHY CLUB.
I'M NOT INTERESTED. AT ALL.
Not at all, huh?
CLINK ガチャン
...
FSHH ジャー…
MAKO?
IS SOMETHING WRONG?
N-NO...
Nothing...
I knew it.

He's mad...

...at me...

...isn't he?

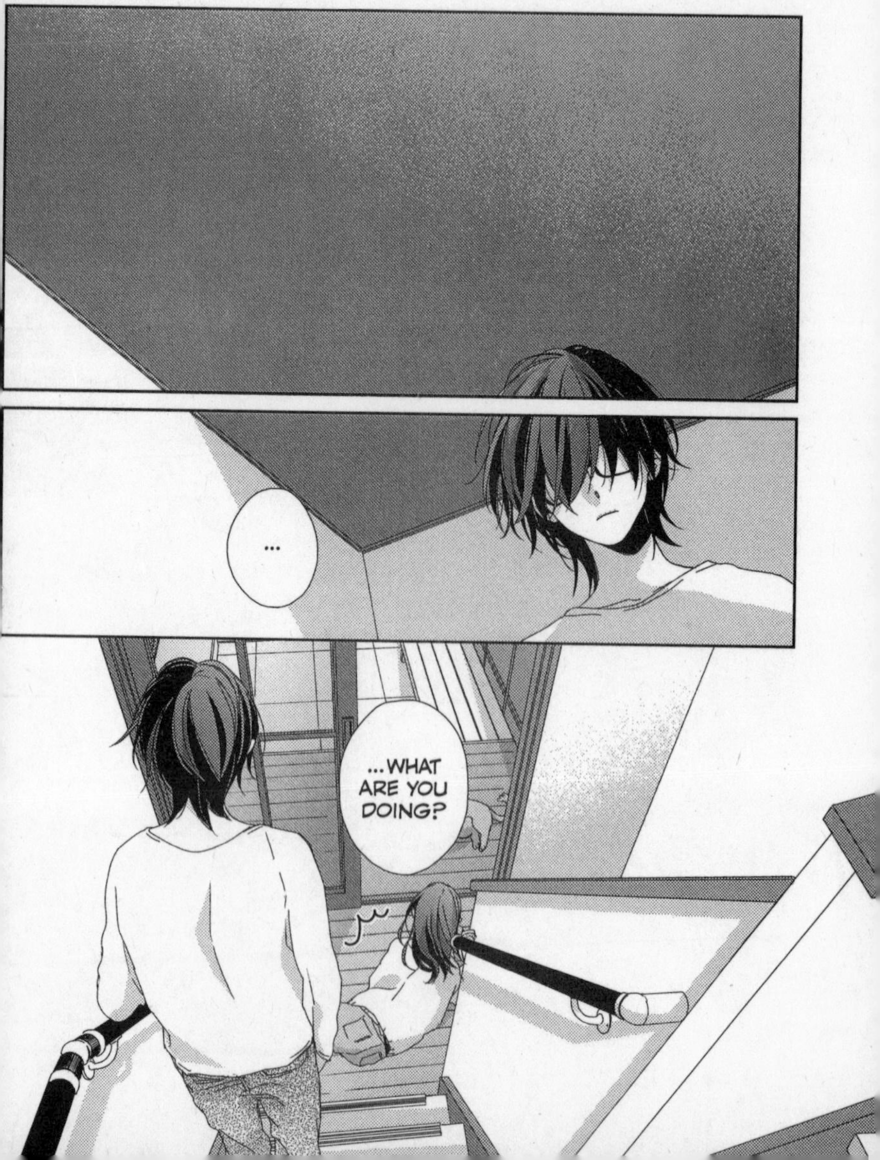
...
...WHAT ARE YOU DOING?

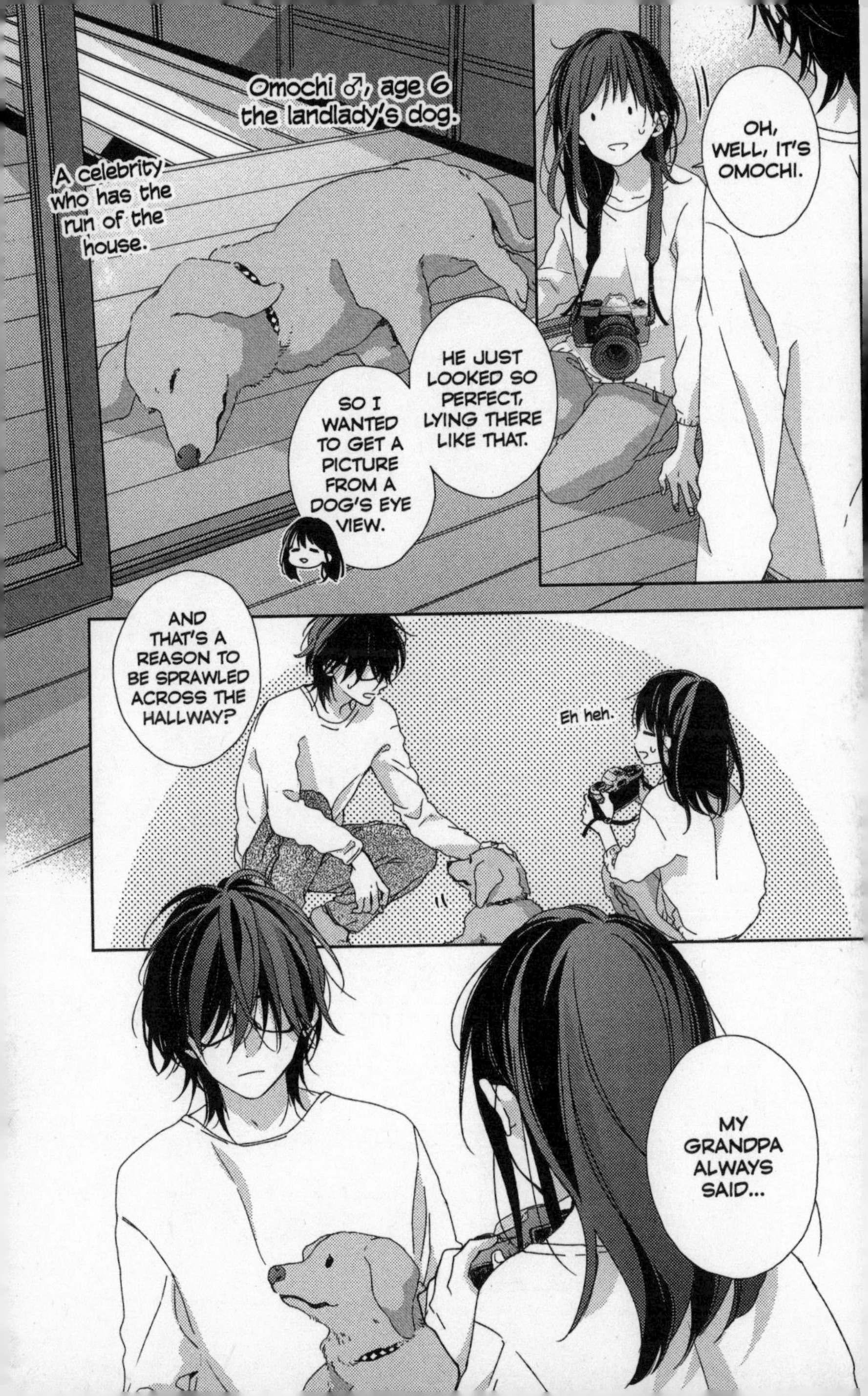
OH, WELL, IT'S OMOCHI.
Omochi ♂, age 6 the landlady's dog.
A celebrity who has the run of the house.
HE JUST LOOKED SO PERFECT, LYING THERE LIKE THAT.
SO I WANTED TO GET A PICTURE FROM A DOG'S EYE VIEW.
AND THAT'S A REASON TO BE SPRAWLED ACROSS THE HALLWAY?
Eh heh.
MY GRANDPA ALWAYS SAID...

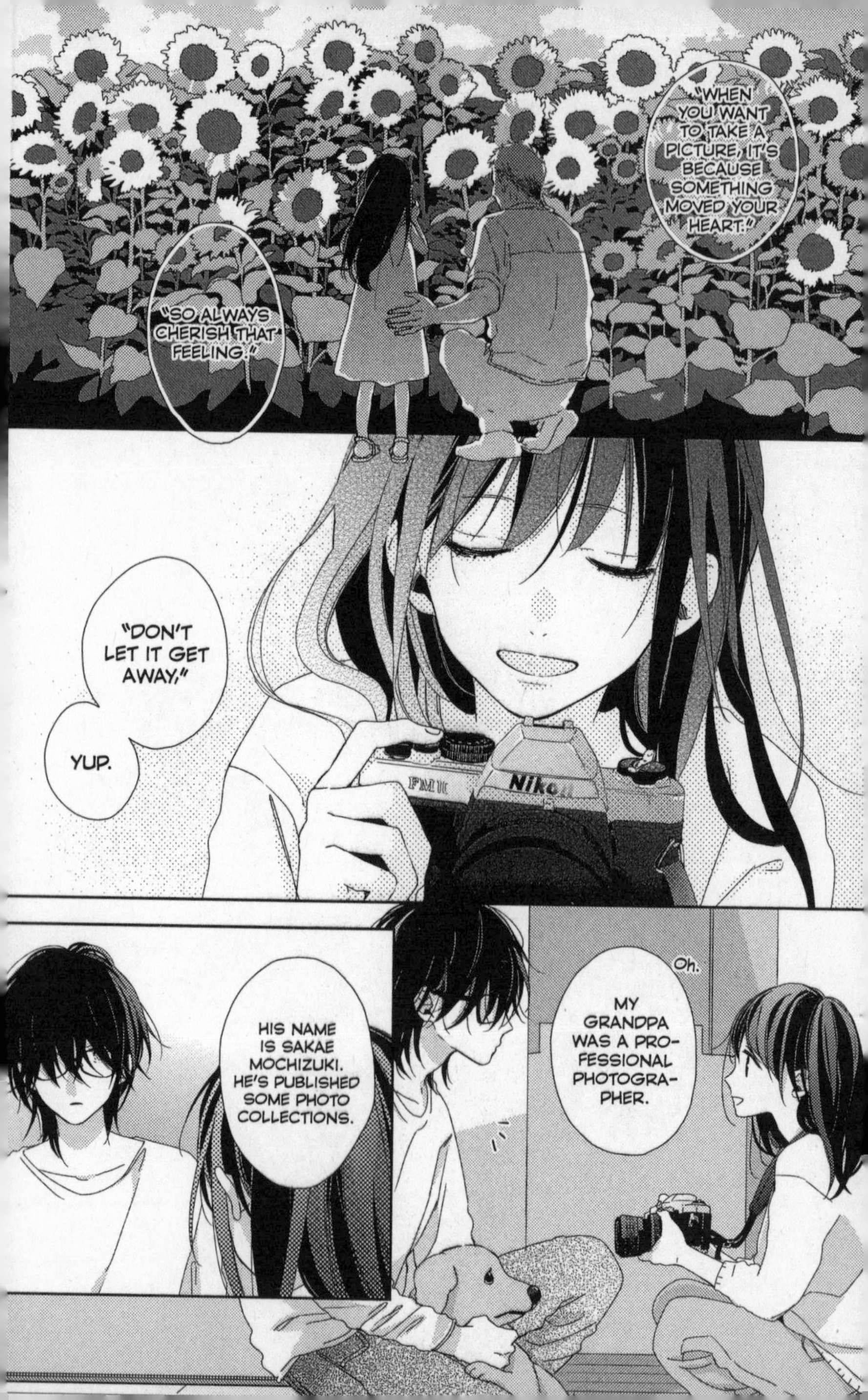
"WHEN YOU WANT TO TAKE A PICTURE, IT'S BECAUSE SOMETHING MOVED YOUR HEART."
"SO ALWAYS CHERISH THAT FEELING."
"DON'T LET IT GET AWAY."
YUP.
FM II
Nikon
Oh.
MY GRANDPA WAS A PROFESSIONAL PHOTOGRAPHER.
HIS NAME IS SAKAE MOCHIZUKI. HE'S PUBLISHED SOME PHOTO COLLECTIONS.

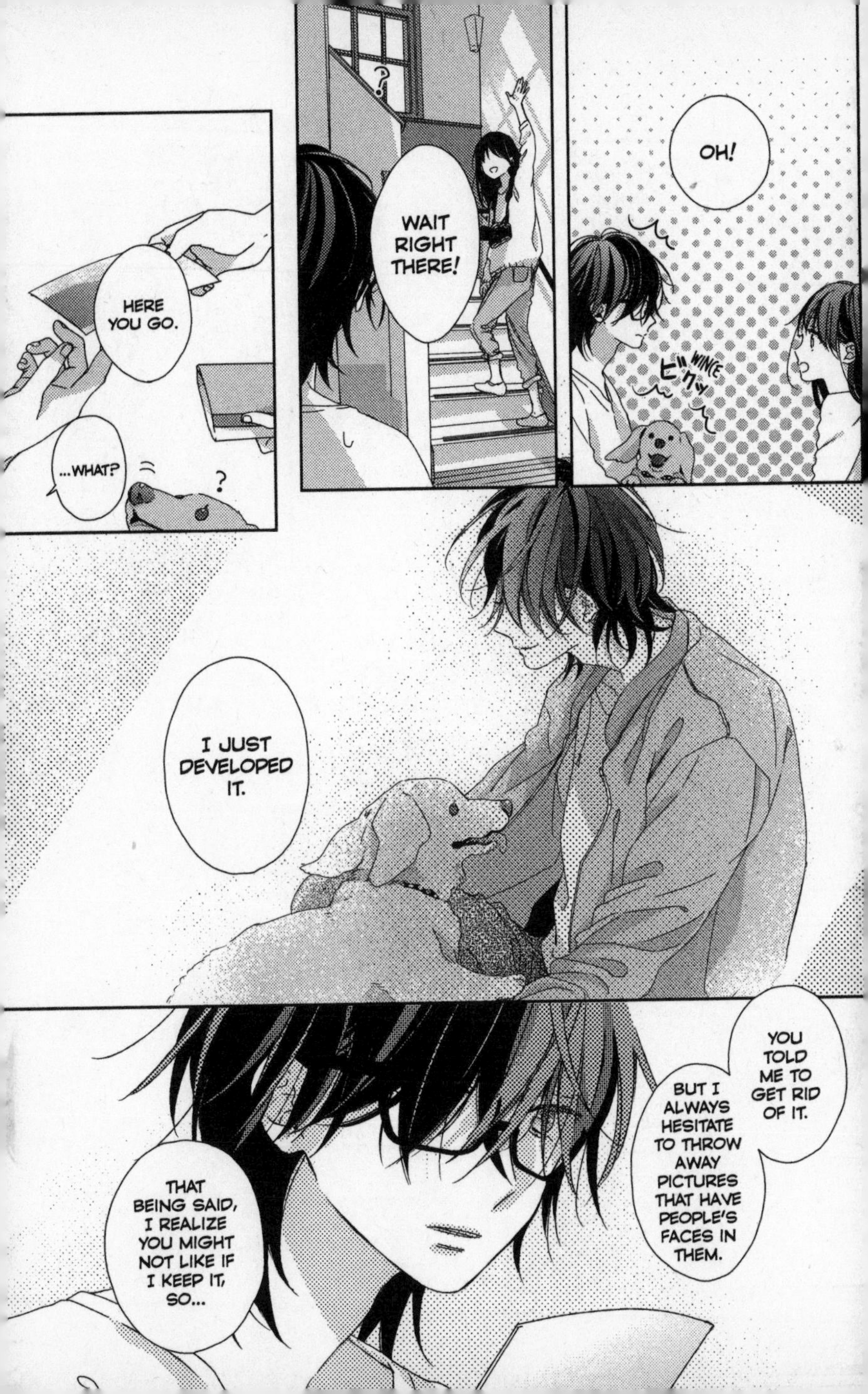
OH!
WINCE
ビクッ
WAIT RIGHT THERE!
HERE YOU GO.
...WHAT?
I JUST DEVELOPED IT.
YOU TOLD ME TO GET RID OF IT.
BUT I ALWAYS HESITATE TO THROW AWAY PICTURES THAT HAVE PEOPLE'S FACES IN THEM.
THAT BEING SAID, I REALIZE YOU MIGHT NOT LIKE IF I KEEP IT, SO...

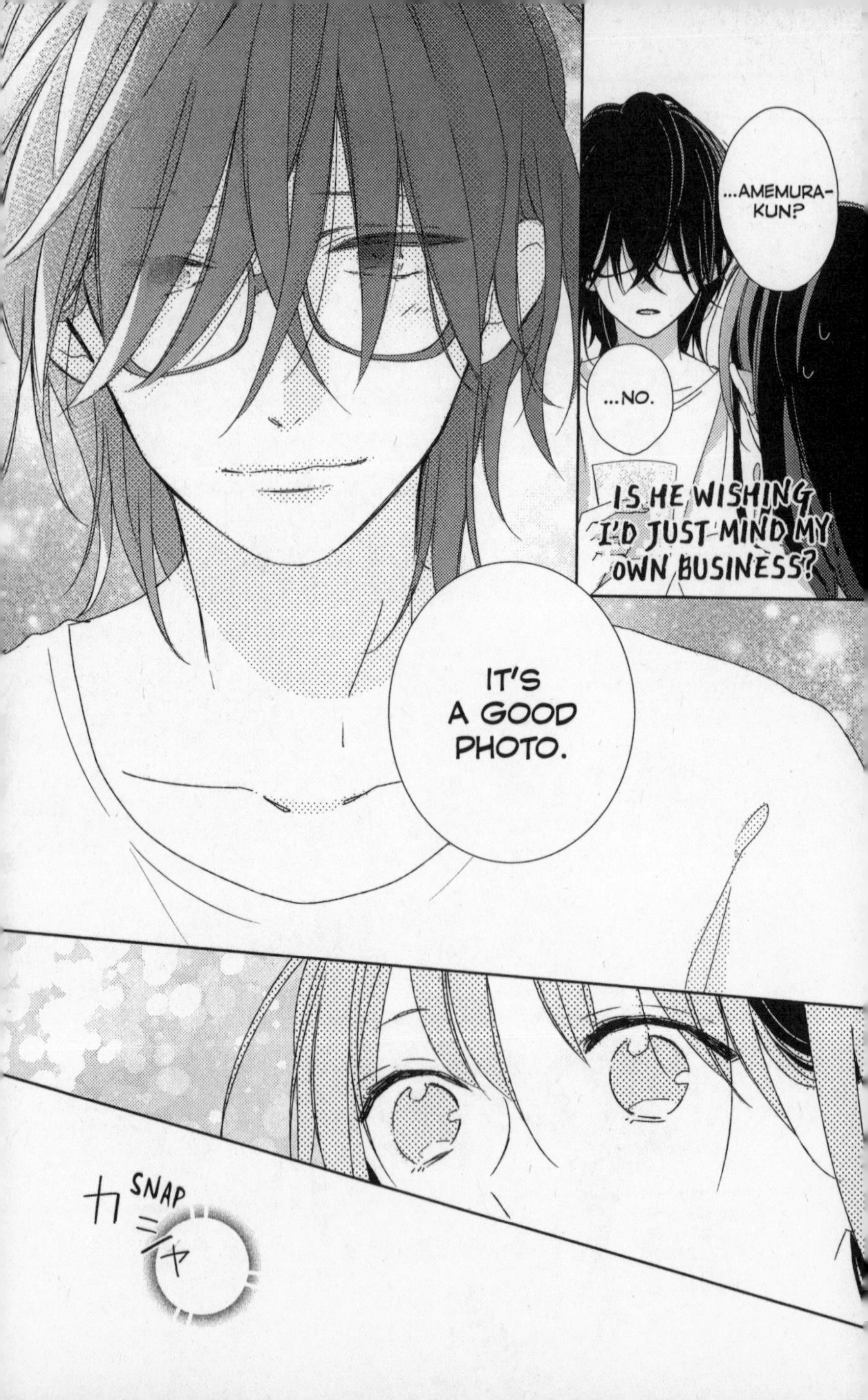
...AMEMURA-KUN?
...NO.
IS HE WISHING I'D JUST MIND MY OWN BUSINESS?
IT'S A GOOD PHOTO.
カシャ
SNAP

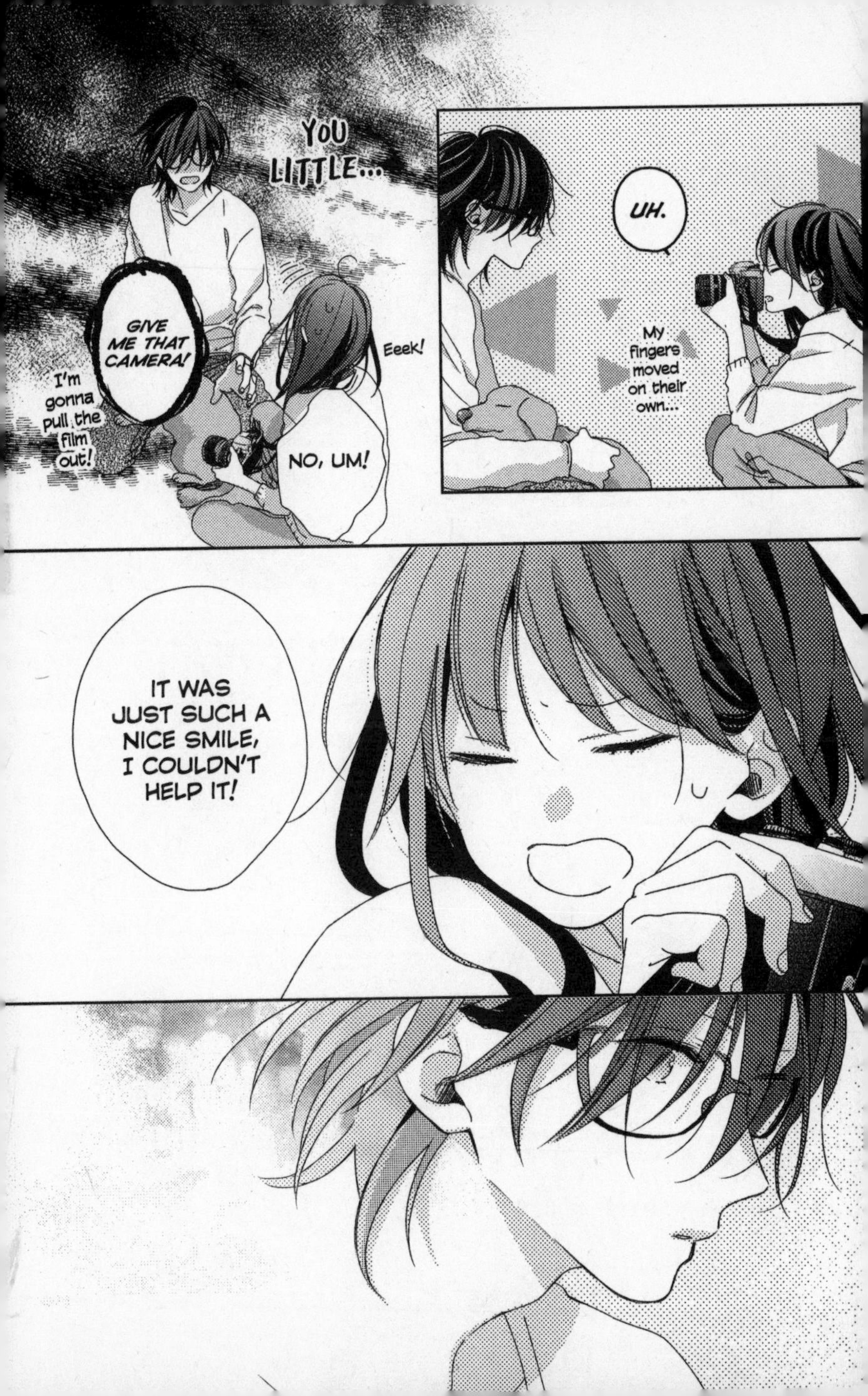
UH.
My fingers moved on their own...
YOU LITTLE...
GIVE ME THAT CAMERA!
I'm gonna pull the film out!
Eeek!
NO, UM!
IT WAS JUST SUCH A NICE SMILE, I COULDN'T HELP IT!

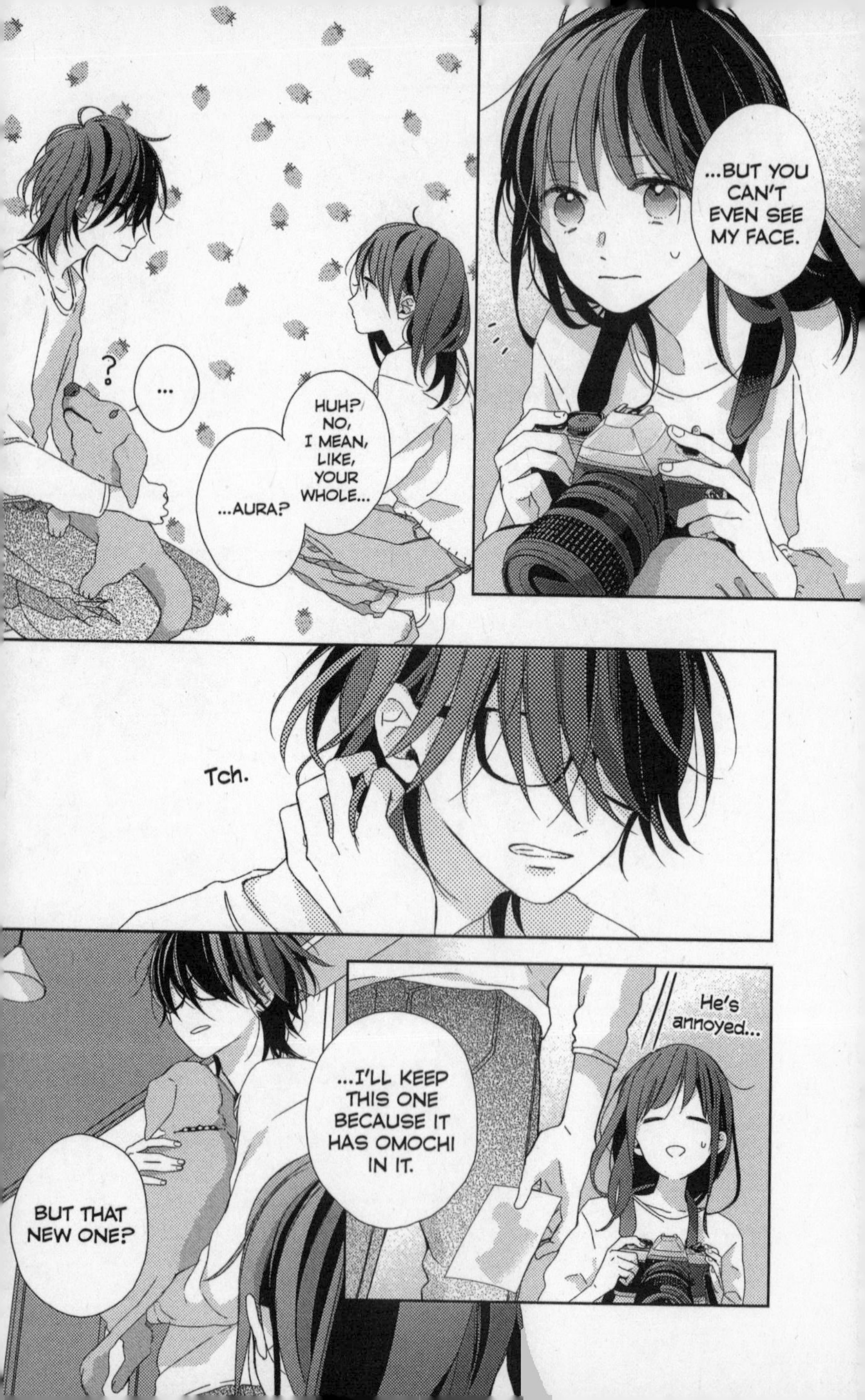
...BUT YOU CAN'T EVEN SEE MY FACE.
?
...
HUH? NO, I MEAN, LIKE, YOUR WHOLE...
...AURA?
Tch.
He's annoyed...
...I'LL KEEP THIS ONE BECAUSE IT HAS OMOCHI IN IT.
BUT THAT NEW ONE?

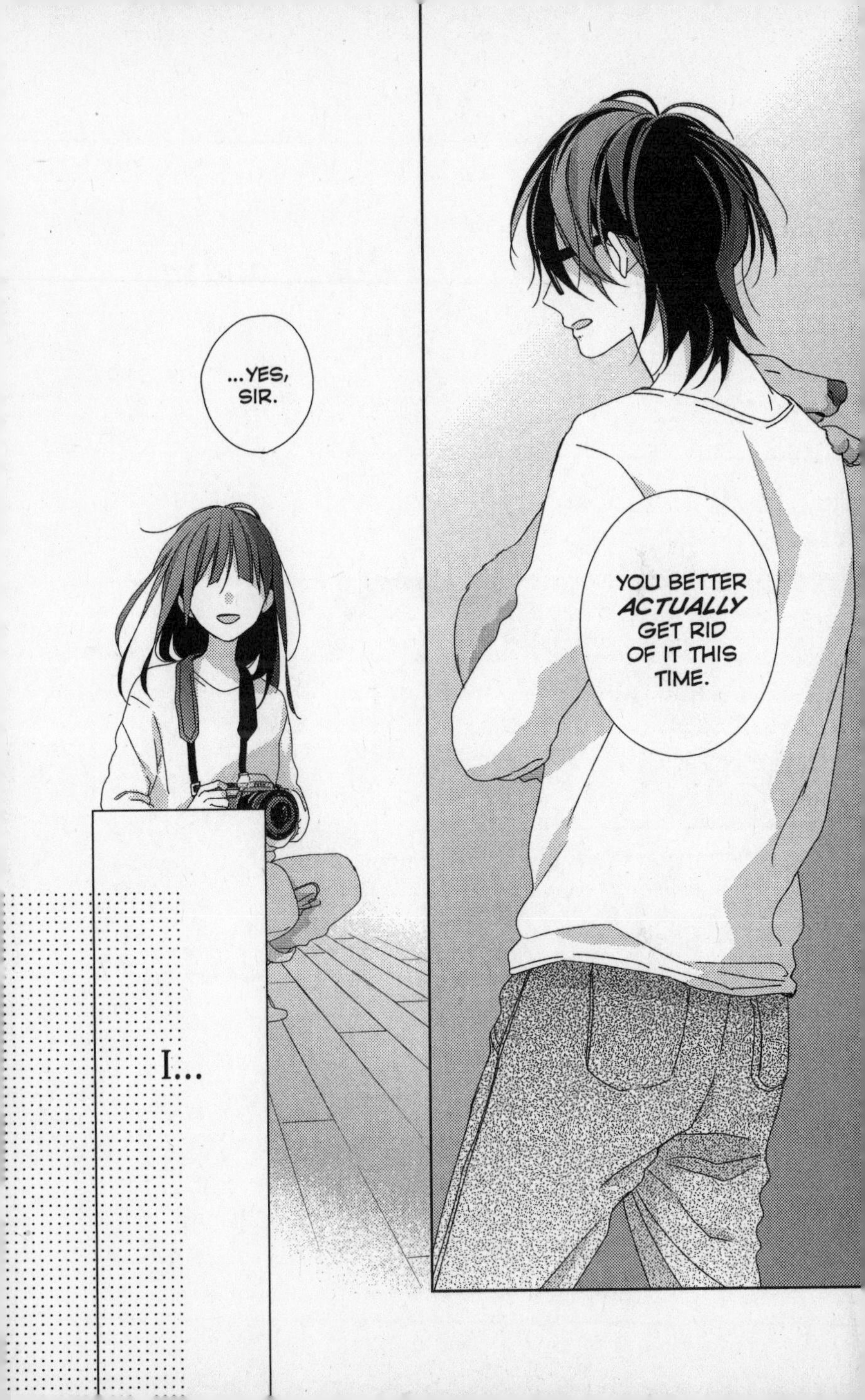
YOU BETTER *ACTUALLY* GET RID OF IT THIS TIME.
...YES, SIR.
I...

I did it again...

Just when I thought things were getting better...

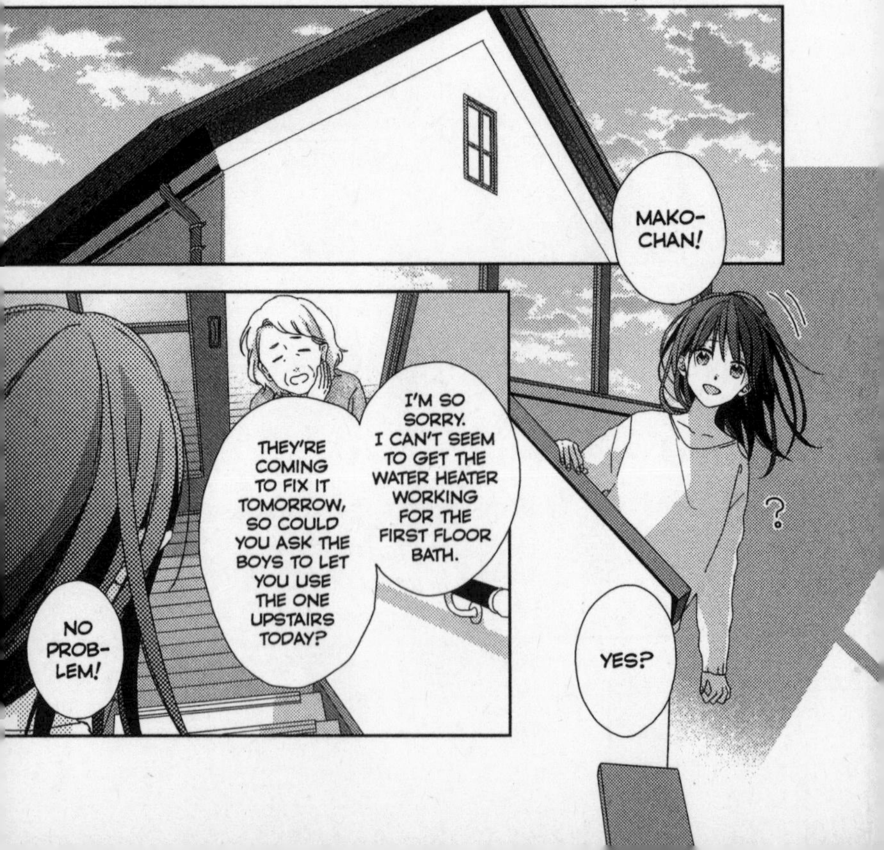
MAKO-CHAN!
YES?
I'M SO SORRY. I CAN'T SEEM TO GET THE WATER HEATER WORKING FOR THE FIRST FLOOR BATH.
THEY'RE COMING TO FIX IT TOMORROW, SO COULD YOU ASK THE BOYS TO LET YOU USE THE ONE UPSTAIRS TODAY?
NO PROB-LEM!

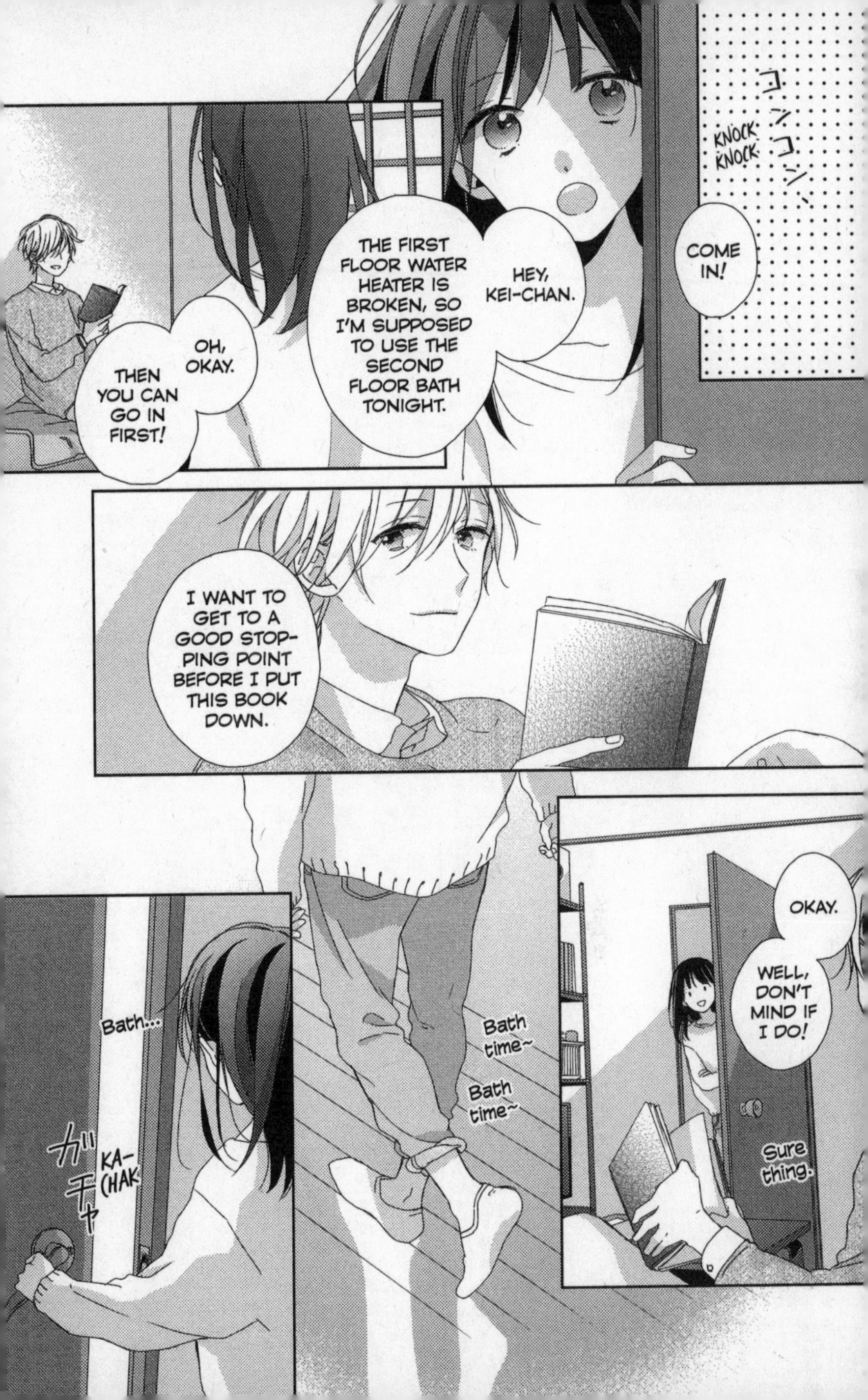
コンコン
KNOCK KNOCK
COME IN!
HEY, KEI-CHAN.
THE FIRST FLOOR WATER HEATER IS BROKEN, SO I'M SUPPOSED TO USE THE SECOND FLOOR BATH TONIGHT.
OH, OKAY.
THEN YOU CAN GO IN FIRST!
I WANT TO GET TO A GOOD STOP-PING POINT BEFORE I PUT THIS BOOK DOWN.
OKAY.
WELL, DON'T MIND IF I DO!
Sure thing.
Bath time~
Bath time~
Bath...
ガチャ
KA-CHAK

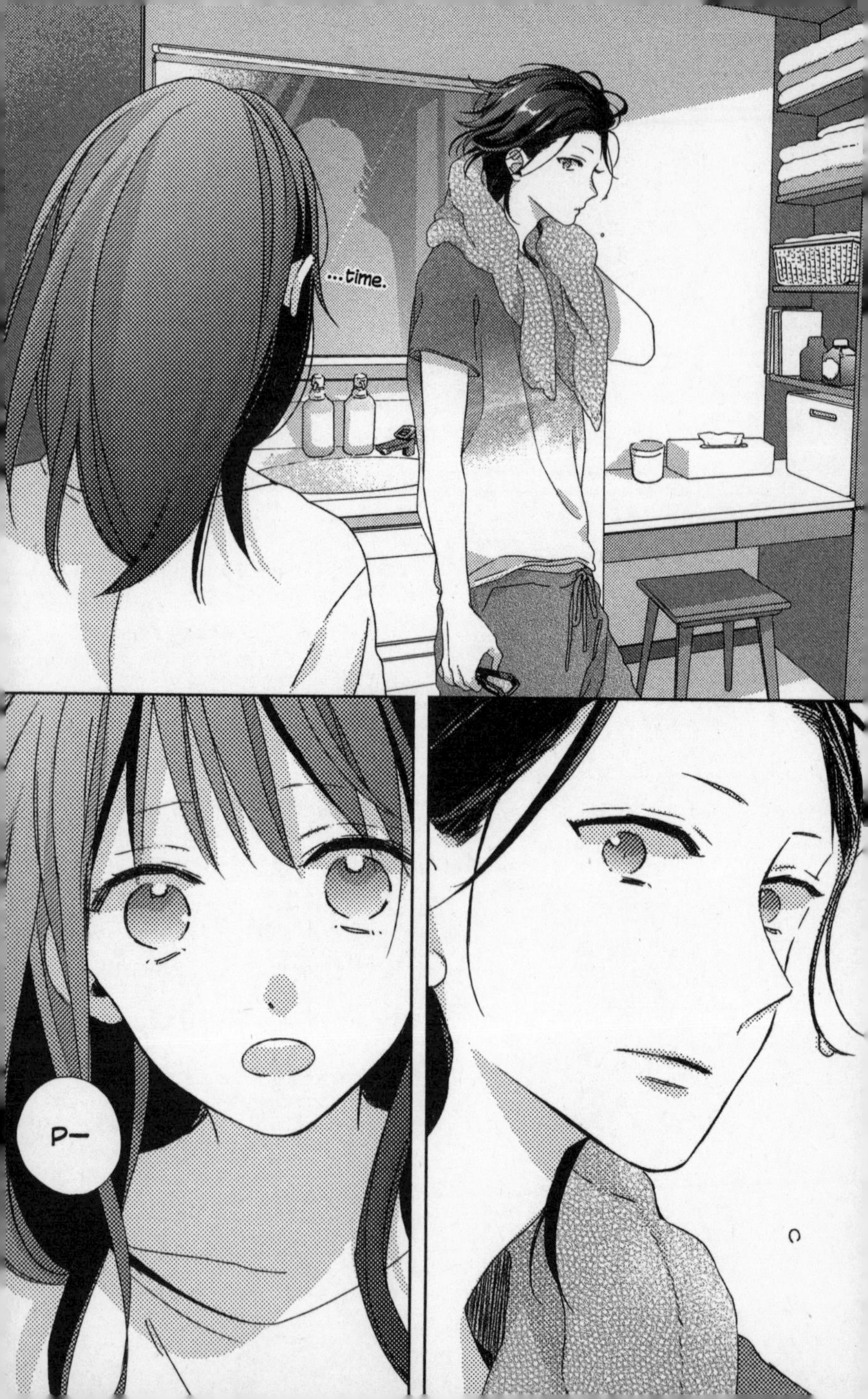
...time.
P–

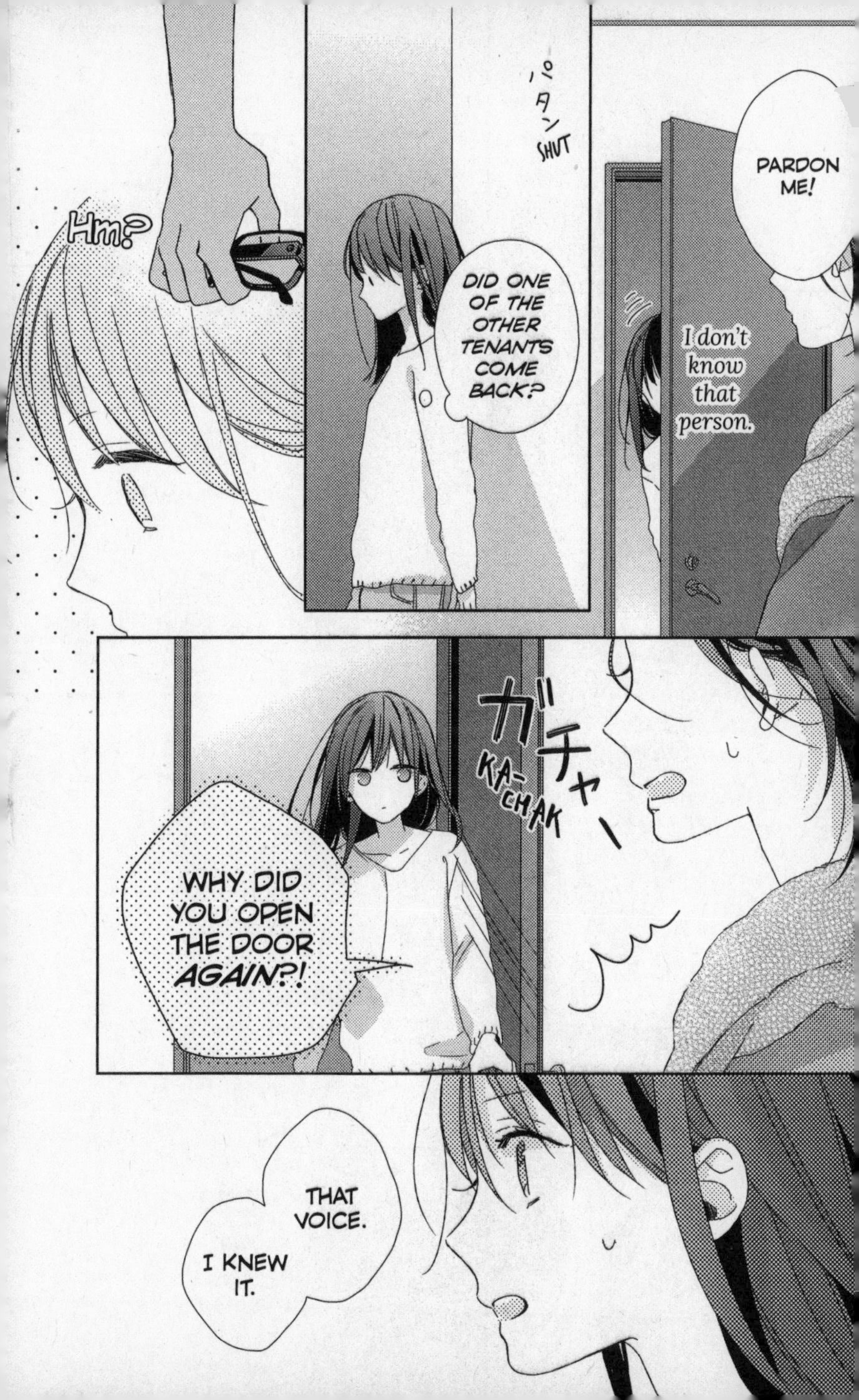
PARDON ME!
I don't know that person.
パタン
SHUT
DID ONE OF THE OTHER TENANTS COME BACK?
Hm?
ガチャー
KA-CHAK
WHY DID YOU OPEN THE DOOR *AGAIN*?!
THAT VOICE.
I KNEW IT.

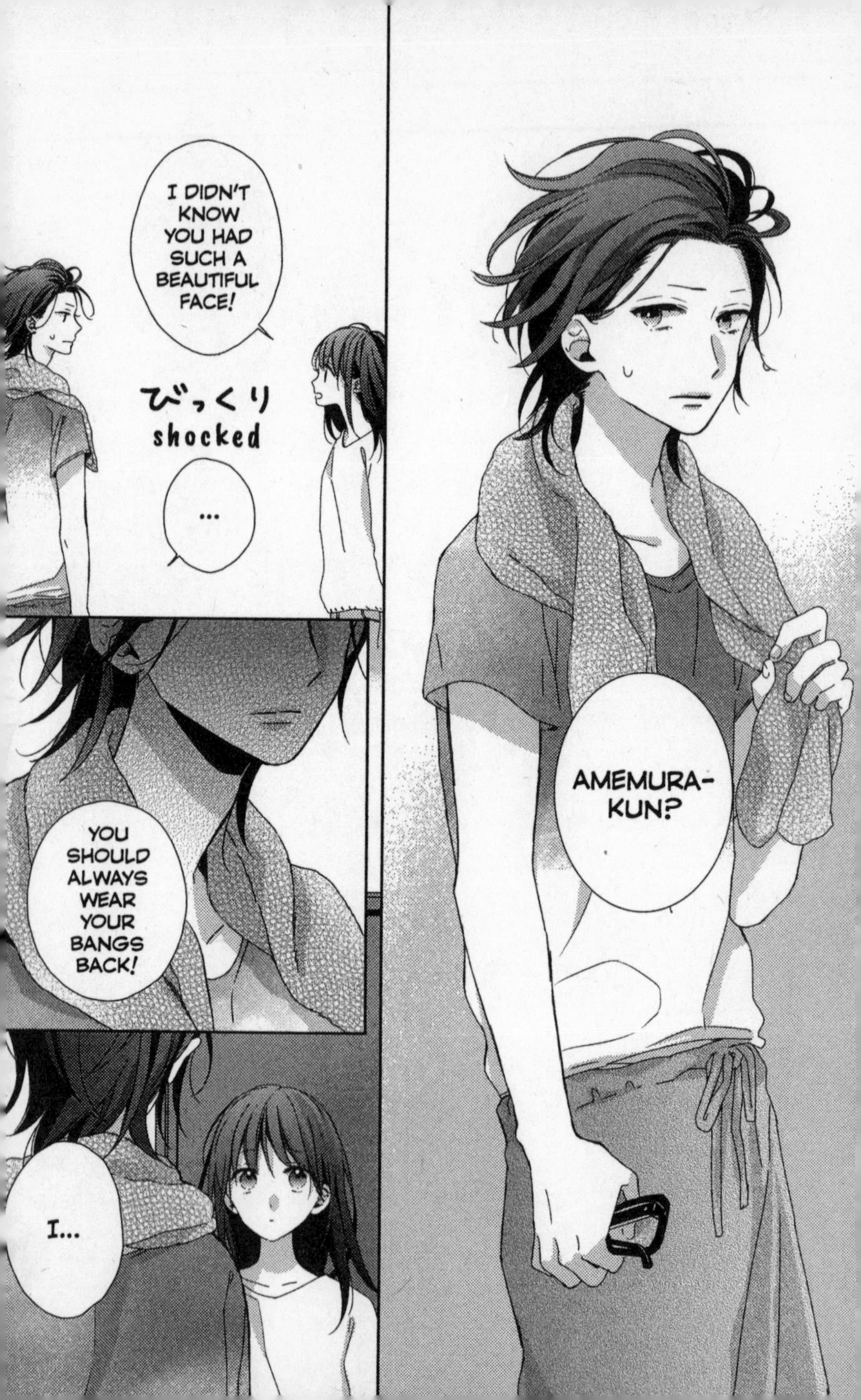
AMEMURA-KUN?
I DIDN'T KNOW YOU HAD SUCH A BEAUTIFUL FACE!
びっくり
shocked
...
YOU SHOULD ALWAYS WEAR YOUR BANGS BACK!
I...

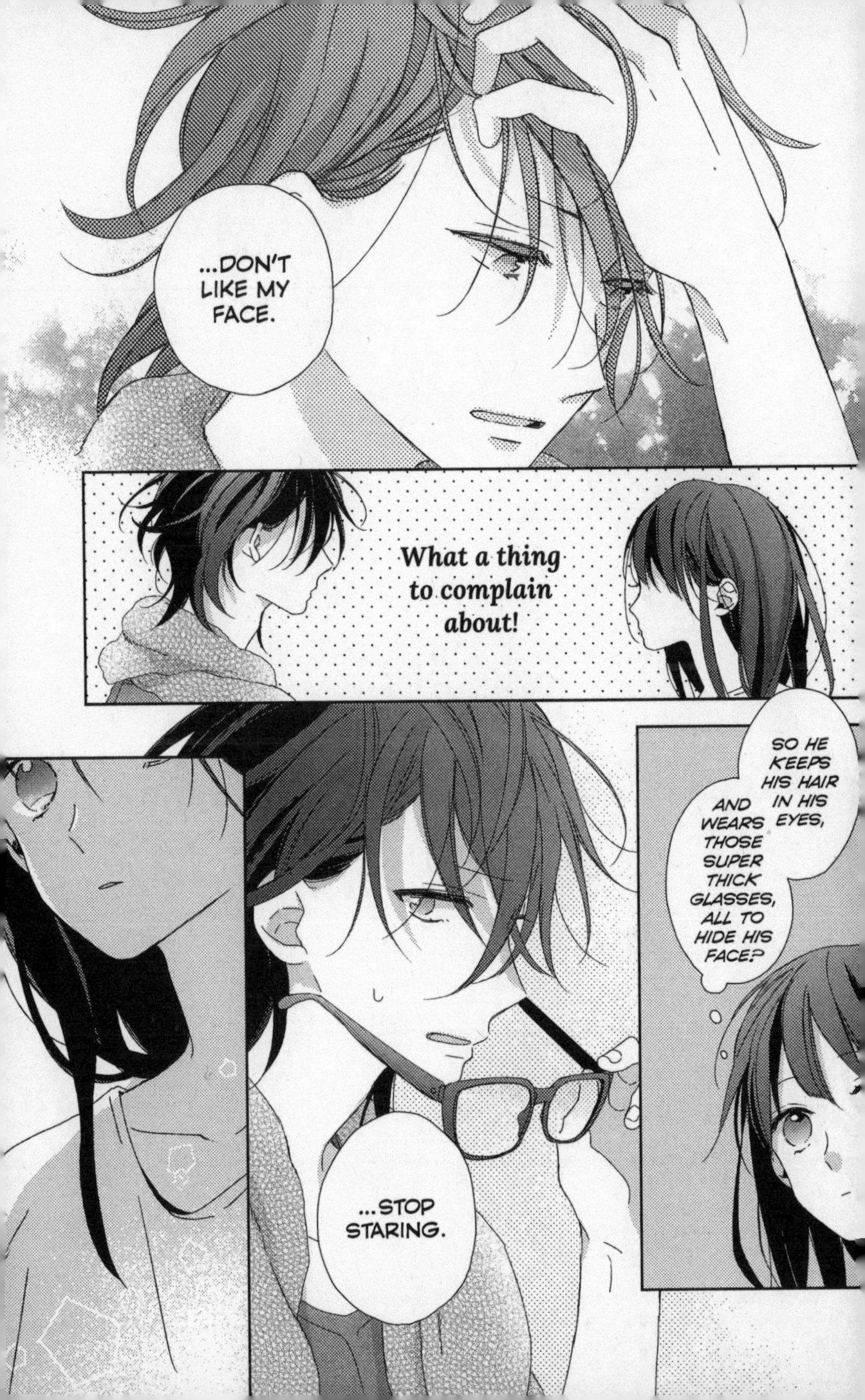
...DON'T LIKE MY FACE.
What a thing to complain about!
SO HE KEEPS HIS HAIR IN HIS EYES,
AND WEARS THOSE SUPER THICK GLASSES, ALL TO HIDE HIS FACE?
...STOP STARING.

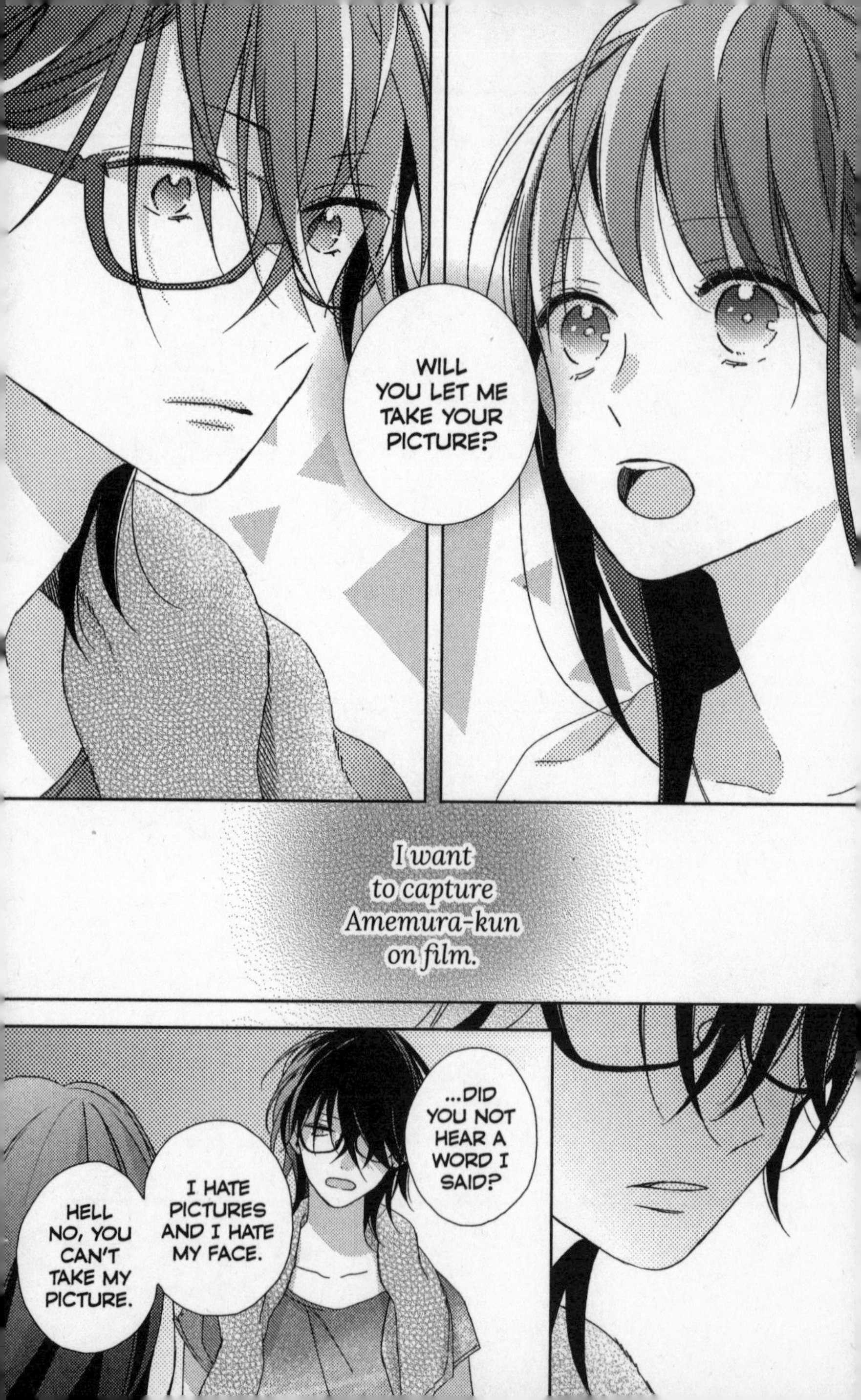
WILL YOU LET ME TAKE YOUR PICTURE?
I want to capture Amemura-kun on film.
...DID YOU NOT HEAR A WORD I SAID?
I HATE PICTURES AND I HATE MY FACE.
HELL NO, YOU CAN'T TAKE MY PICTURE.

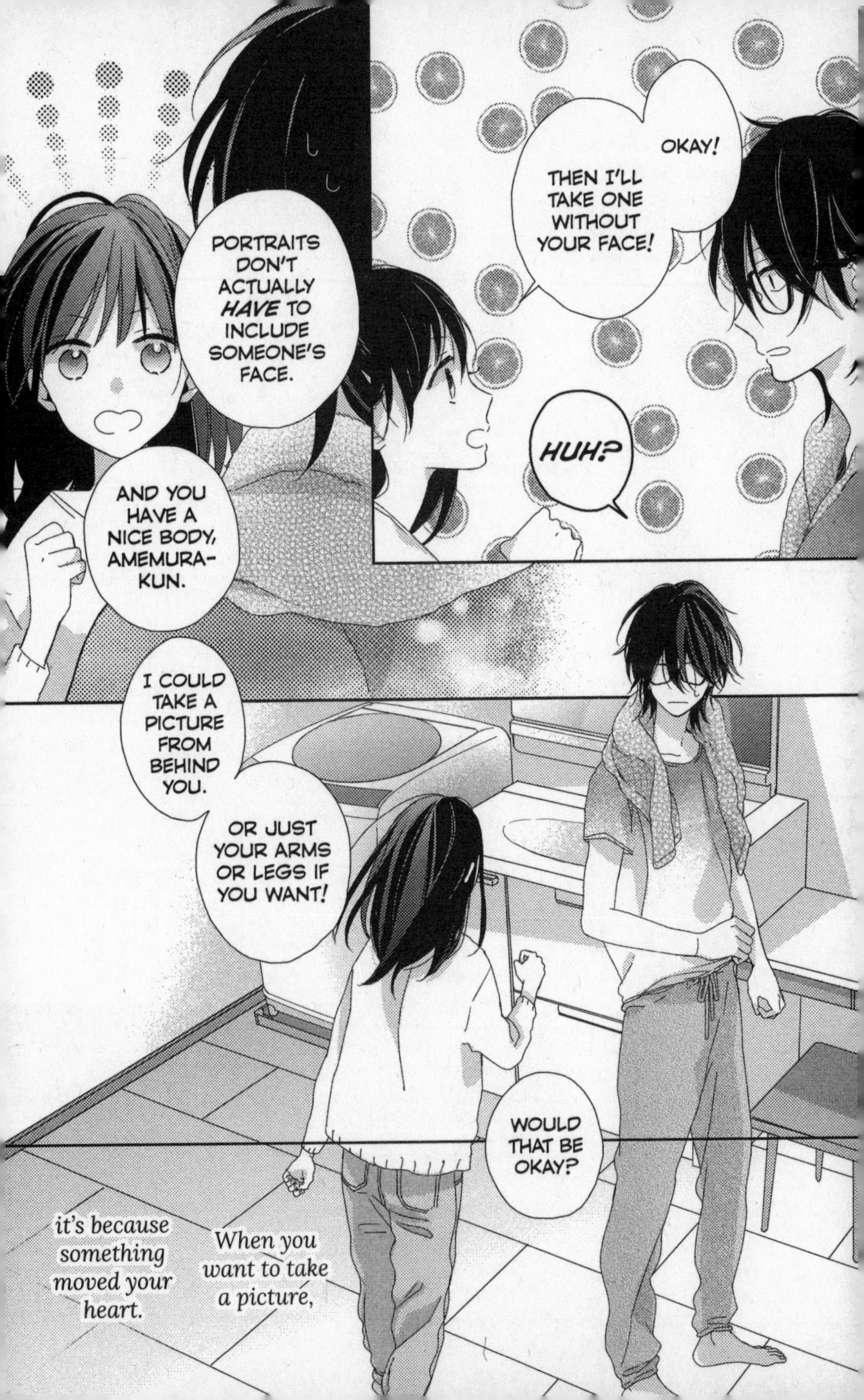
OKAY!
THEN I'LL TAKE ONE WITHOUT YOUR FACE!
HUH?
PORTRAITS DON'T ACTUALLY *HAVE* TO INCLUDE SOMEONE'S FACE.
AND YOU HAVE A NICE BODY, AMEMURA-KUN.
I COULD TAKE A PICTURE FROM BEHIND YOU.
OR JUST YOUR ARMS OR LEGS IF YOU WANT!
WOULD THAT BE OKAY?
When you want to take a picture,
it's because something moved your heart.

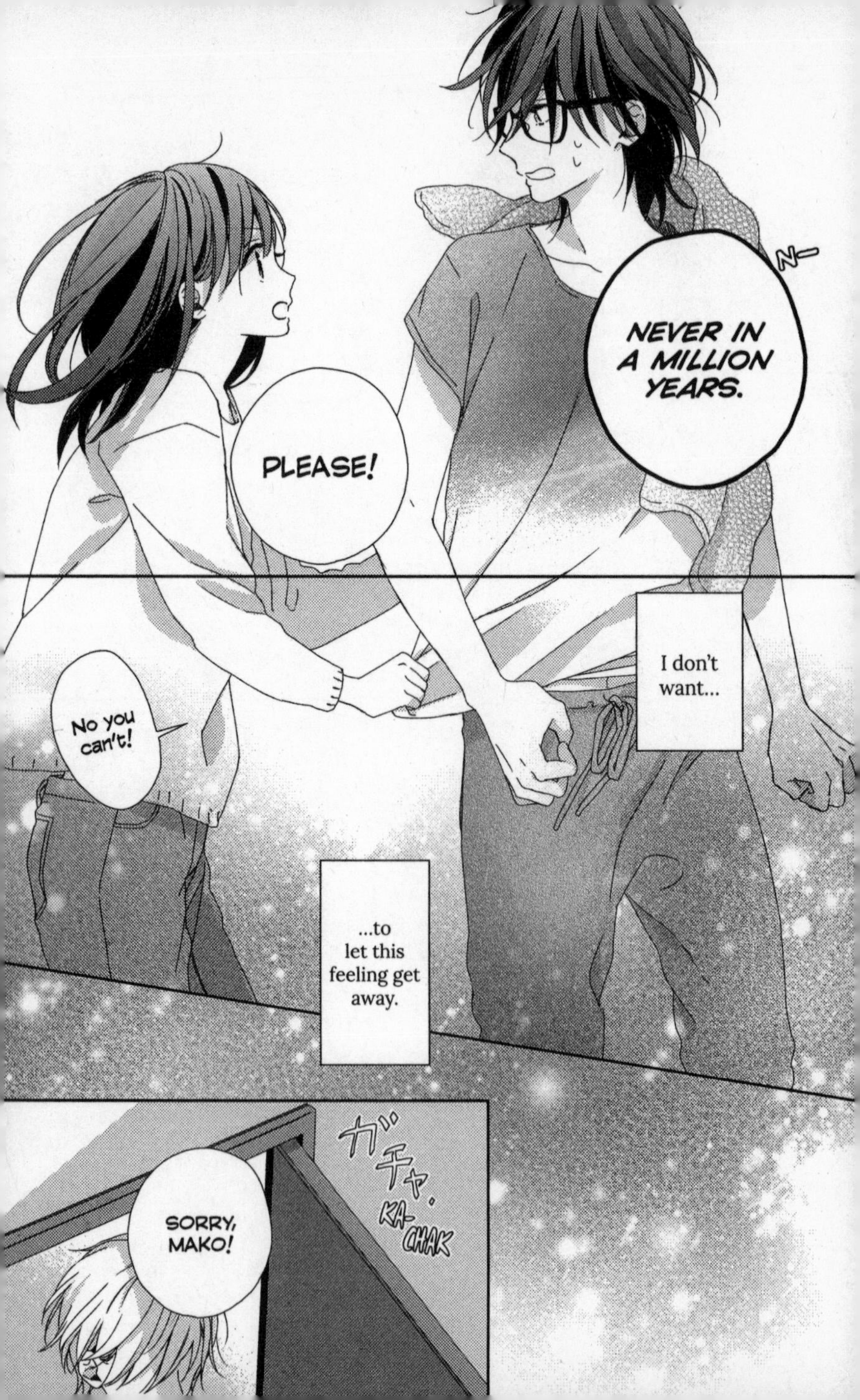
N—
NEVER IN A MILLION YEARS.
PLEASE!
I don't want...
No you can't!
...to let this feeling get away.
ガチャ
KA-CHAK
SORRY, MAKO!

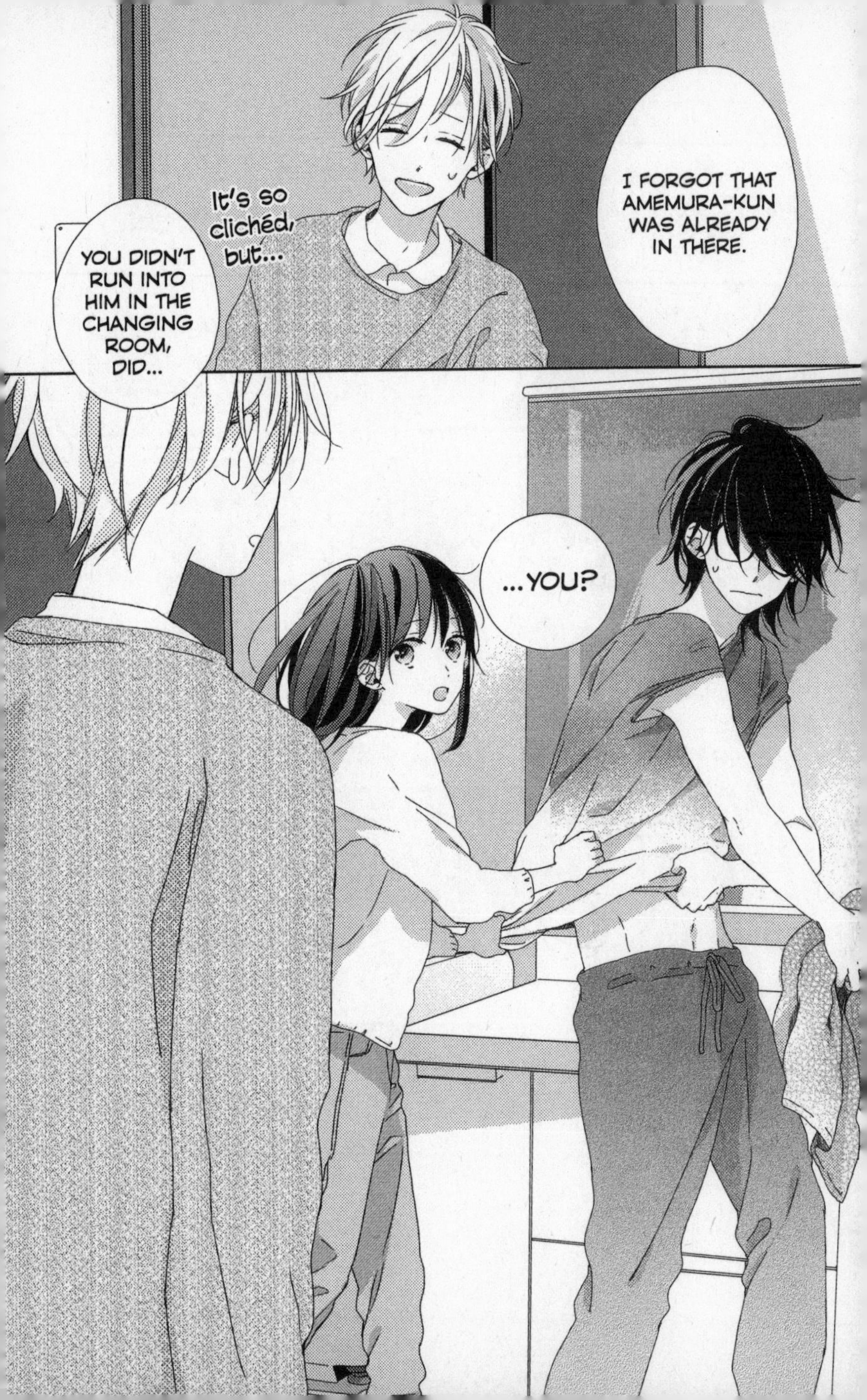
I FORGOT THAT AMEMURA-KUN WAS ALREADY IN THERE.
It's so clichéd, but...
YOU DIDN'T RUN INTO HIM IN THE CHANGING ROOM, DID...
...YOU?

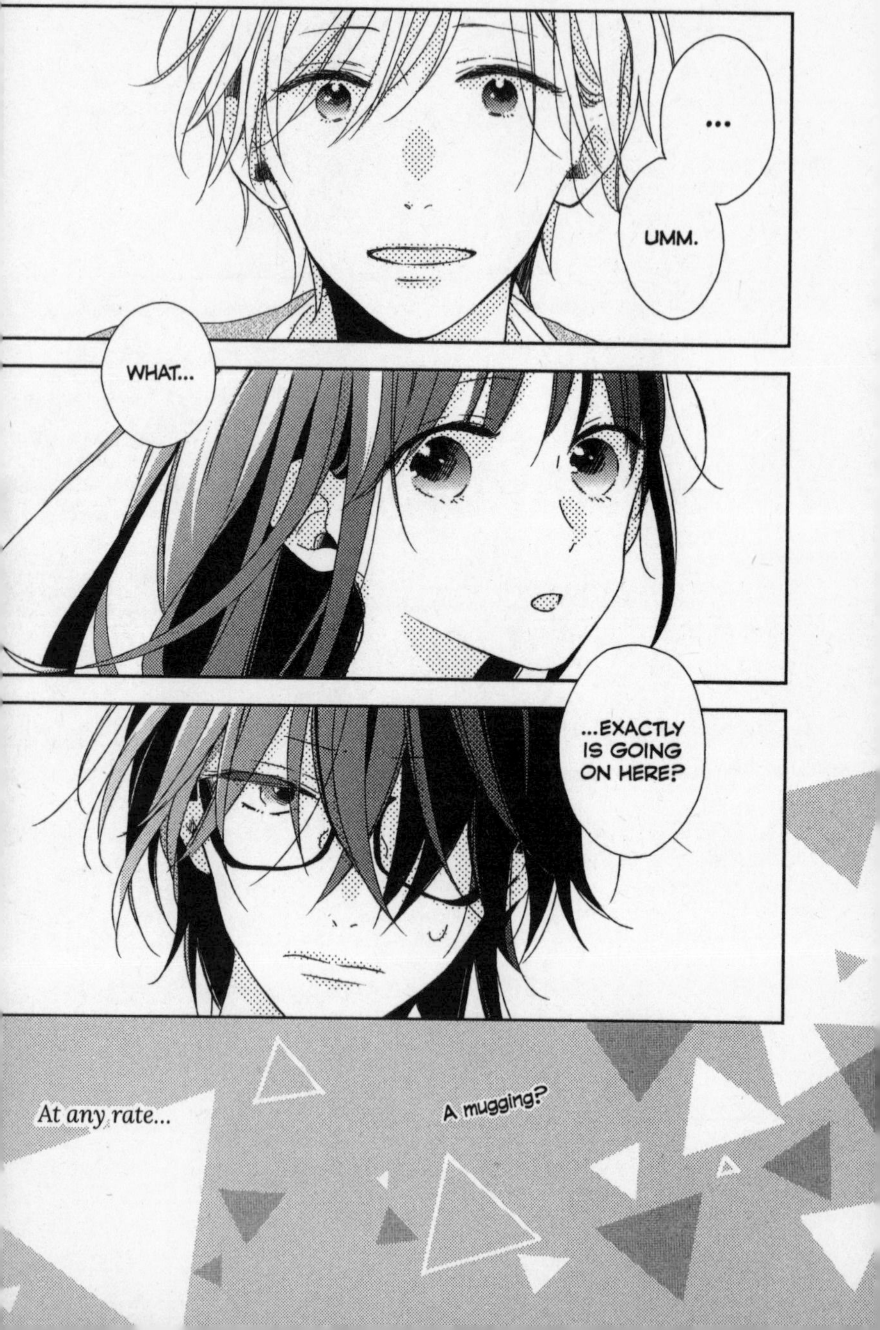
...
UMM.
WHAT...
...EXACTLY IS GOING ON HERE?
A mugging?
At any rate...

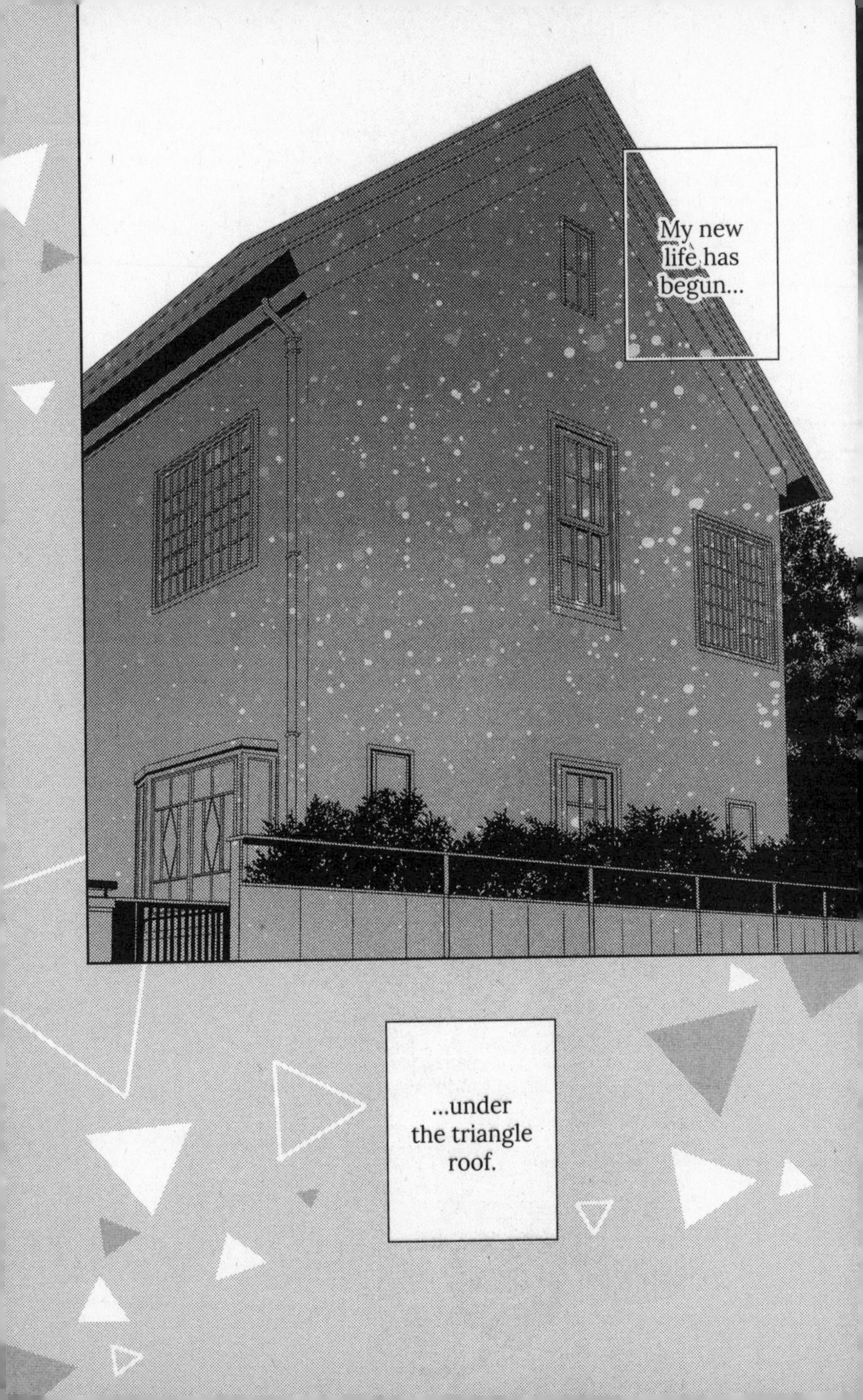
My new life has begun...
...under the triangle roof.

LOVE IN FOCUS

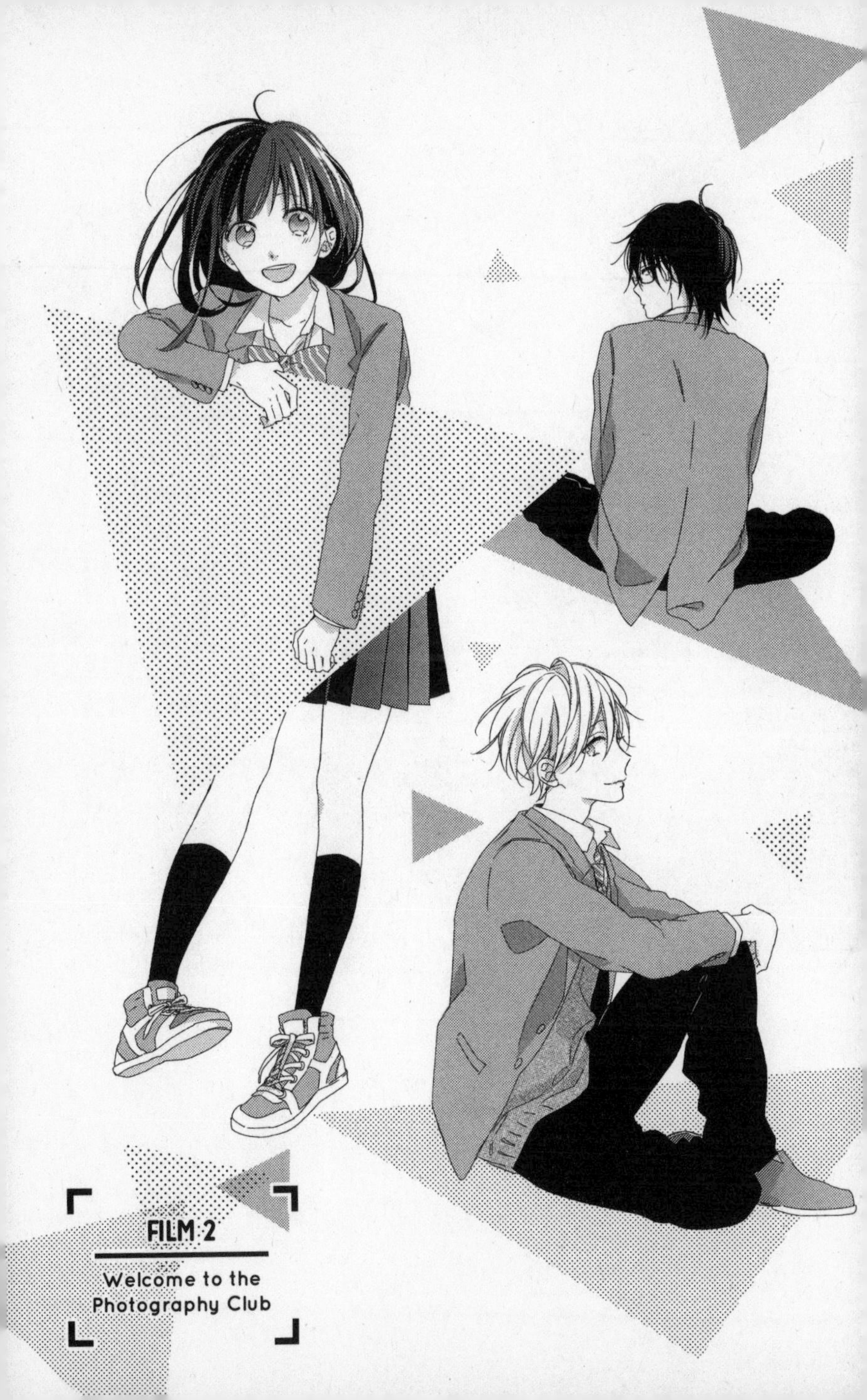

FILM 2

Welcome to the Photography Club

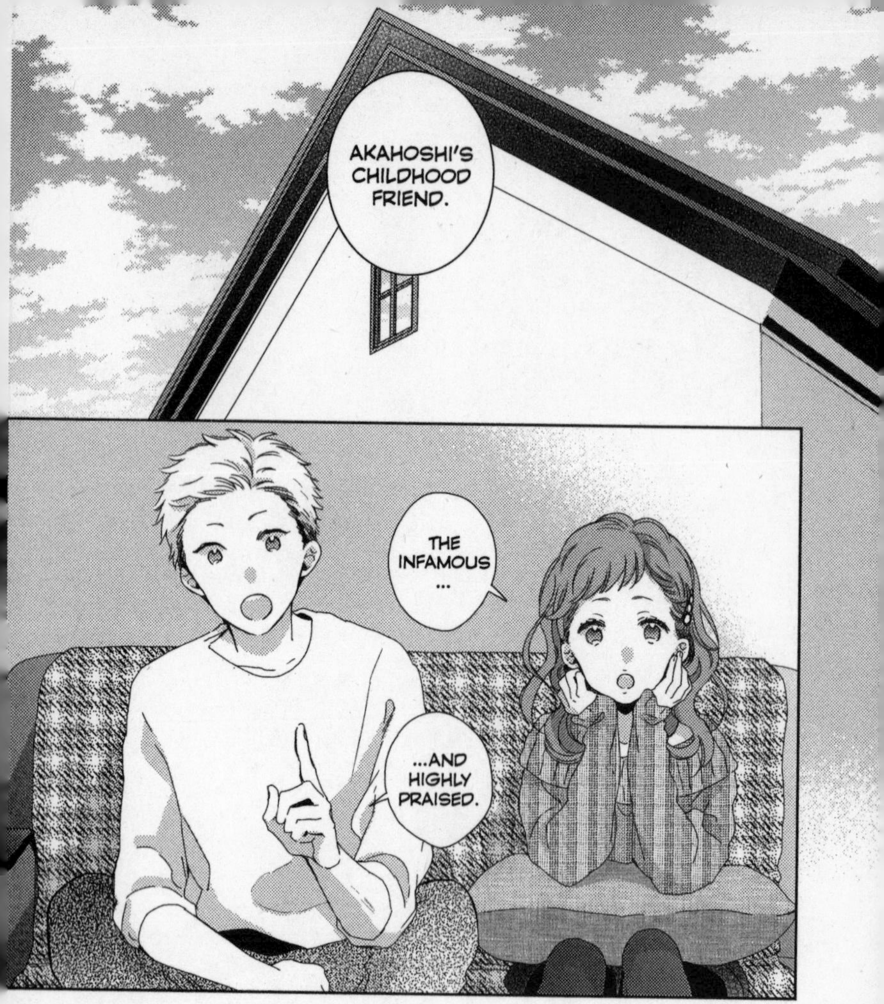
AKAHOSHI'S CHILDHOOD FRIEND.
THE INFAMOUS ...
...AND HIGHLY PRAISED.

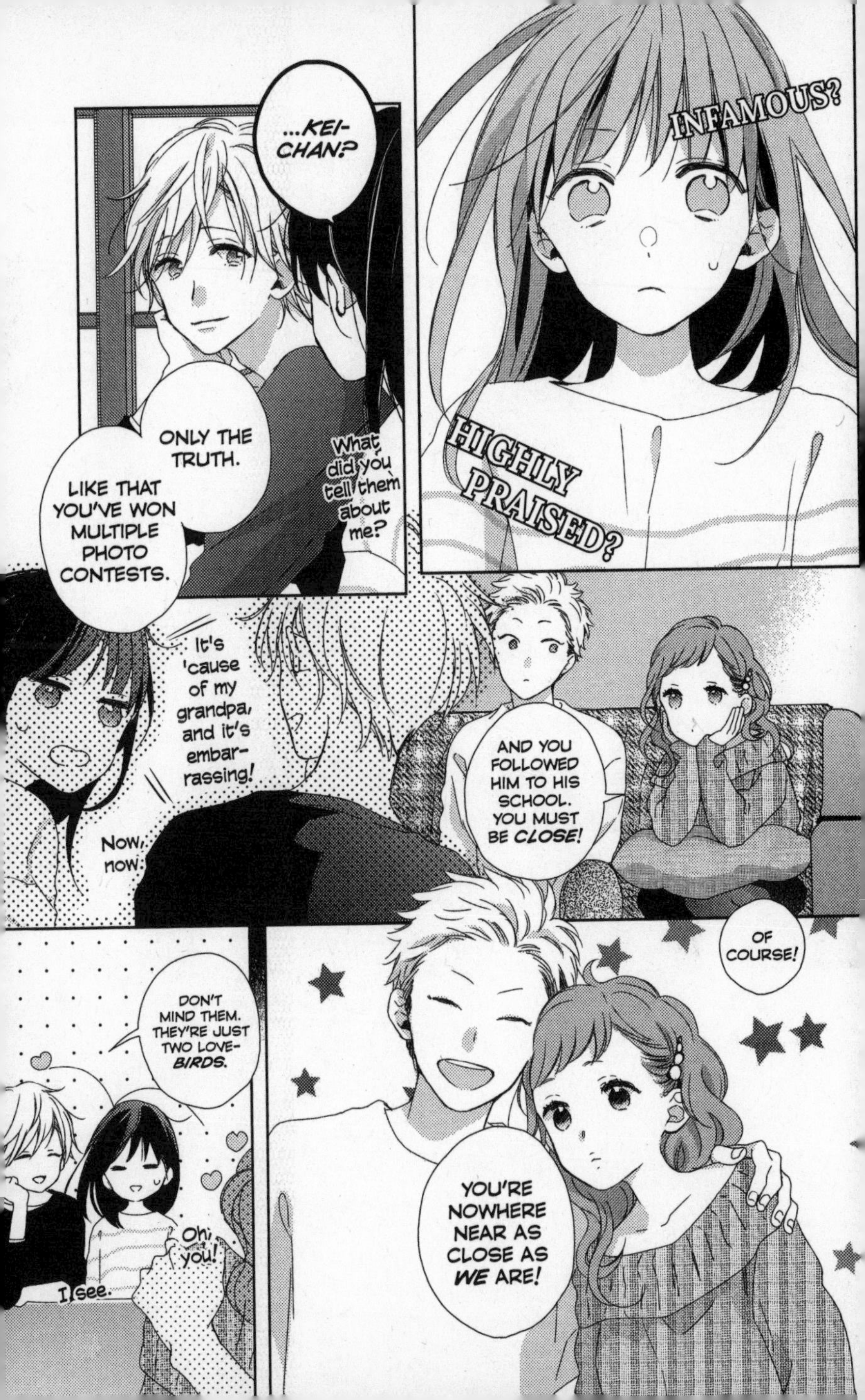
INFAMOUS?
HIGHLY PRAISED?
...KEI-CHAN?
What did you tell them about me?
ONLY THE TRUTH.
LIKE THAT YOU'VE WON MULTIPLE PHOTO CONTESTS.
AND YOU FOLLOWED HIM TO HIS SCHOOL. YOU MUST BE *CLOSE*!
It's 'cause of my grandpa, and it's embarrassing!
Now, now.
OF COURSE!
YOU'RE NOWHERE NEAR AS CLOSE AS *WE* ARE!
DON'T MIND THEM. THEY'RE JUST TWO LOVE-*BIRDS*.
Oh, you!
I see.

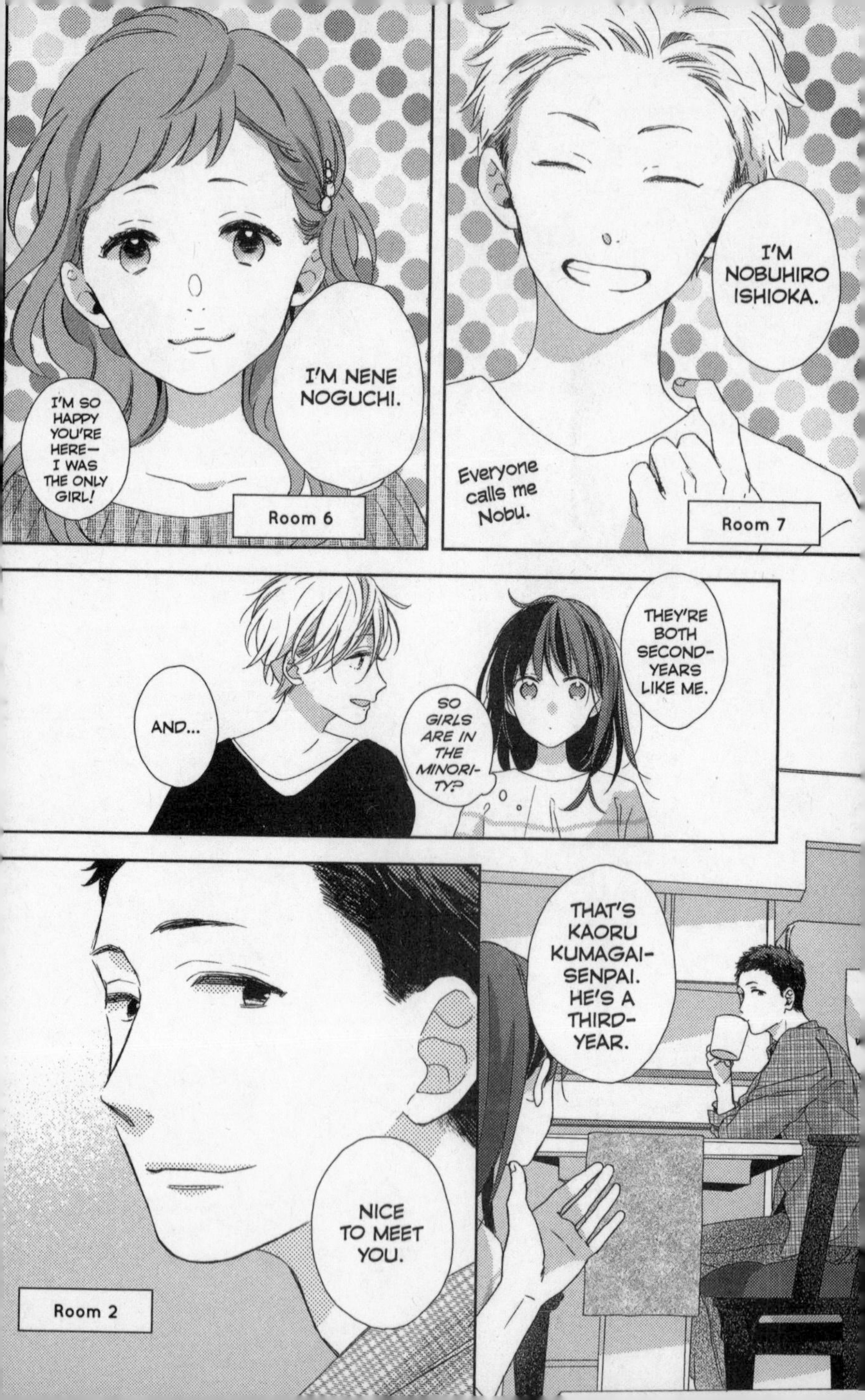
I'M NOBUHIRO ISHIOKA.
Everyone calls me Nobu.
Room 7
I'M NENE NOGUCHI.
I'M SO HAPPY YOU'RE HERE—I WAS THE ONLY GIRL!
Room 6
THEY'RE BOTH SECOND-YEARS LIKE ME.
SO GIRLS ARE IN THE MINORITY?
AND...
THAT'S KAORU KUMAGAI-SENPAI. HE'S A THIRD-YEAR.
NICE TO MEET YOU.
Room 2

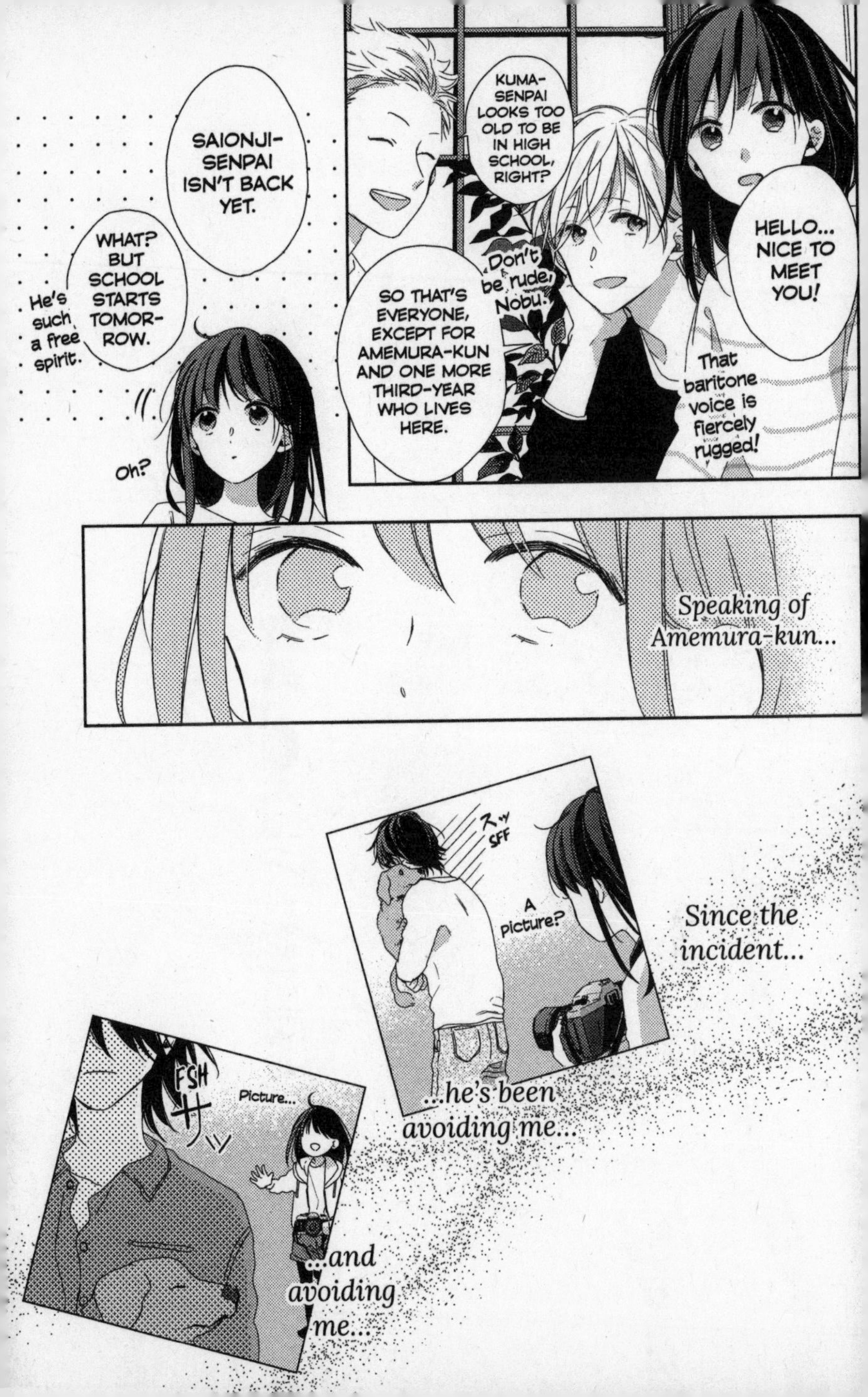
HELLO... NICE TO MEET YOU!
KUMA-SENPAI LOOKS TOO OLD TO BE IN HIGH SCHOOL, RIGHT?
That baritone voice is fiercely rugged!
Don't be rude, Nobu.
SO THAT'S EVERYONE, EXCEPT FOR AMEMURA-KUN AND ONE MORE THIRD-YEAR WHO LIVES HERE.
SAIONJI-SENPAI ISN'T BACK YET.
WHAT? BUT SCHOOL STARTS TOMORROW.
He's such a free spirit.
Oh?
Speaking of Amemura-kun...
Since the incident...
SFF
A picture?
...he's been avoiding me...
FSH
Picture...
...and avoiding me...

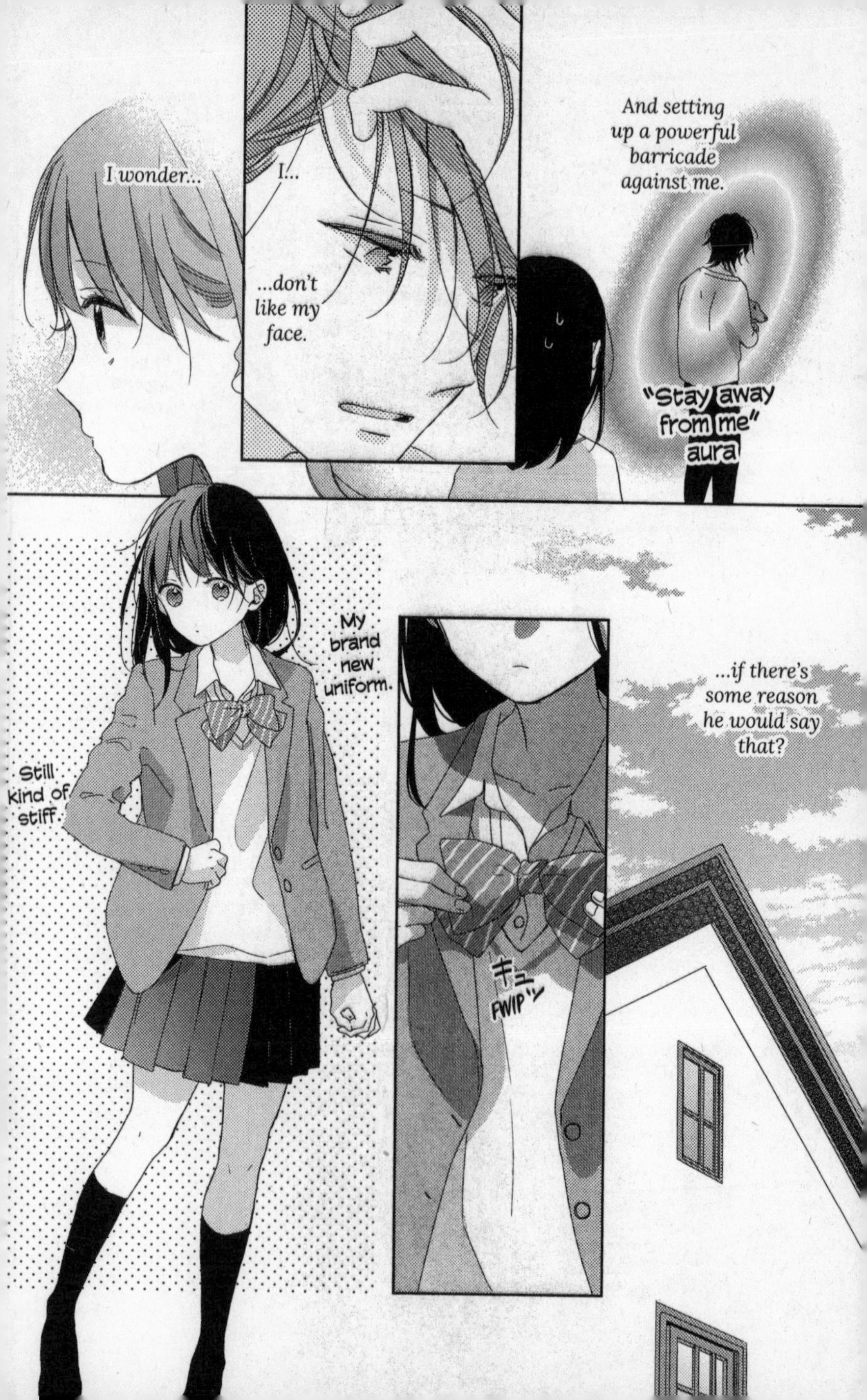
And setting up a powerful barricade against me.
"Stay away from me" aura
I...
...don't like my face.
I wonder...
...if there's some reason he would say that?
キュッ
FWIP
My brand new uniform.
Still kind of stiff.

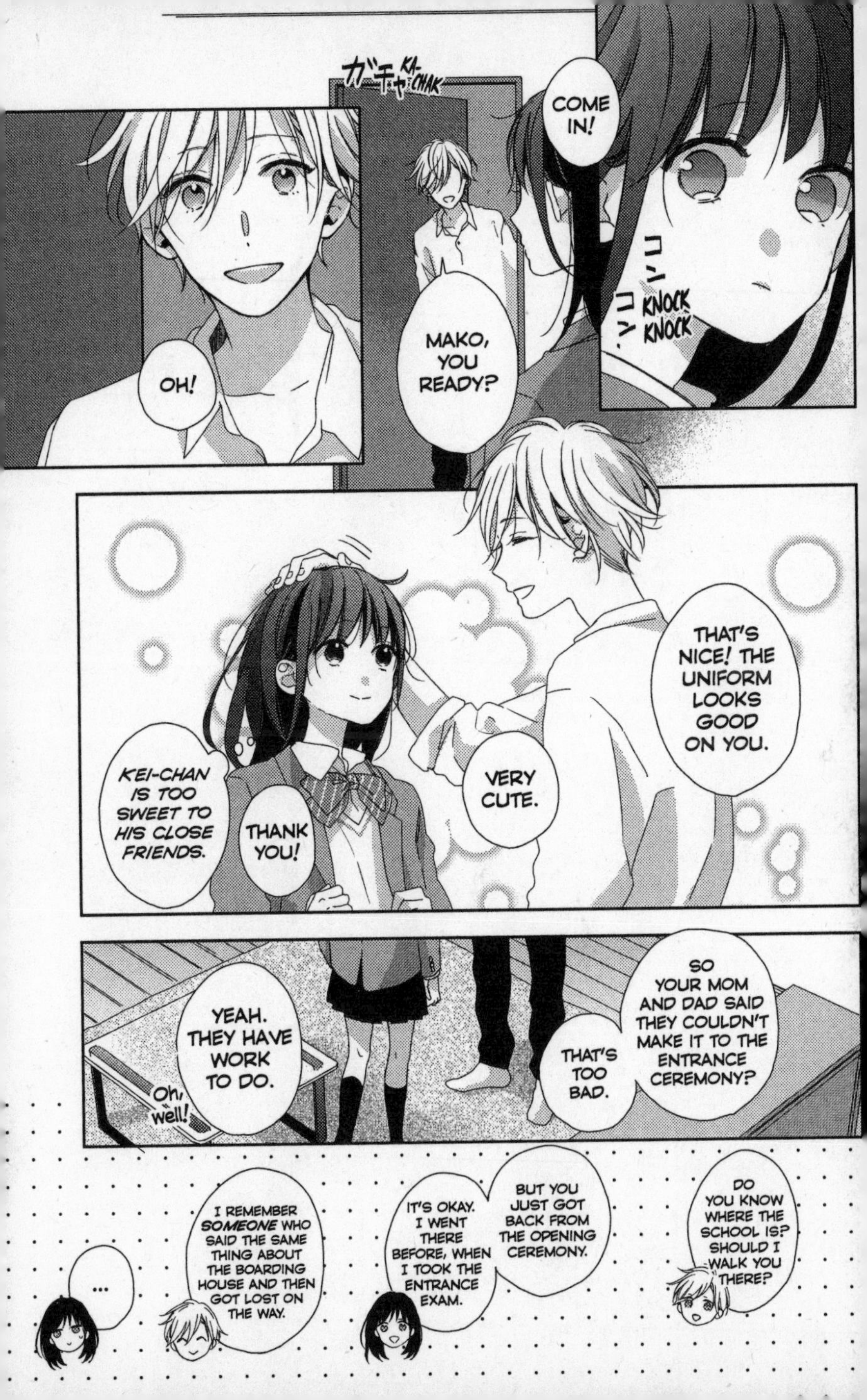
コンコン
KNOCK KNOCK
COME IN!
ガチャ
KA-CHAK
MAKO, YOU READY?
OH!
THAT'S NICE! THE UNIFORM LOOKS GOOD ON YOU.
VERY CUTE.
THANK YOU!
KEI-CHAN IS TOO SWEET TO HIS CLOSE FRIENDS.
SO YOUR MOM AND DAD SAID THEY COULDN'T MAKE IT TO THE ENTRANCE CEREMONY?
THAT'S TOO BAD.
YEAH. THEY HAVE WORK TO DO.
Oh, well!
DO YOU KNOW WHERE THE SCHOOL IS? SHOULD I WALK YOU THERE?
BUT YOU JUST GOT BACK FROM THE OPENING CEREMONY.
IT'S OKAY. I WENT THERE BEFORE, WHEN I TOOK THE ENTRANCE EXAM.
I REMEMBER SOMEONE WHO SAID THE SAME THING ABOUT THE BOARDING HOUSE AND THEN GOT LOST ON THE WAY.
...

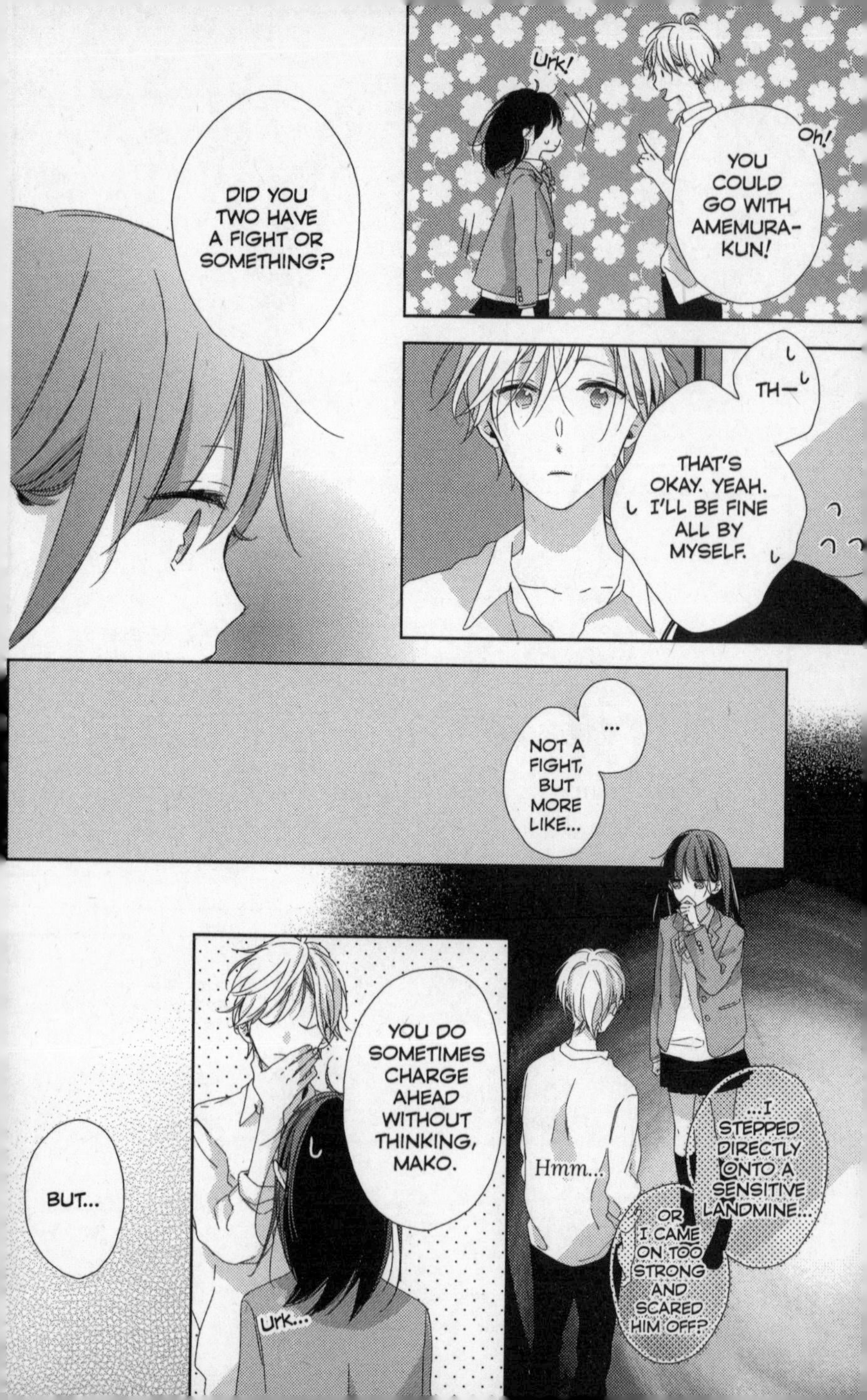
Oh!
YOU COULD GO WITH AMEMURA-KUN!
Urk!
TH—
THAT'S OKAY. YEAH. I'LL BE FINE ALL BY MYSELF.
DID YOU TWO HAVE A FIGHT OR SOMETHING?
...
NOT A FIGHT, BUT MORE LIKE...
...I STEPPED DIRECTLY ONTO A SENSITIVE LANDMINE...
OR I CAME ON TOO STRONG AND SCARED HIM OFF?
Hmm...
YOU DO SOMETIMES CHARGE AHEAD WITHOUT THINKING, MAKO.
Urk...
BUT...

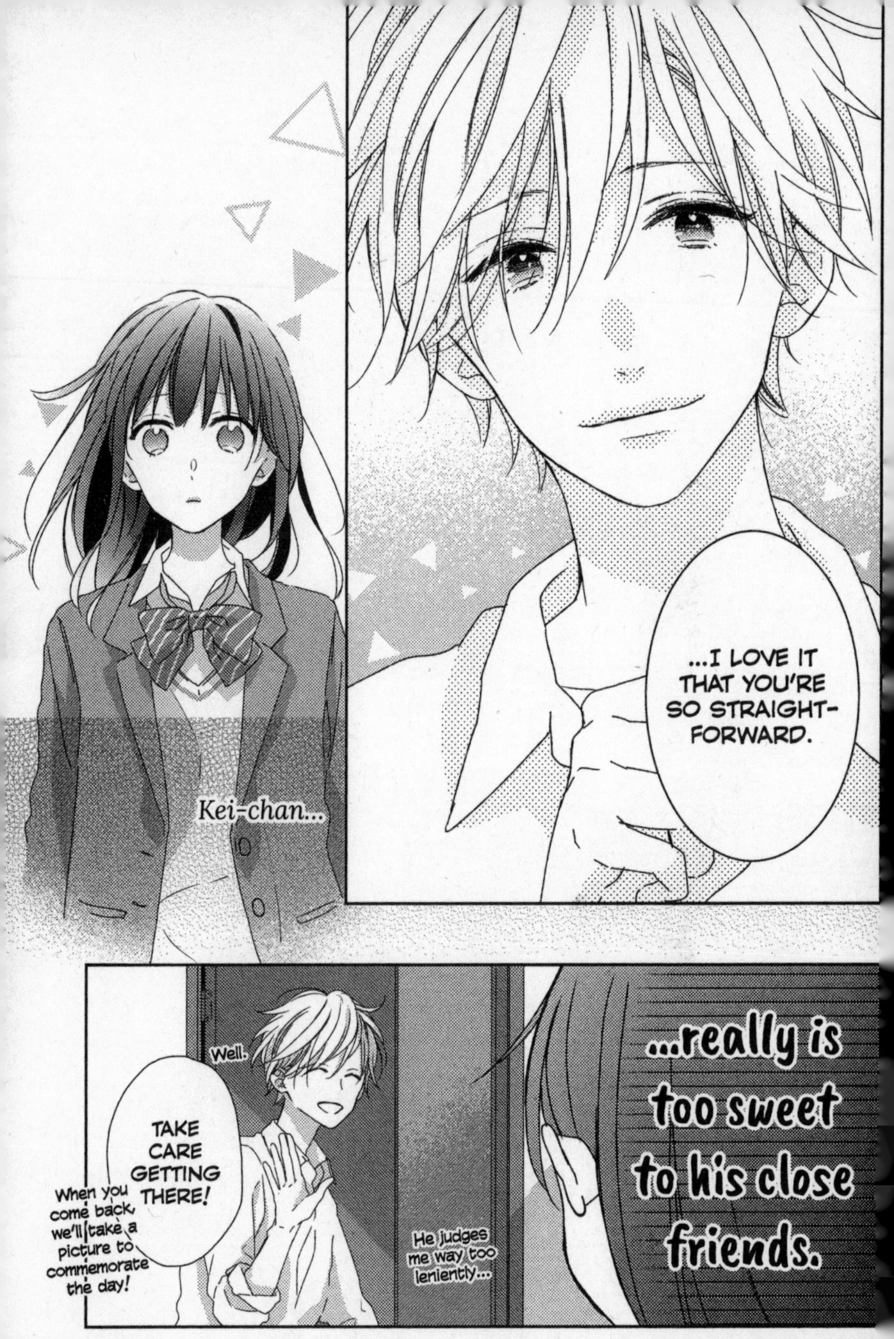
...I LOVE IT THAT YOU'RE SO STRAIGHT-FORWARD.
Kei-chan...
...really is too sweet to his close friends.
He judges me way too leniently...
Well.
TAKE CARE GETTING THERE!
When you come back, we'll take a picture to commemorate the day!

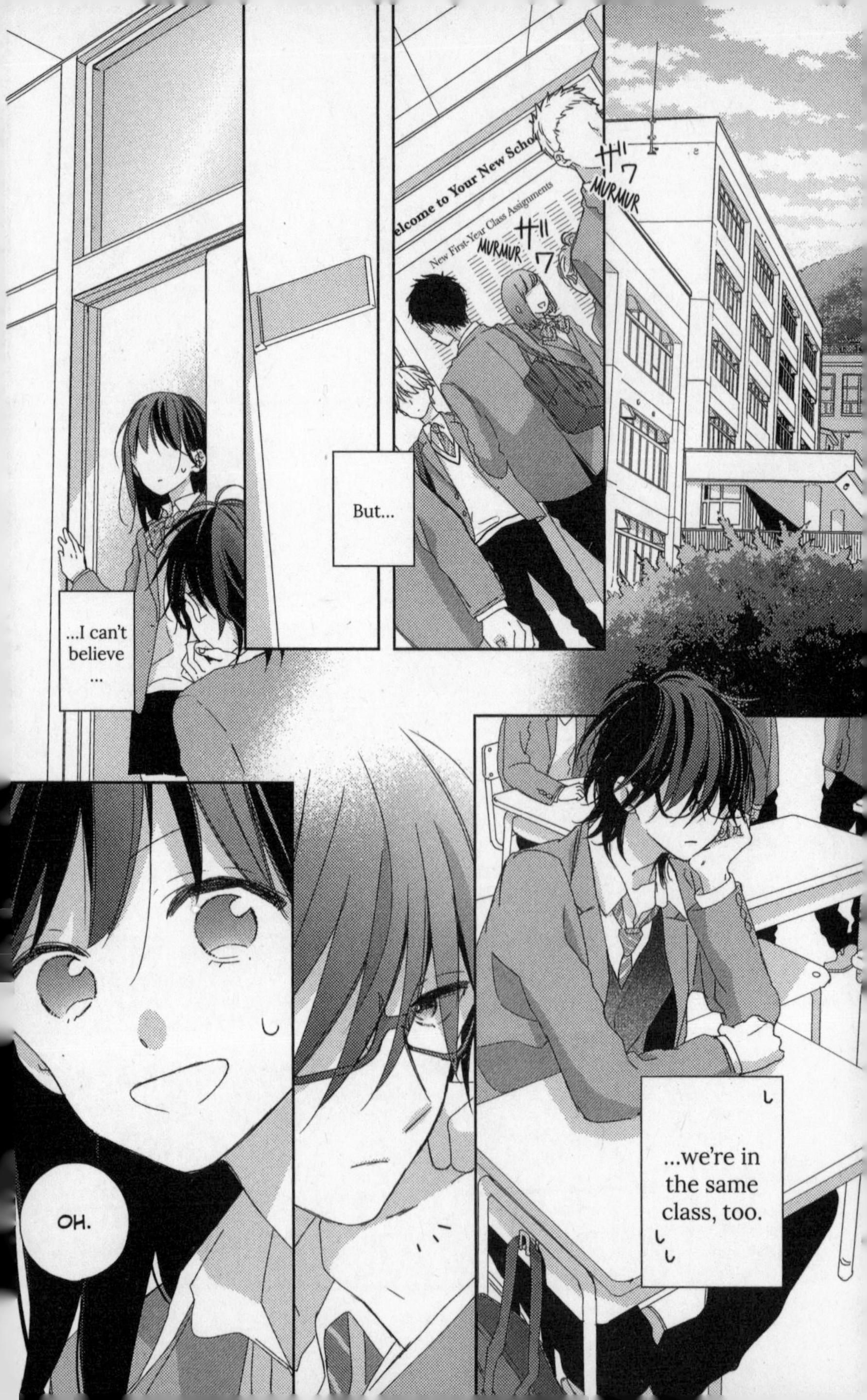

elcome to Your New Scho
New First-Year Class Assignments
ザワ
MURMUR
ザワ
MURMUR
But...
...I can't believe ...
...we're in the same class, too.
OH.

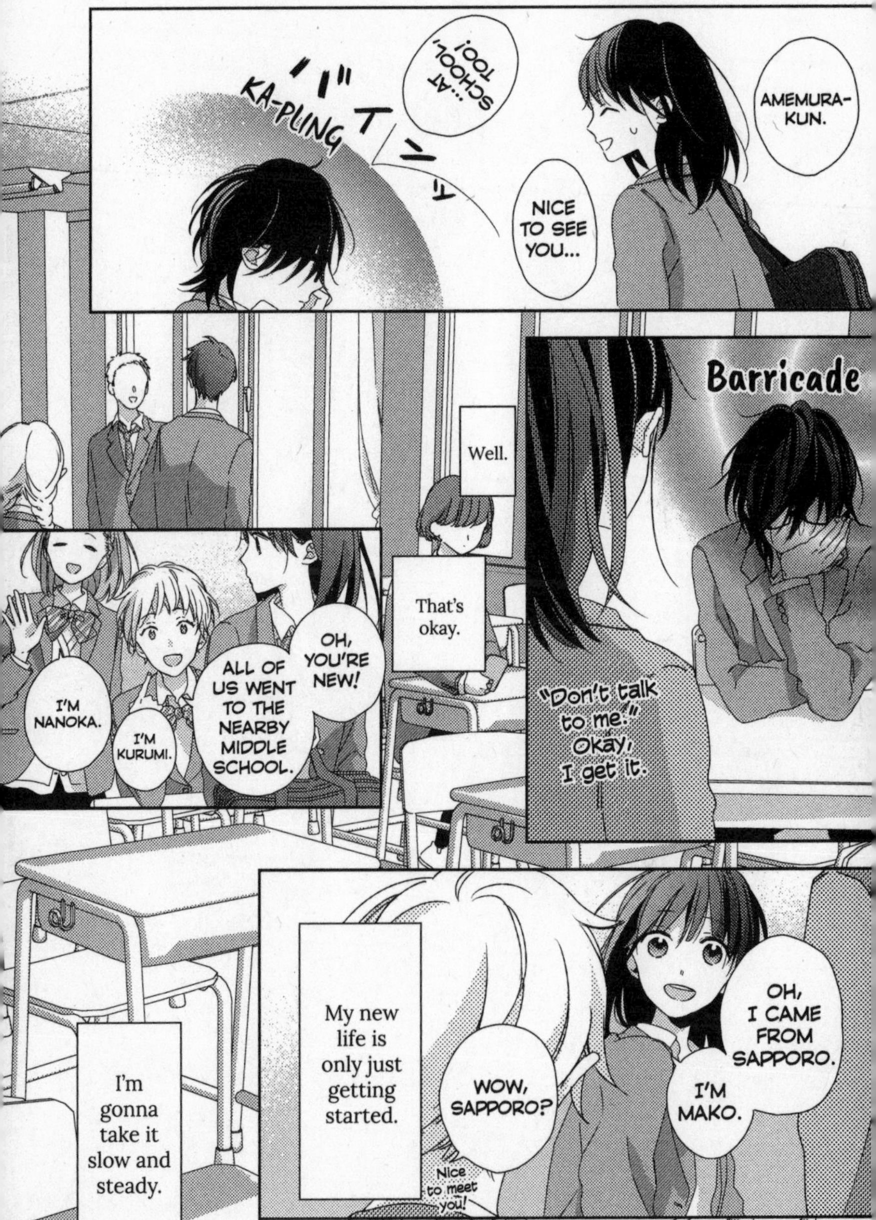
AMEMURA-KUN.
NICE TO SEE YOU...
...AT SCHOOL, TOO!
KA-PLING
Barricade
“Don't talk to me.” Okay, I get it.
Well.
That's okay.
OH, YOU'RE NEW!
ALL OF US WENT TO THE NEARBY MIDDLE SCHOOL.
I'M KURUMI.
I'M NANOKA.
OH, I CAME FROM SAPPORO.
I'M MAKO.
WOW, SAPPORO?
Nice to meet you!
My new life is only just getting started.
I'm gonna take it slow and steady.

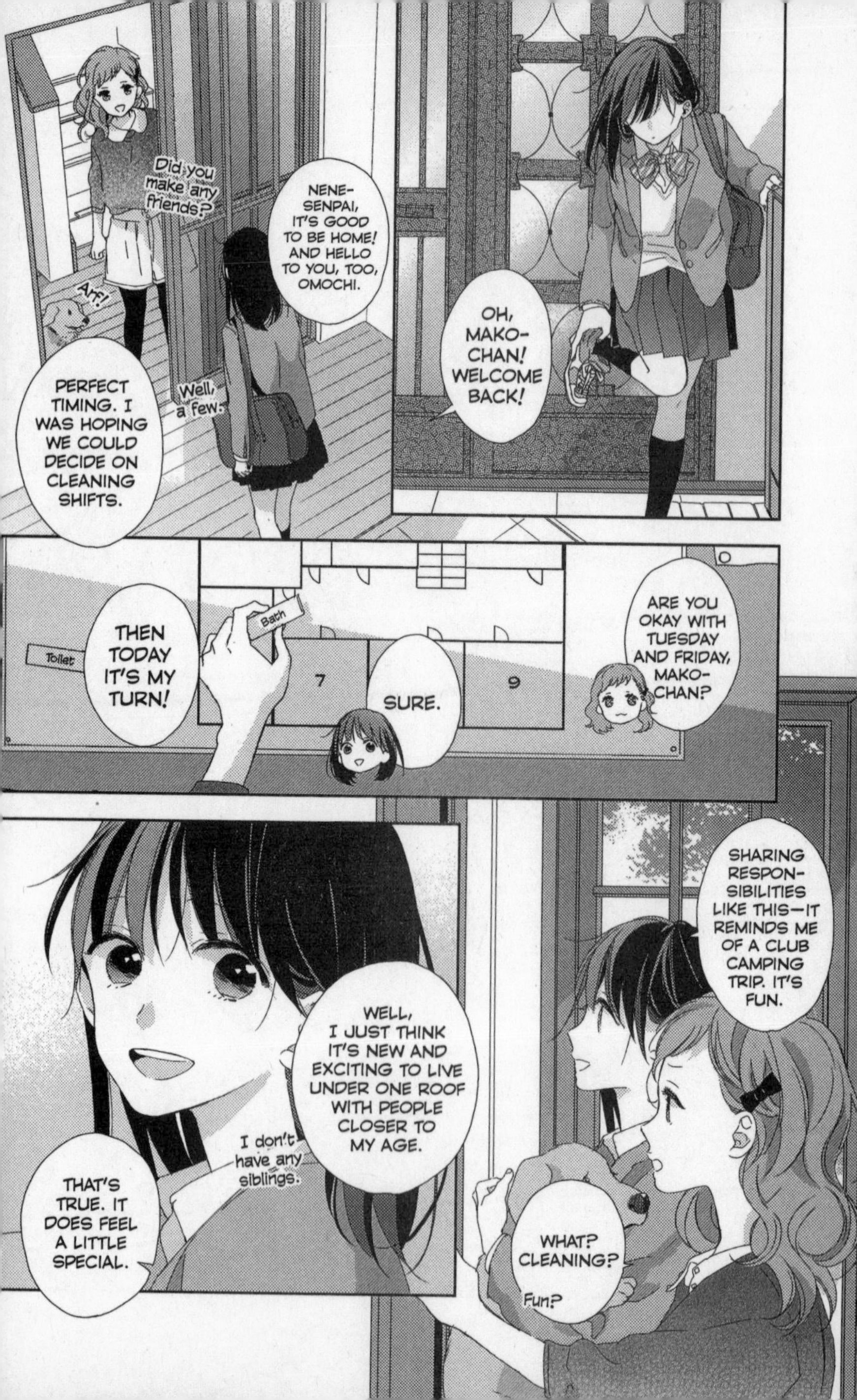
OH, MAKO-CHAN! WELCOME BACK!
NENE-SENPAI, IT'S GOOD TO BE HOME! AND HELLO TO YOU, TOO, OMOCHI.
Did you make any friends?
Arf!
Well, a few.
PERFECT TIMING. I WAS HOPING WE COULD DECIDE ON CLEANING SHIFTS.
ARE YOU OKAY WITH TUESDAY AND FRIDAY, MAKO-CHAN?
9
SURE.
7
Bath
Toilet
THEN TODAY IT'S MY TURN!
SHARING RESPON-SIBILITIES LIKE THIS—IT REMINDS ME OF A CLUB CAMPING TRIP. IT'S FUN.
WHAT? CLEANING?
Fun?
WELL, I JUST THINK IT'S NEW AND EXCITING TO LIVE UNDER ONE ROOF WITH PEOPLE CLOSER TO MY AGE.
I don't have any siblings.
THAT'S TRUE. IT DOES FEEL A LITTLE SPECIAL.

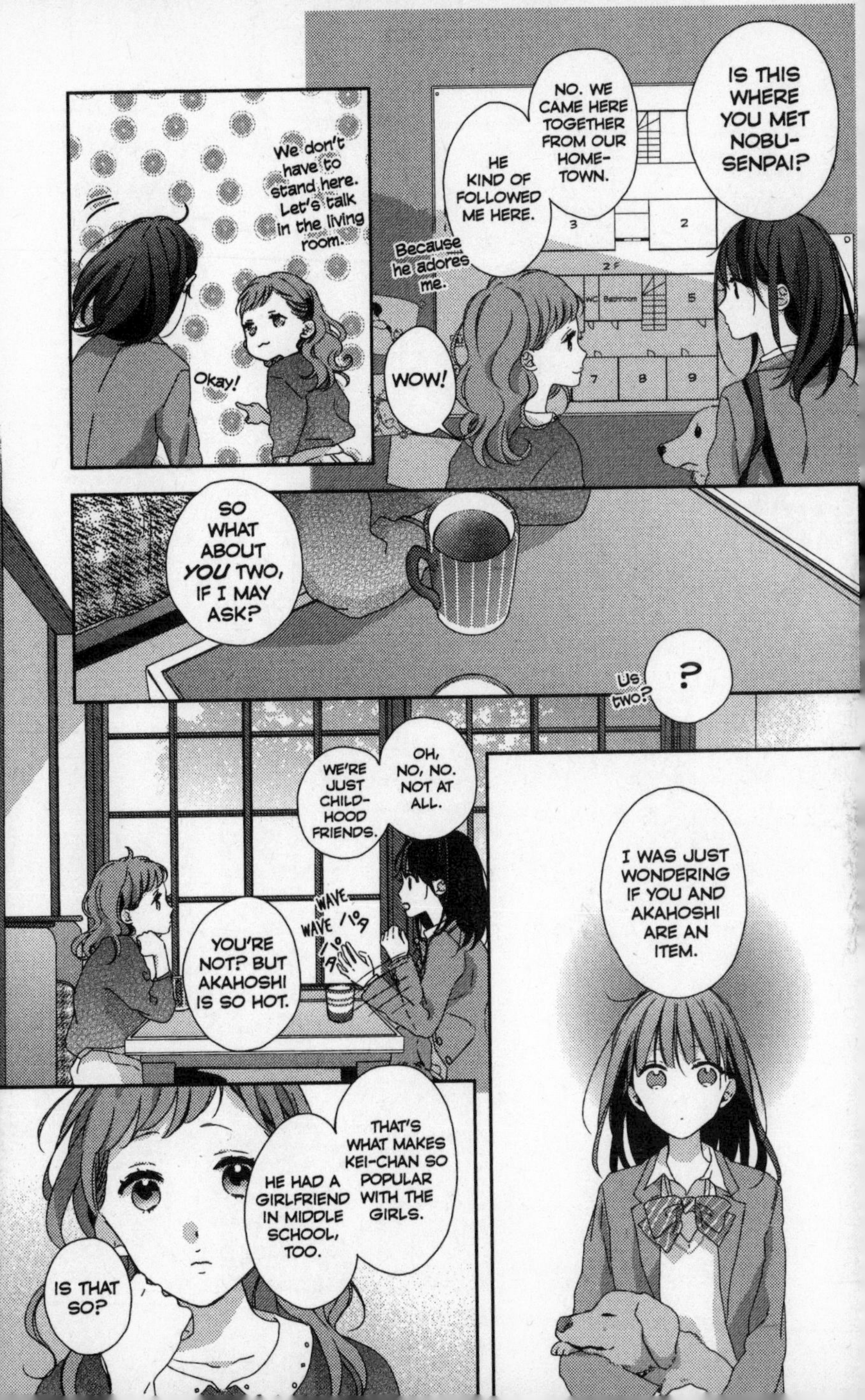
IS THIS WHERE YOU MET NOBU-SENPAI?
NO. WE CAME HERE TOGETHER FROM OUR HOME-TOWN.
HE KIND OF FOLLOWED ME HERE.
Because he adores me.
WOW!
We don't have to stand here. Let's talk in the living room.
Okay!
SO WHAT ABOUT *YOU* TWO, IF I MAY ASK?
?
Us two?
I WAS JUST WONDERING IF YOU AND AKAHOSHI ARE AN ITEM.
OH, NO, NO. NOT AT ALL.
WE'RE JUST CHILD-HOOD FRIENDS.
WAVE WAVE パタパタ
YOU'RE NOT? BUT AKAHOSHI IS SO HOT.
THAT'S WHAT MAKES KEI-CHAN SO POPULAR WITH THE GIRLS.
HE HAD A GIRLFRIEND IN MIDDLE SCHOOL, TOO.
IS THAT SO?

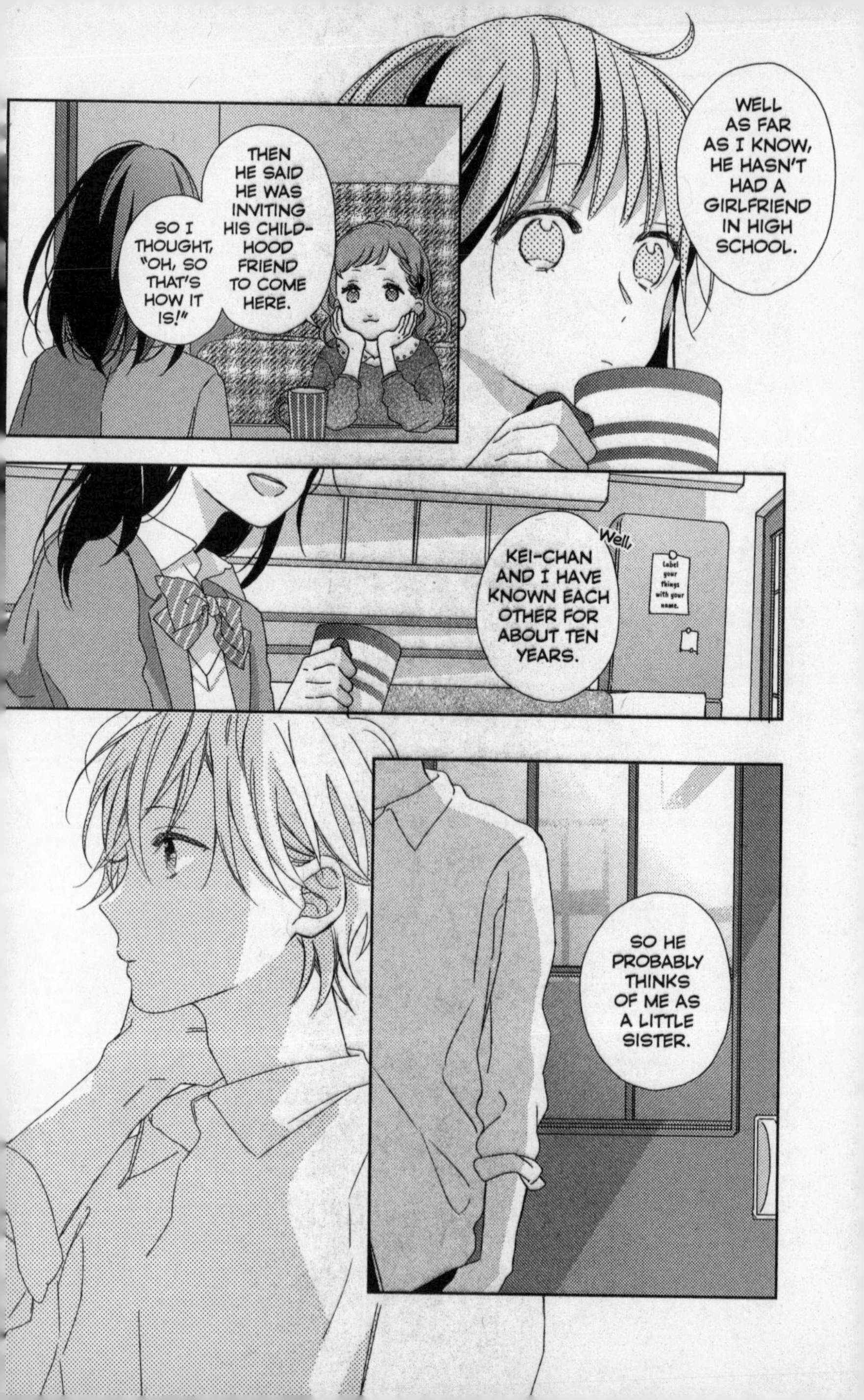
WELL AS FAR AS I KNOW, HE HASN'T HAD A GIRLFRIEND IN HIGH SCHOOL.
THEN HE SAID HE WAS INVITING HIS CHILD-HOOD FRIEND TO COME HERE.
SO I THOUGHT, "OH, SO THAT'S HOW IT IS!"
Well,
KEI-CHAN AND I HAVE KNOWN EACH OTHER FOR ABOUT TEN YEARS.
Label your things with your name.
SO HE PROBABLY THINKS OF ME AS A LITTLE SISTER.

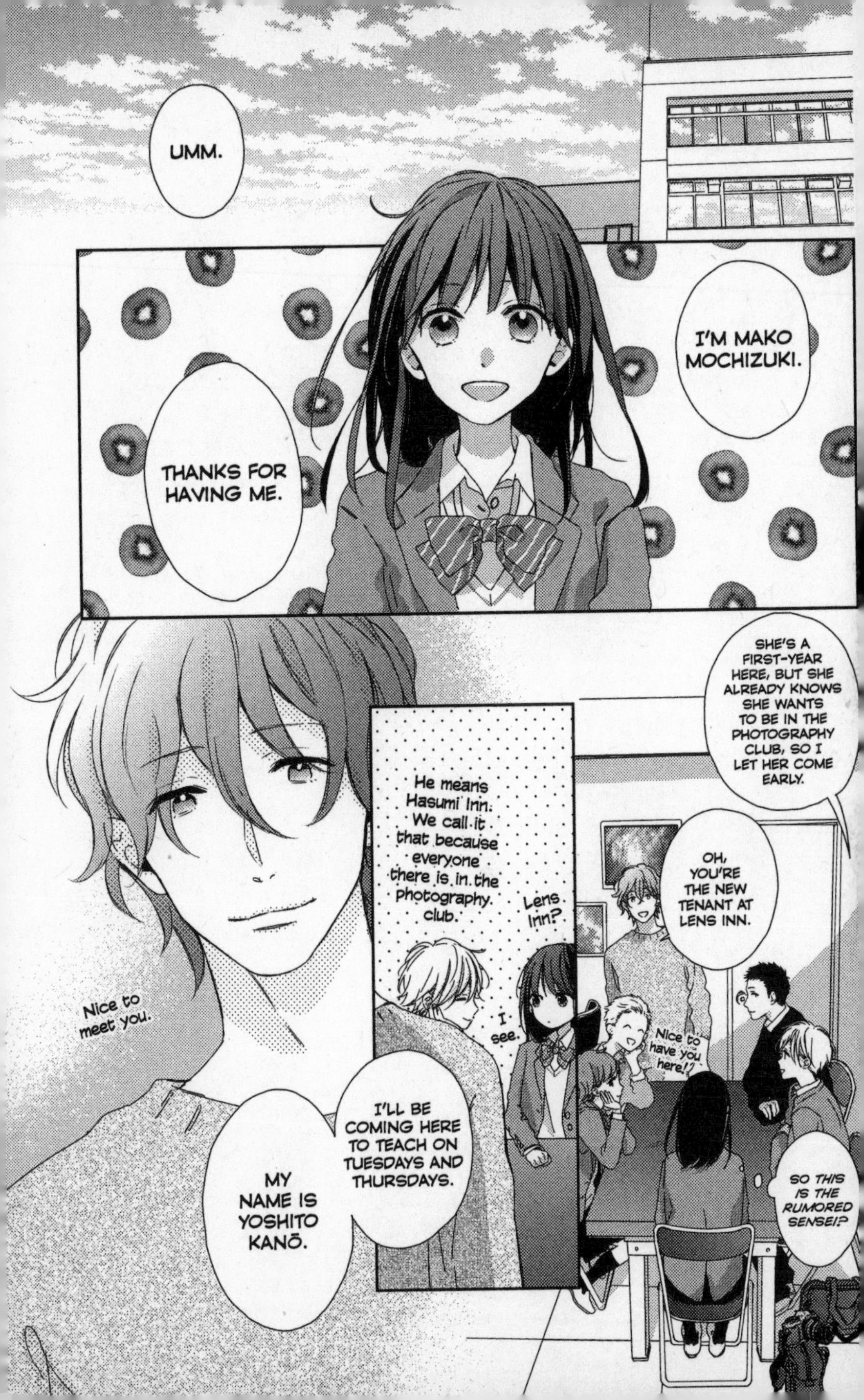
UMM.
I'M MAKO MOCHIZUKI.
THANKS FOR HAVING ME.
SHE'S A FIRST-YEAR HERE, BUT SHE ALREADY KNOWS SHE WANTS TO BE IN THE PHOTOGRAPHY CLUB, SO I LET HER COME EARLY.
OH, YOU'RE THE NEW TENANT AT LENS INN.
Nice to have you here!?
SO THIS IS THE RUMORED SENSEI!?
Lens Inn?
He means Hasumi Inn. We call it that because everyone there is in the photography club.
I see.
I'LL BE COMING HERE TO TEACH ON TUESDAYS AND THURSDAYS.
MY NAME IS YOSHITO KANŌ.
Nice to meet you.

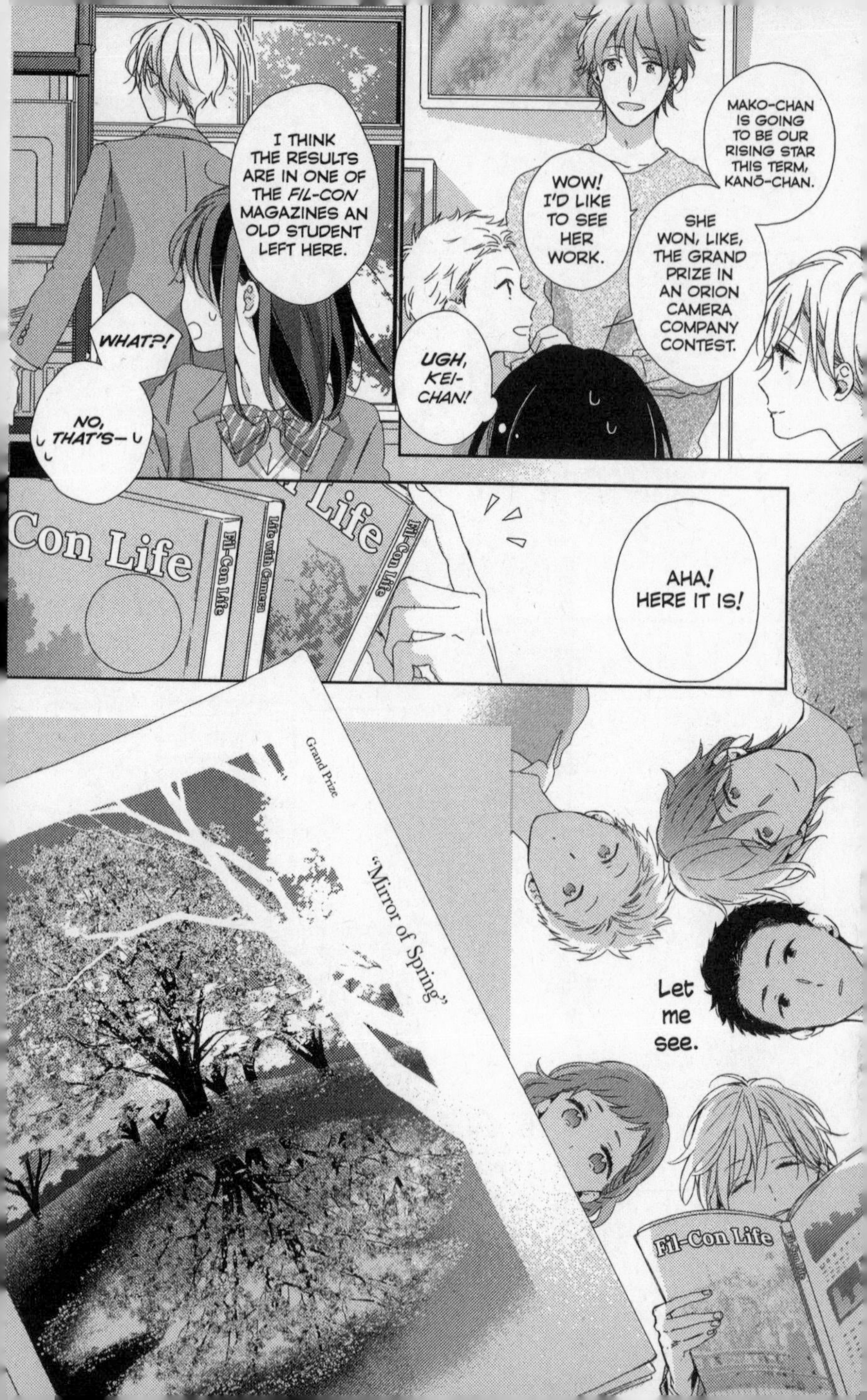
MAKO-CHAN IS GOING TO BE OUR RISING STAR THIS TERM, KANŌ-CHAN.
SHE WON, LIKE, THE GRAND PRIZE IN AN ORION CAMERA COMPANY CONTEST.
WOW! I'D LIKE TO SEE HER WORK.
UGH, KEI-CHAN!
I THINK THE RESULTS ARE IN ONE OF THE *FIL-CON* MAGAZINES AN OLD STUDENT LEFT HERE.
WHAT?!
NO, THAT'S—
AHA! HERE IT IS!
Life
Fil-Con Life
Life with Camera
Fil-Con Life
Con Life
Let me see.
Fil-Con Life
Grand Prize
'Mirror of Spring'

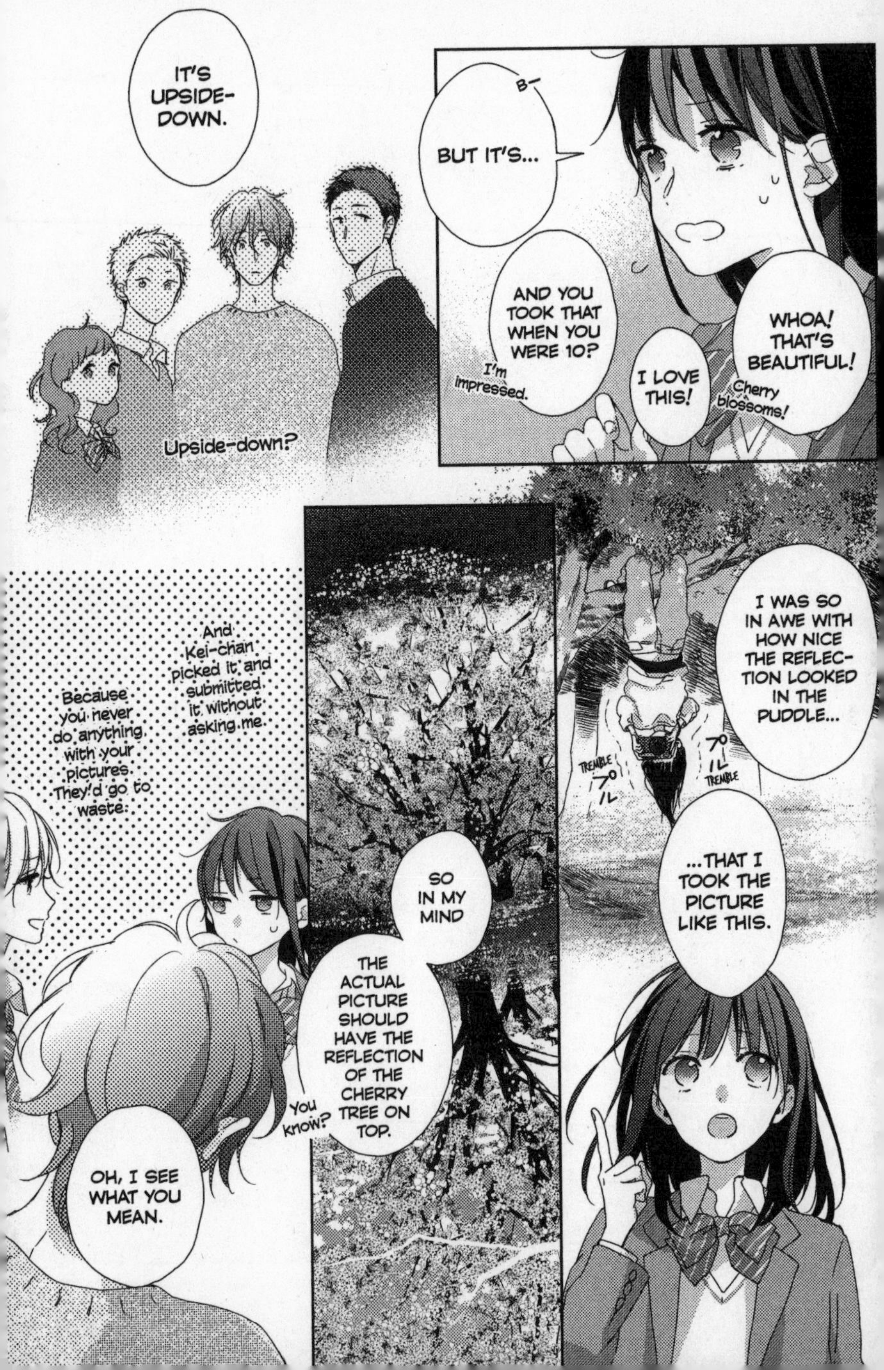
B—
BUT IT'S...
WHOA! THAT'S BEAUTIFUL!
Cherry blossoms!
I LOVE THIS!
AND YOU TOOK THAT WHEN YOU WERE 10?
I'm impressed.
IT'S UPSIDE-DOWN.
Upside-down?
I WAS SO IN AWE WITH HOW NICE THE REFLECTION LOOKED IN THE PUDDLE...
TREMBLE
TREMBLE
...THAT I TOOK THE PICTURE LIKE THIS.
SO IN MY MIND
THE ACTUAL PICTURE SHOULD HAVE THE REFLECTION OF THE CHERRY TREE ON TOP.
You know?
And Kei-chan picked it and submitted it without asking me.
Because you never do anything with your pictures. They'd go to waste.
OH, I SEE WHAT YOU MEAN.

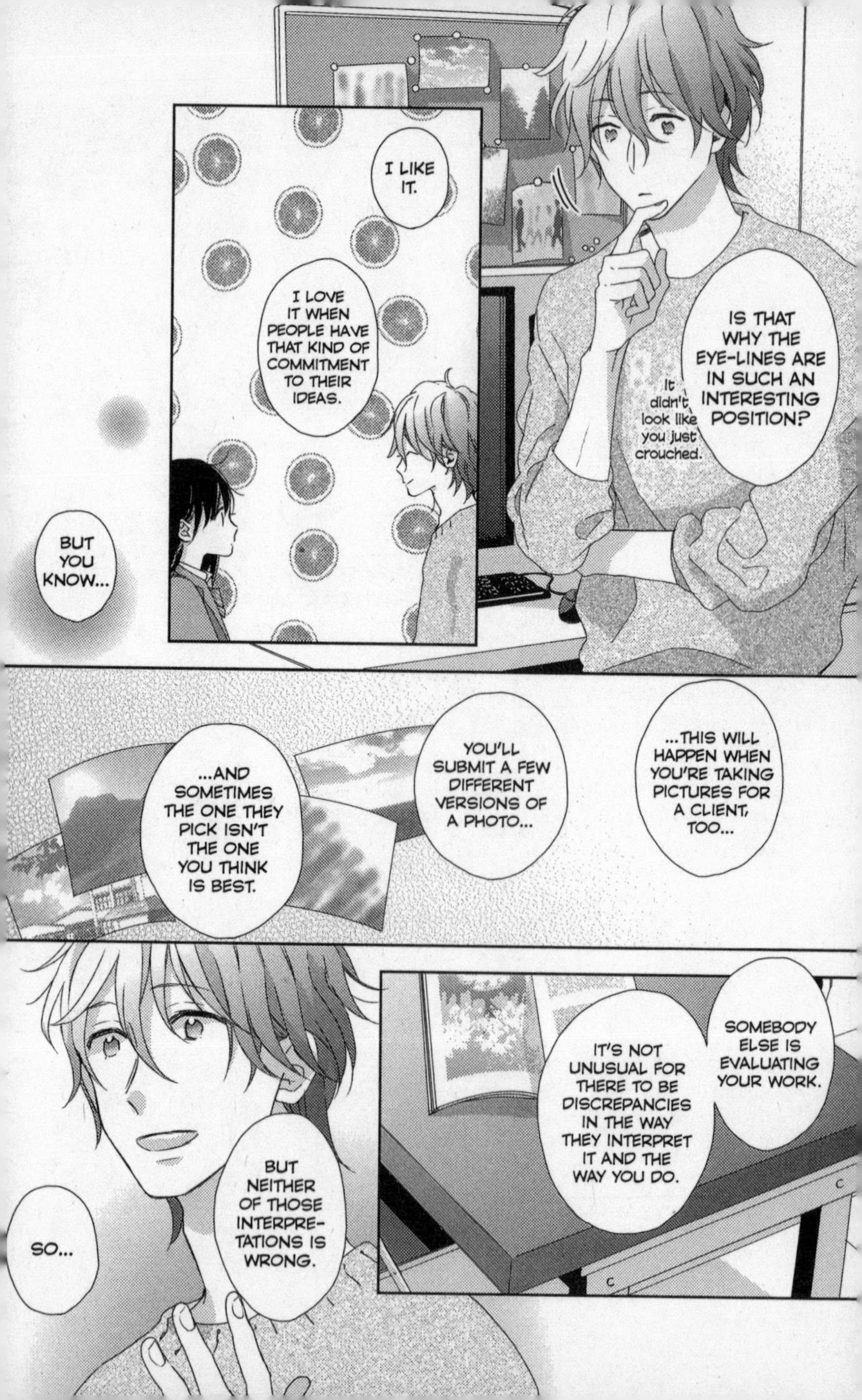
IS THAT WHY THE EYE-LINES ARE IN SUCH AN INTERESTING POSITION?
It didn't look like you just crouched.
I LIKE IT.
I LOVE IT WHEN PEOPLE HAVE THAT KIND OF COMMITMENT TO THEIR IDEAS.
BUT YOU KNOW...
...THIS WILL HAPPEN WHEN YOU'RE TAKING PICTURES FOR A CLIENT, TOO...
YOU'LL SUBMIT A FEW DIFFERENT VERSIONS OF A PHOTO...
...AND SOMETIMES THE ONE THEY PICK ISN'T THE ONE YOU THINK IS BEST.
SOMEBODY ELSE IS EVALUATING YOUR WORK.
IT'S NOT UNUSUAL FOR THERE TO BE DISCREPANCIES IN THE WAY THEY INTERPRET IT AND THE WAY YOU DO.
BUT NEITHER OF THOSE INTERPRETATIONS IS WRONG.
SO...

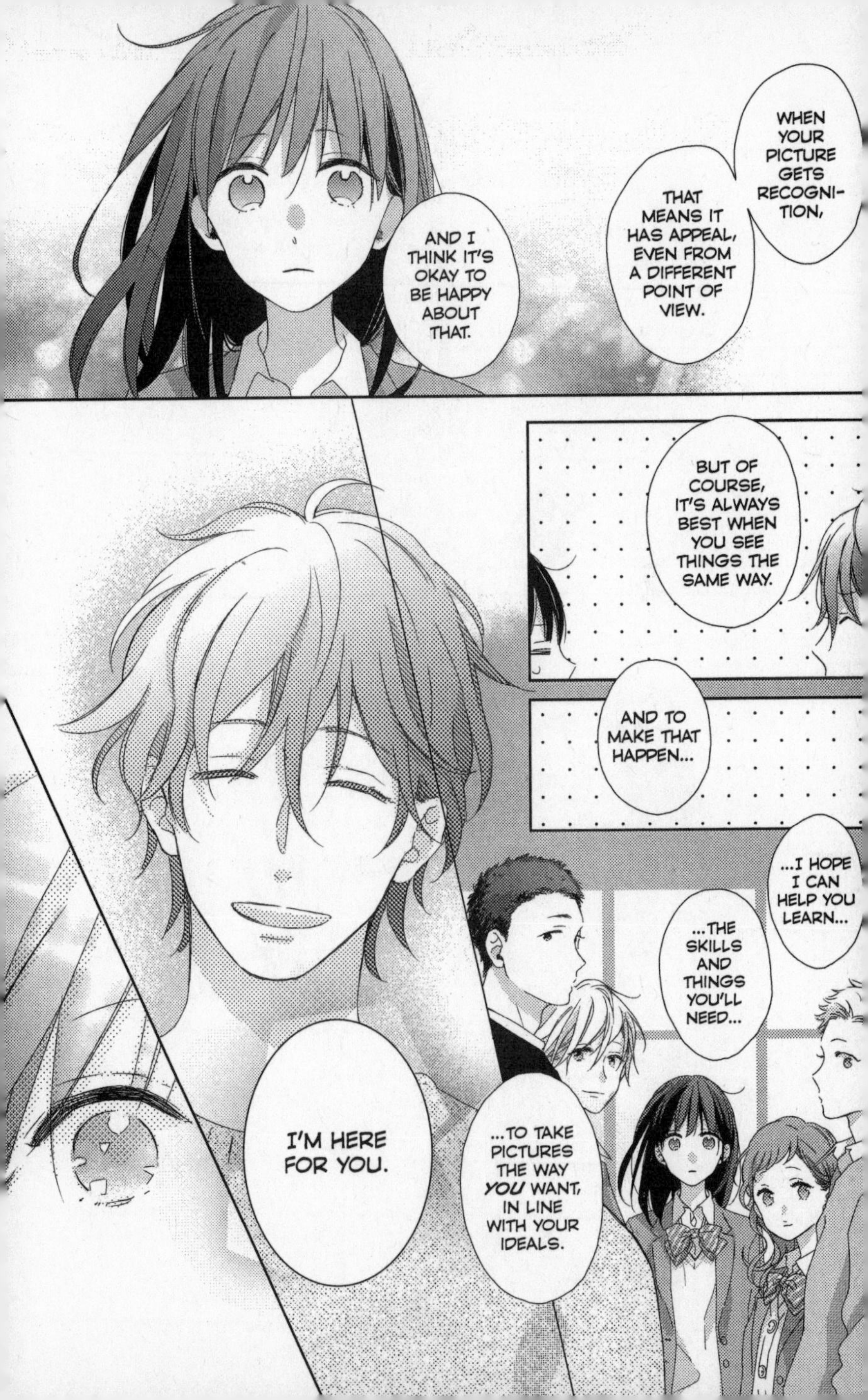
WHEN YOUR PICTURE GETS RECOGNITION,
THAT MEANS IT HAS APPEAL, EVEN FROM A DIFFERENT POINT OF VIEW.
AND I THINK IT'S OKAY TO BE HAPPY ABOUT THAT.
BUT OF COURSE, IT'S ALWAYS BEST WHEN YOU SEE THINGS THE SAME WAY.
AND TO MAKE THAT HAPPEN...
...I HOPE I CAN HELP YOU LEARN...
...THE SKILLS AND THINGS YOU'LL NEED...
...TO TAKE PICTURES THE WAY *YOU* WANT, IN LINE WITH YOUR IDEALS.
I'M HERE FOR YOU.

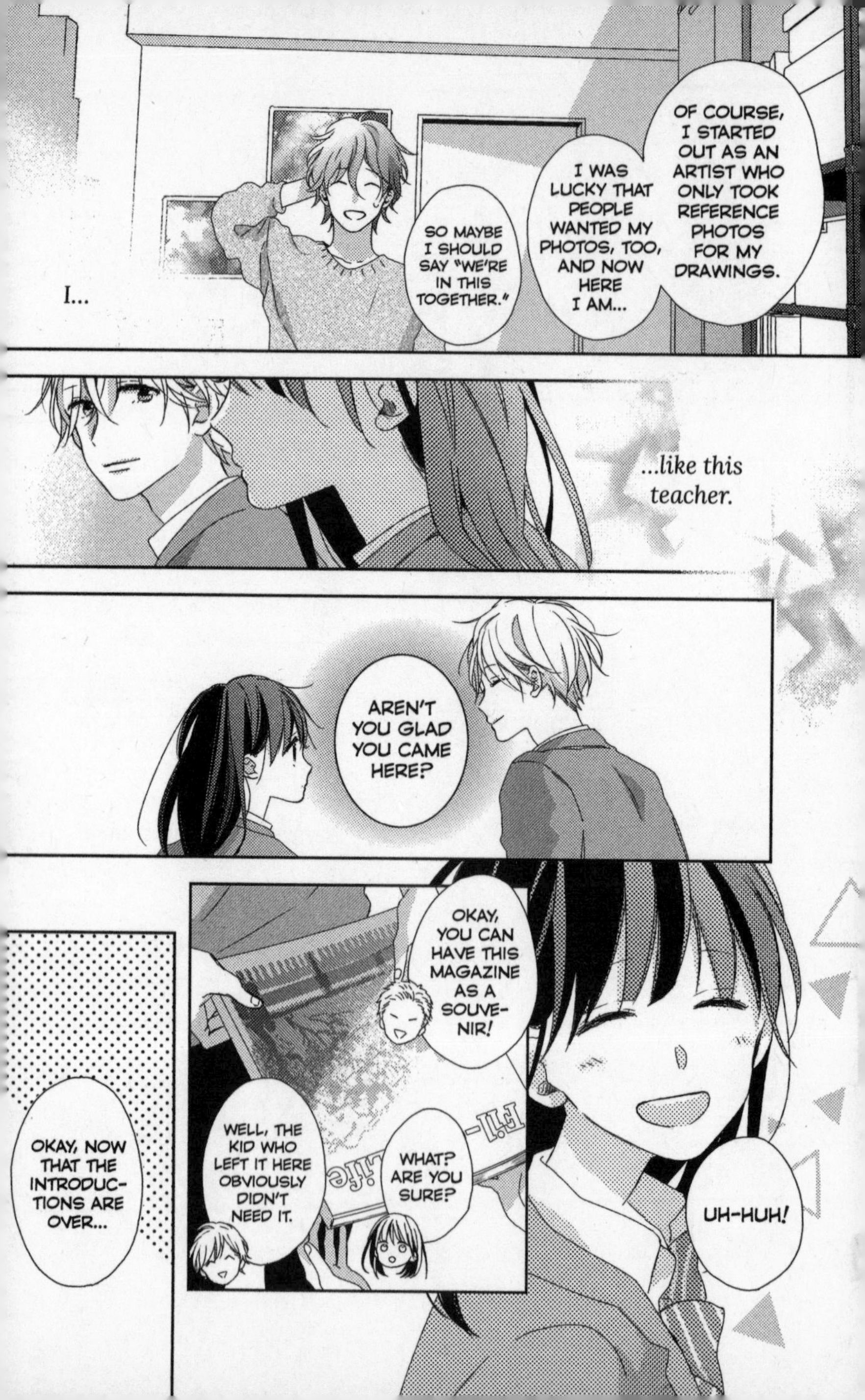
OF COURSE, I STARTED OUT AS AN ARTIST WHO ONLY TOOK REFERENCE PHOTOS FOR MY DRAWINGS.
I WAS LUCKY THAT PEOPLE WANTED MY PHOTOS, TOO, AND NOW HERE I AM...
SO MAYBE I SHOULD SAY "WE'RE IN THIS TOGETHER."
I...
...like this teacher.
AREN'T YOU GLAD YOU CAME HERE?
UH-HUH!
OKAY, YOU CAN HAVE THIS MAGAZINE AS A SOUVENIR!
WHAT? ARE YOU SURE?
WELL, THE KID WHO LEFT IT HERE OBVIOUSLY DIDN'T NEED IT.
OKAY, NOW THAT THE INTRODUCTIONS ARE OVER...

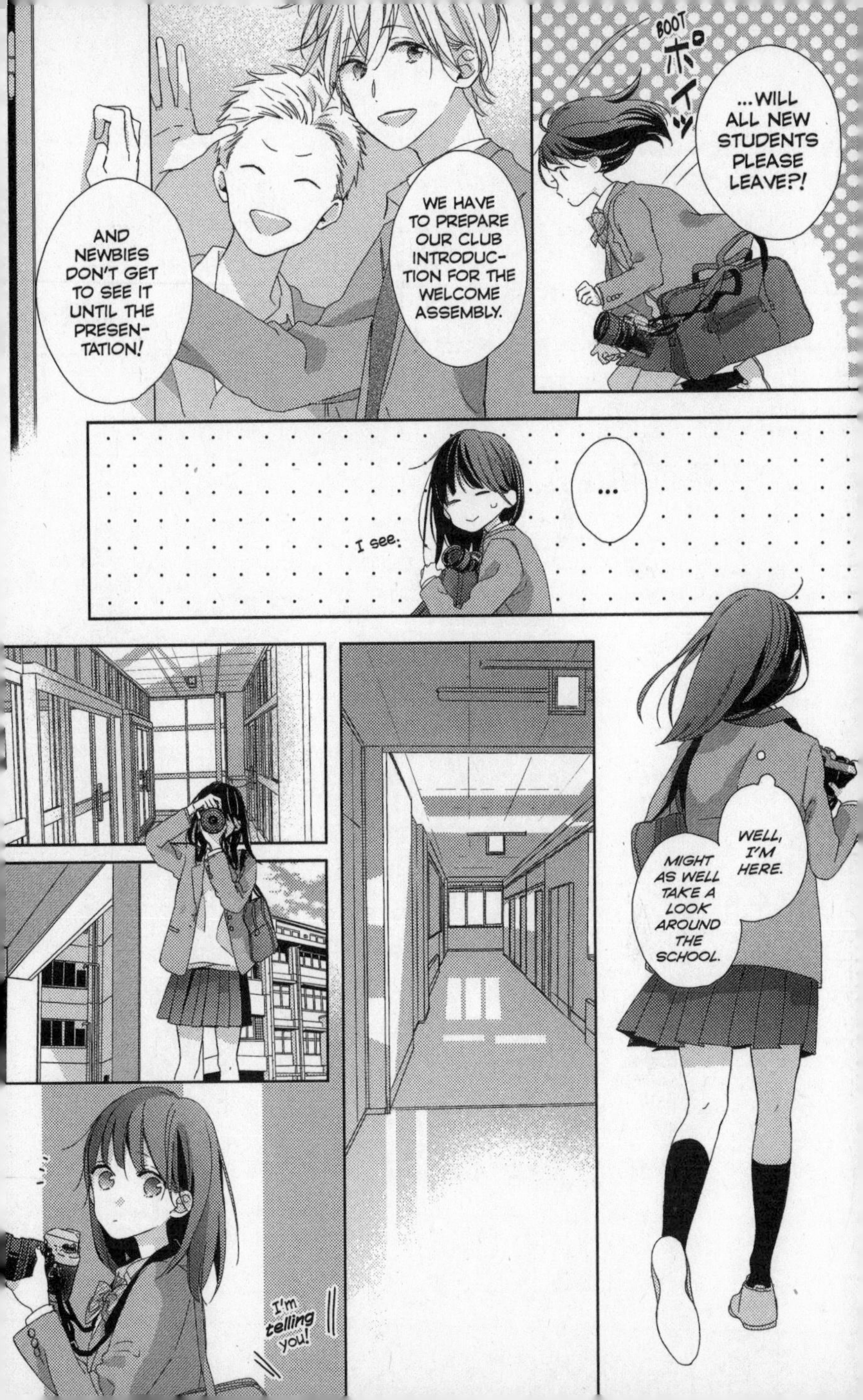
BOOT
ポイッ
...WILL ALL NEW STUDENTS PLEASE LEAVE?!
WE HAVE TO PREPARE OUR CLUB INTRODUCTION FOR THE WELCOME ASSEMBLY.
AND NEWBIES DON'T GET TO SEE IT UNTIL THE PRESENTATION!
...
I see.
WELL, I'M HERE.
MIGHT AS WELL TAKE A LOOK AROUND THE SCHOOL.
I'm telling you!

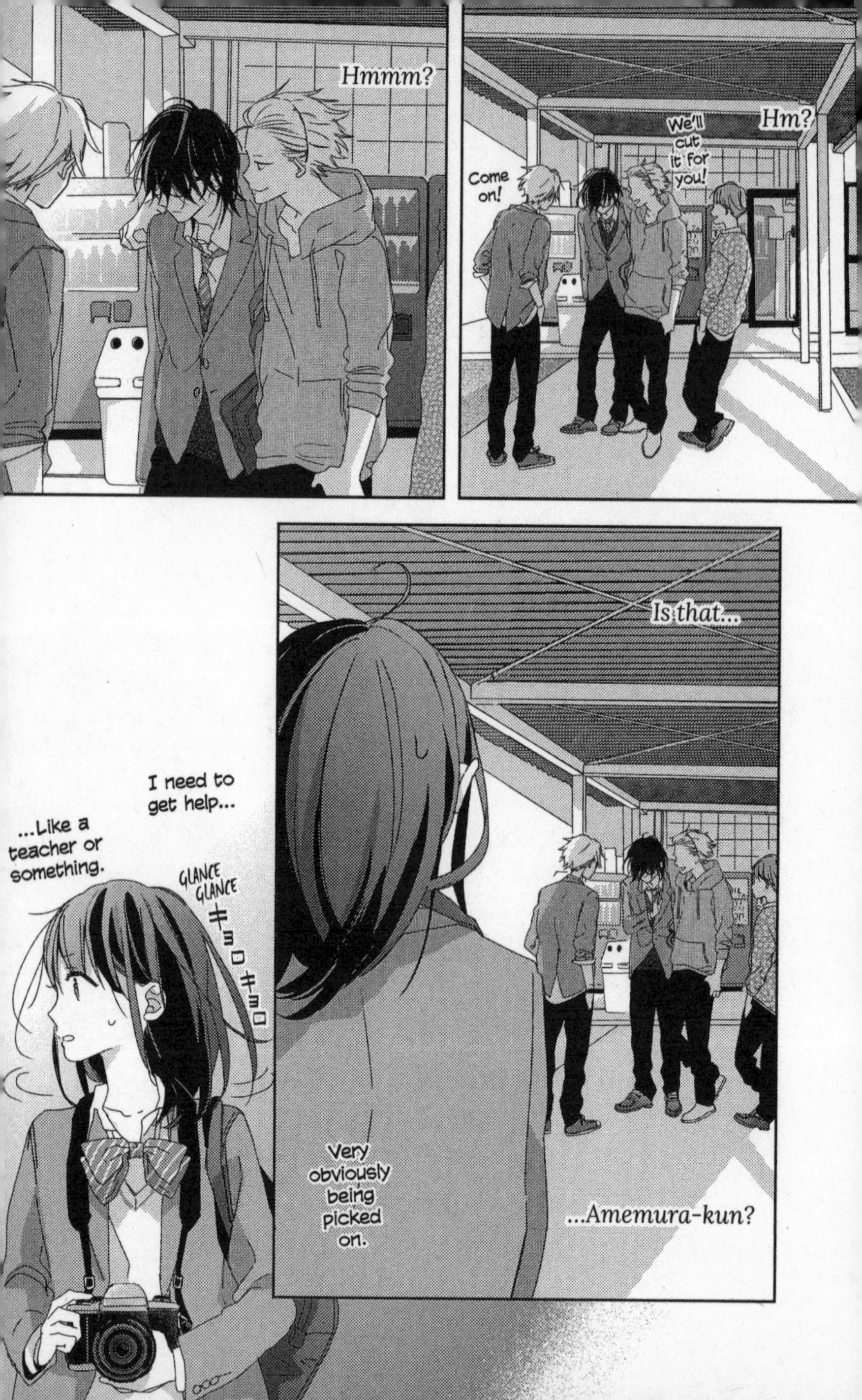
Hm?
We'll cut it for you!
Come on!
Hmmm?
Is that...
...Amemura-kun?
Very obviously being picked on.
I need to get help...
...Like a teacher or something.
GLANCE GLANCE
キョロキョロ

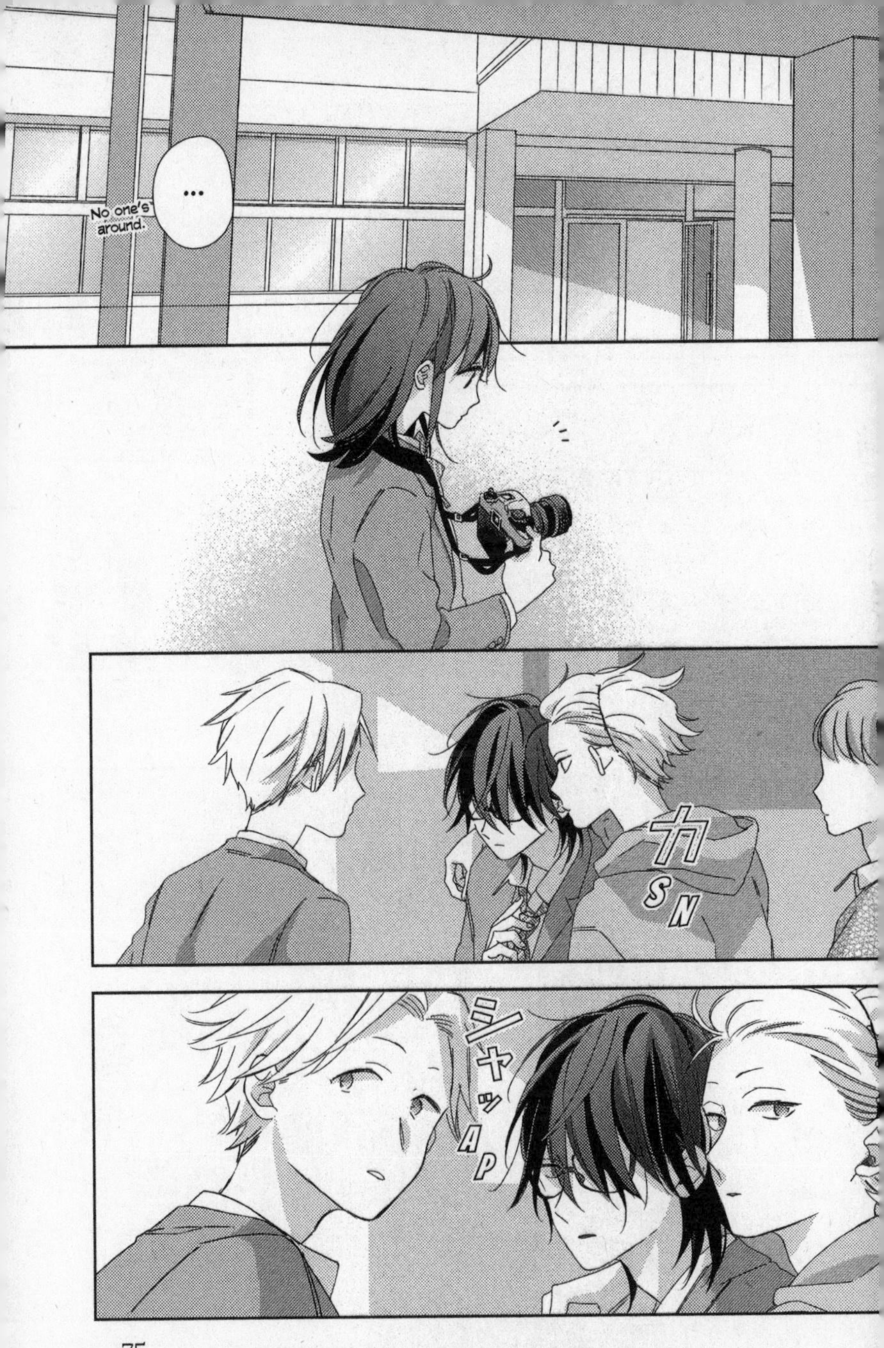
...
No one's around.
カ
SN
シャッ
AP

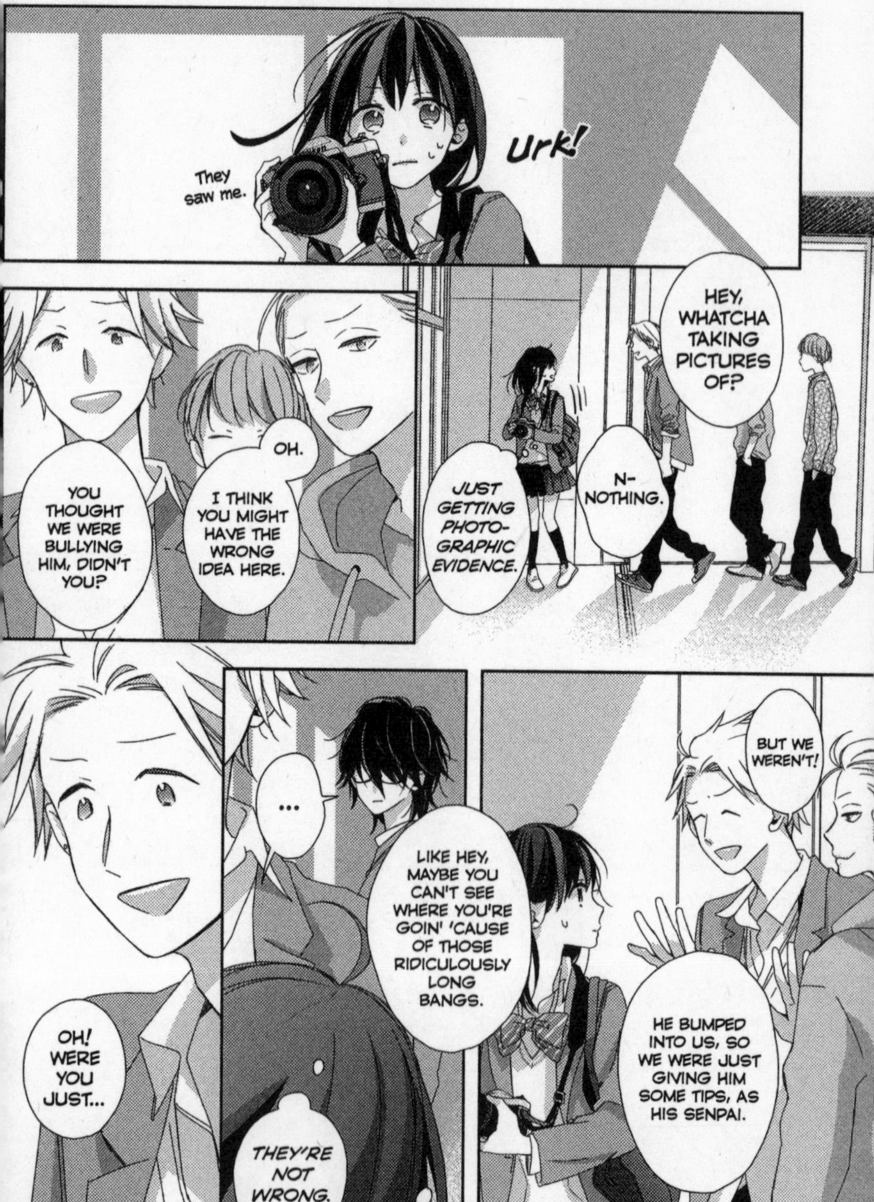
Urk!
They saw me.
HEY, WHATCHA TAKING PICTURES OF?
N-NOTHING.
JUST GETTING PHOTOGRAPHIC EVIDENCE.
OH.
I THINK YOU MIGHT HAVE THE WRONG IDEA HERE.
YOU THOUGHT WE WERE BULLYING HIM, DIDN'T YOU?
BUT WE WEREN'T!
HE BUMPED INTO US, SO WE WERE JUST GIVING HIM SOME TIPS, AS HIS SENPAI.
...
LIKE HEY, MAYBE YOU CAN'T SEE WHERE YOU'RE GOIN' 'CAUSE OF THOSE RIDICULOUSLY LONG BANGS.
THEY'RE NOT WRONG.
OH! WERE YOU JUST...

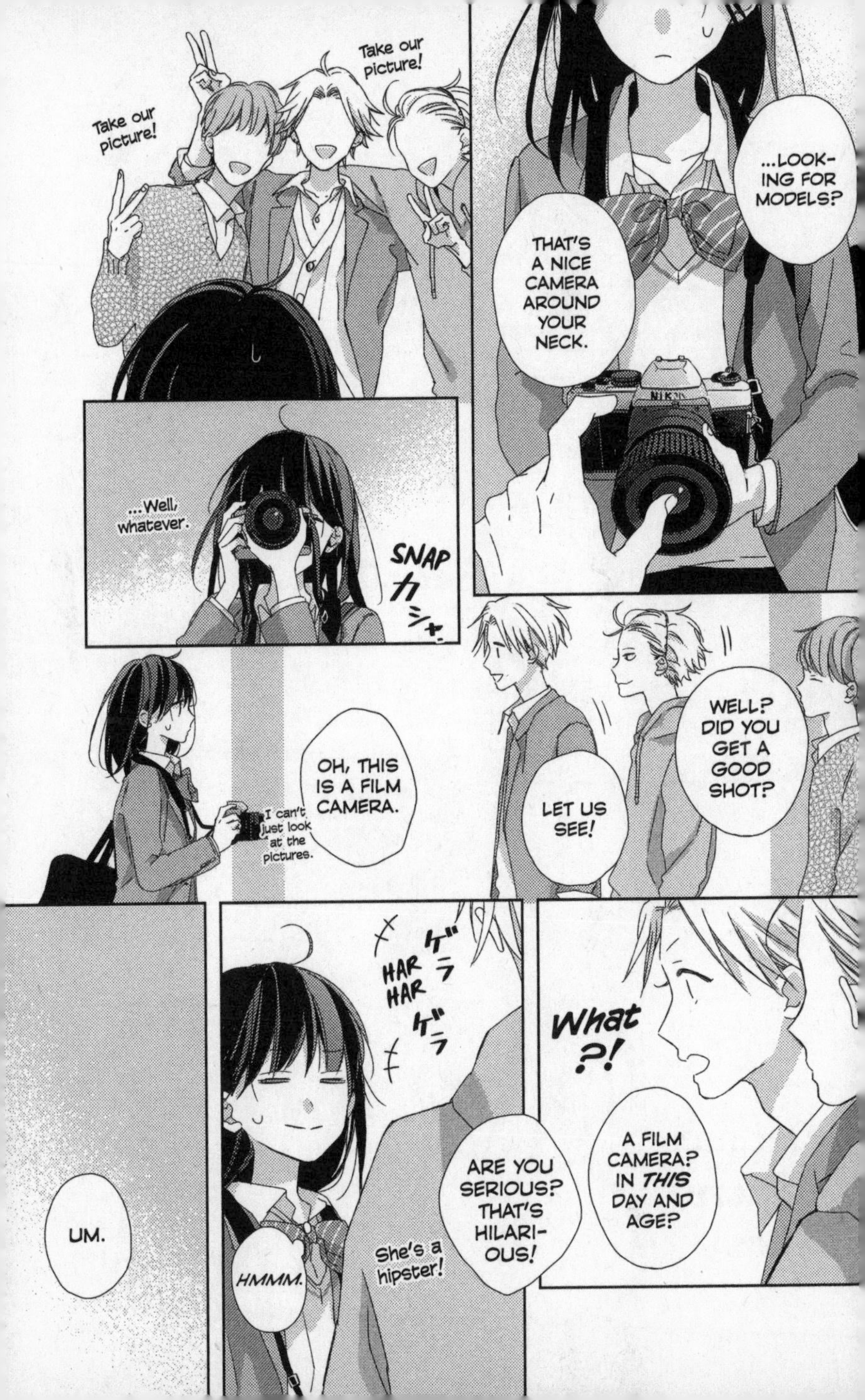
...LOOKING FOR MODELS?
THAT'S A NICE CAMERA AROUND YOUR NECK.
Take our picture!
Take our picture!
...Well, whatever.
SNAP
カシャ
WELL? DID YOU GET A GOOD SHOT?
LET US SEE!
OH, THIS IS A FILM CAMERA.
I can't just look at the pictures.
What?!
A FILM CAMERA? IN *THIS* DAY AND AGE?
HAR HAR
ゲラゲラ
ARE YOU SERIOUS? THAT'S HILARIOUS!
She's a hipster!
HMMM.
UM.

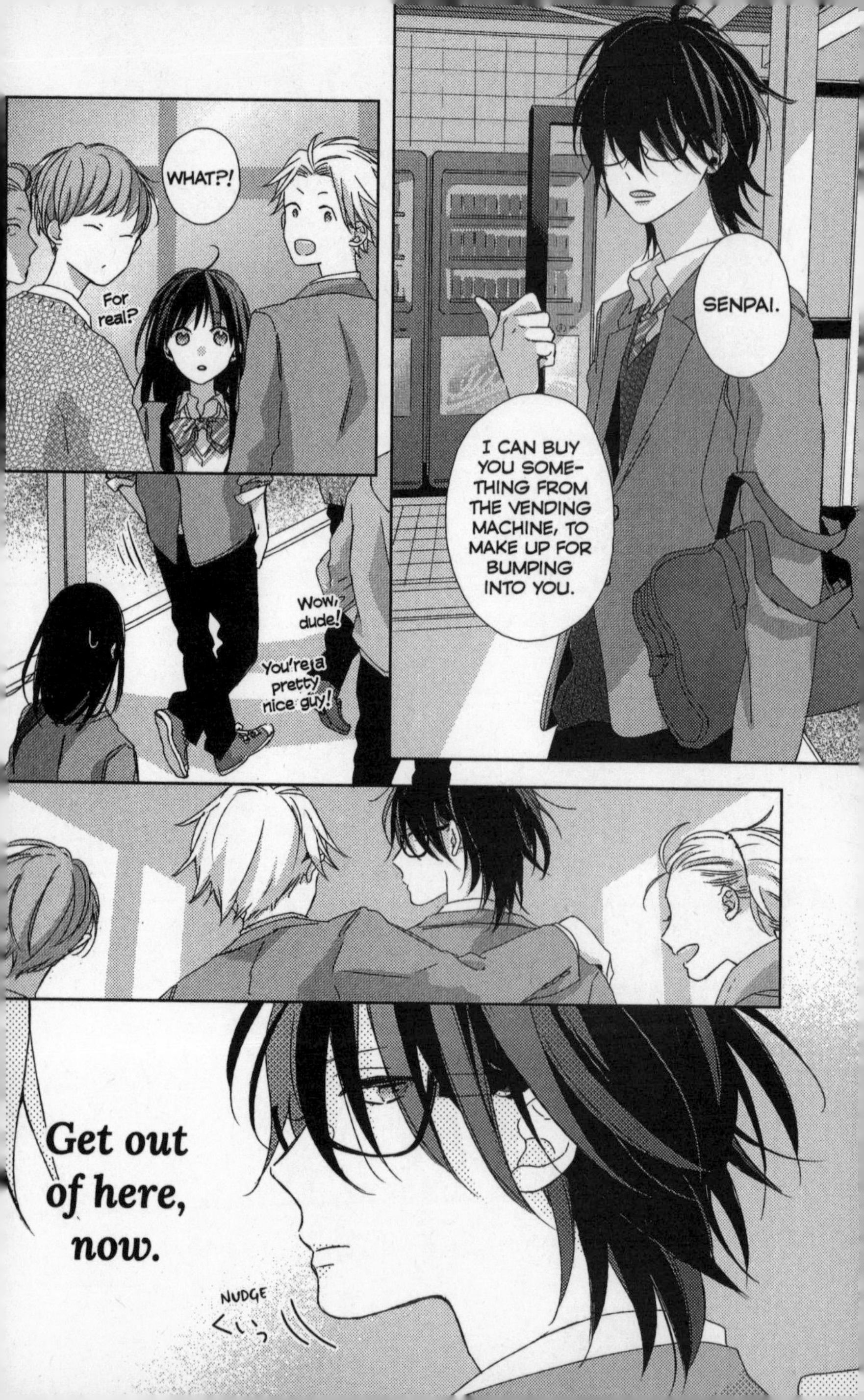
SENPAI.
I CAN BUY YOU SOME-THING FROM THE VENDING MACHINE, TO MAKE UP FOR BUMPING INTO YOU.
WHAT?!
For real?
Wow, dude!
You're a pretty nice guy!
Get out of here, now.
NUDGE
くいっ

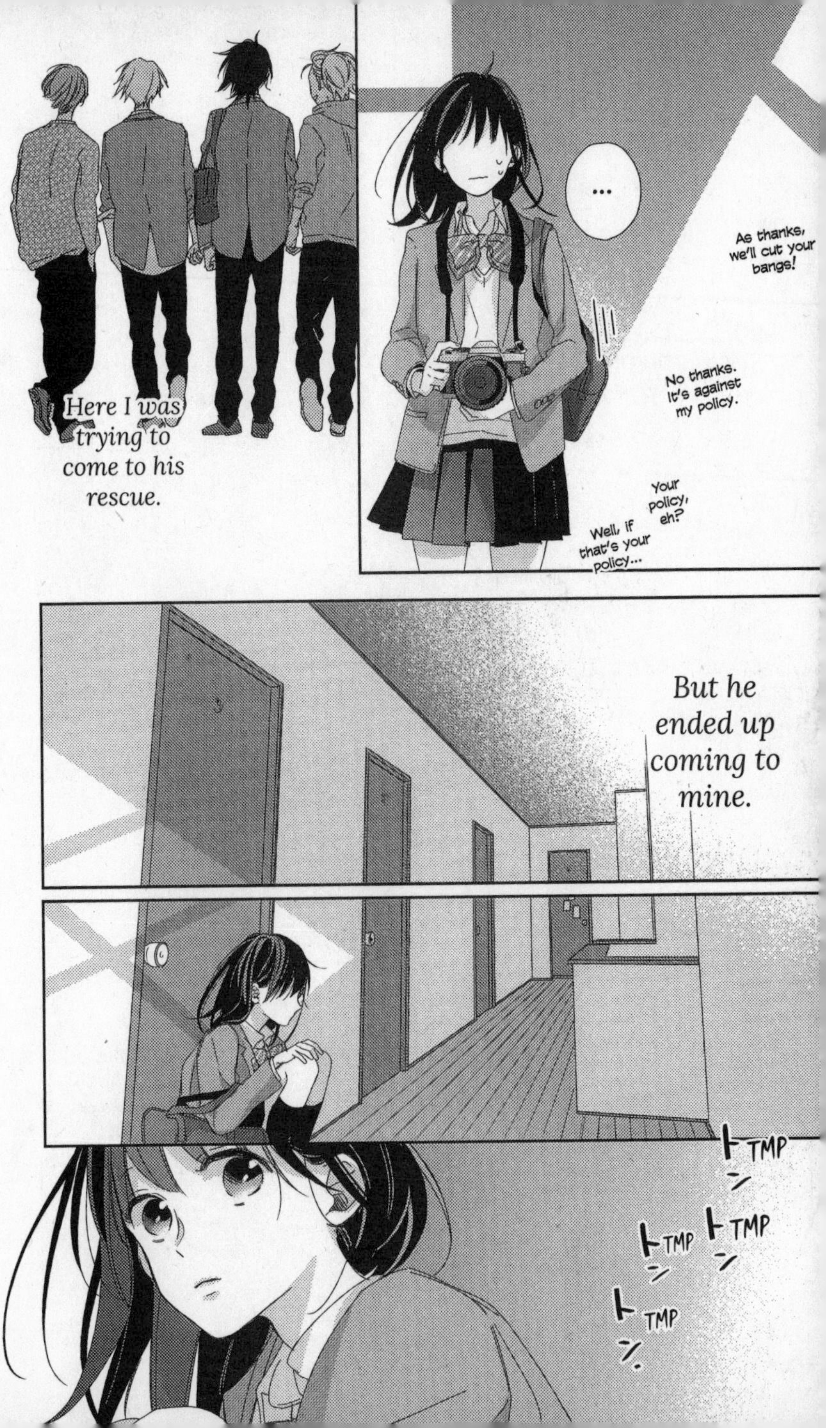
...
As thanks, we'll cut your bangs!
No thanks. It's against my policy.
Your policy, eh?
Well, if that's your policy...
Here I was trying to come to his rescue.
But he ended up coming to mine.
TMP
TMP
TMP
TMP

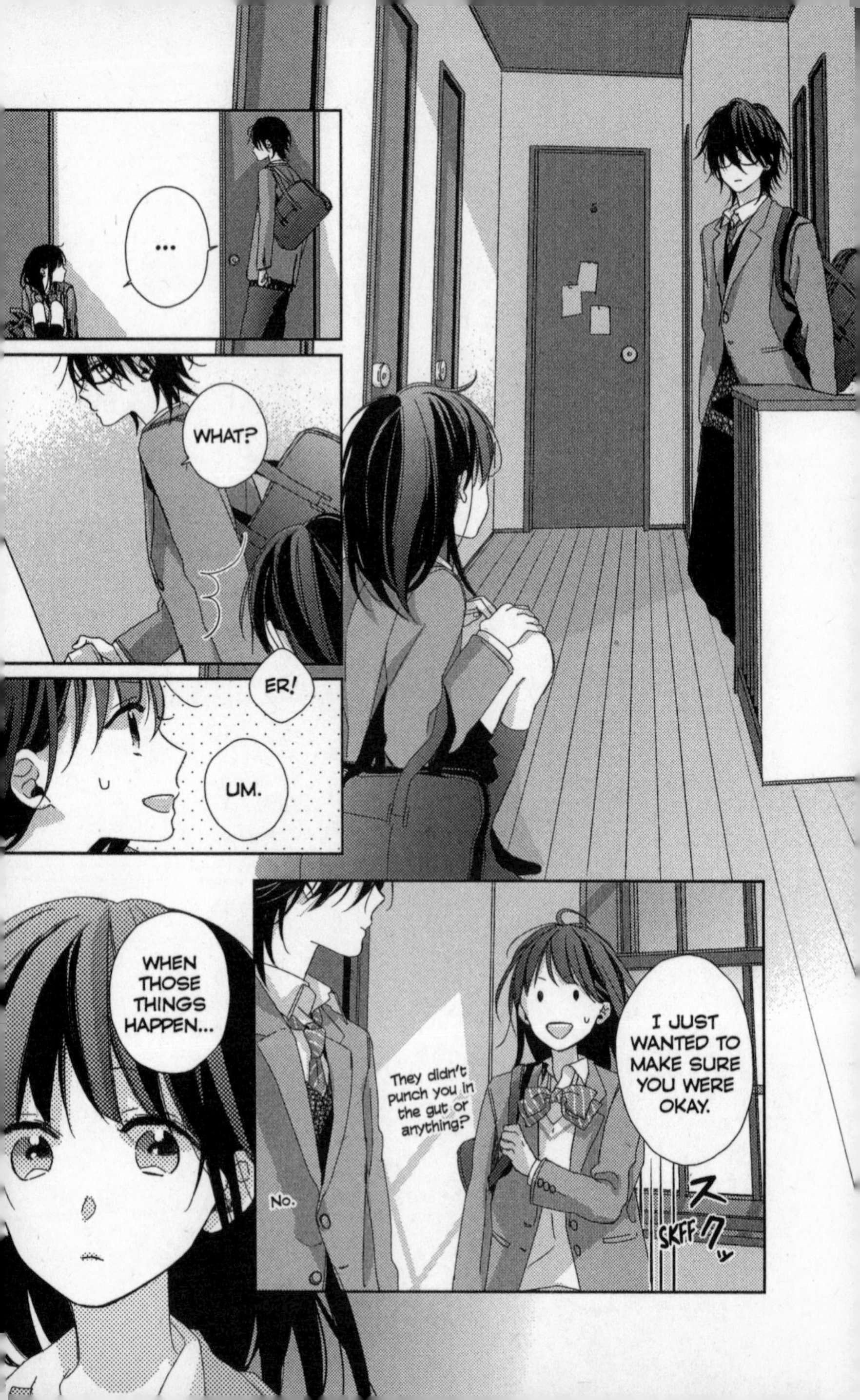
...
WHAT?
ER!
UM.
I JUST WANTED TO MAKE SURE YOU WERE OKAY.
スクッ
SKFF
They didn't punch you in the gut or anything?
No.
WHEN THOSE THINGS HAPPEN...

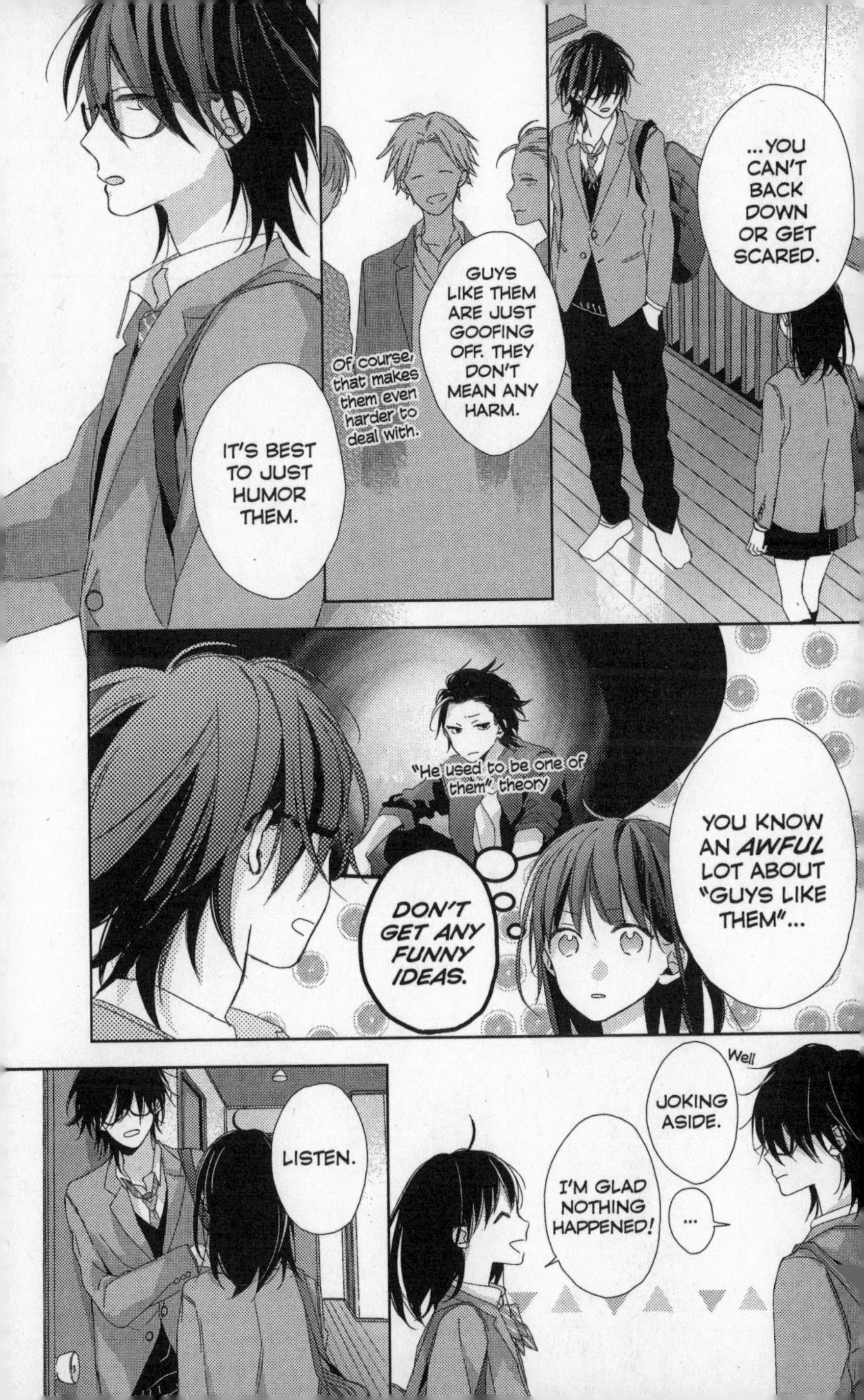
...YOU CAN'T BACK DOWN OR GET SCARED.
GUYS LIKE THEM ARE JUST GOOFING OFF. THEY DON'T MEAN ANY HARM.
Of course, that makes them even harder to deal with.
IT'S BEST TO JUST HUMOR THEM.
YOU KNOW AN AWFUL LOT ABOUT "GUYS LIKE THEM"...
"He used to be one of them" theory
DON'T GET ANY FUNNY IDEAS.
Well
JOKING ASIDE.
...
I'M GLAD NOTHING HAPPENED!
LISTEN.

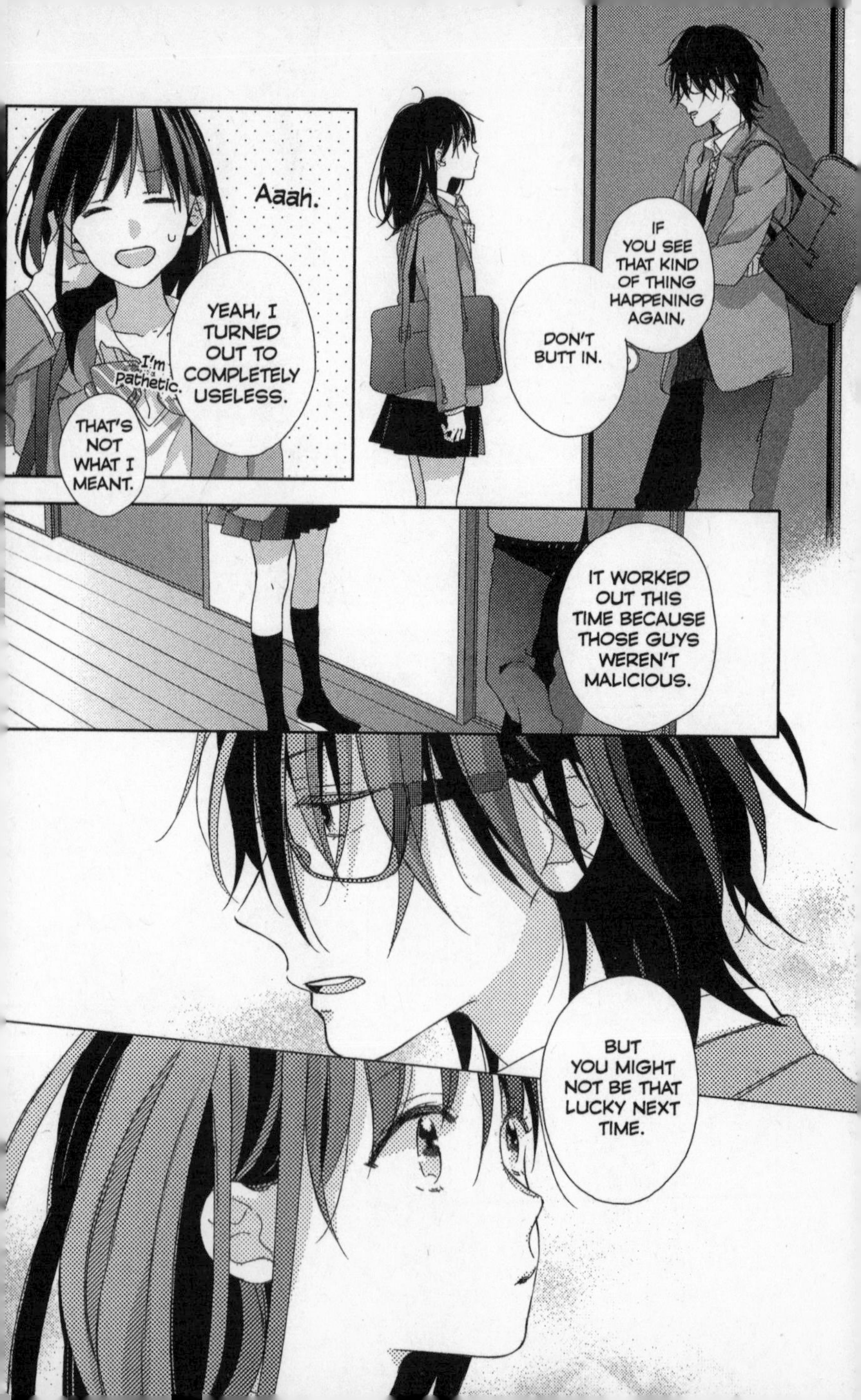
IF YOU SEE THAT KIND OF THING HAPPENING AGAIN,
DON'T BUTT IN.
Aaah.
YEAH, I TURNED OUT TO COMPLETELY USELESS.
I'm Pathetic.
THAT'S NOT WHAT I MEANT.
IT WORKED OUT THIS TIME BECAUSE THOSE GUYS WEREN'T MALICIOUS.
BUT YOU MIGHT NOT BE THAT LUCKY NEXT TIME.

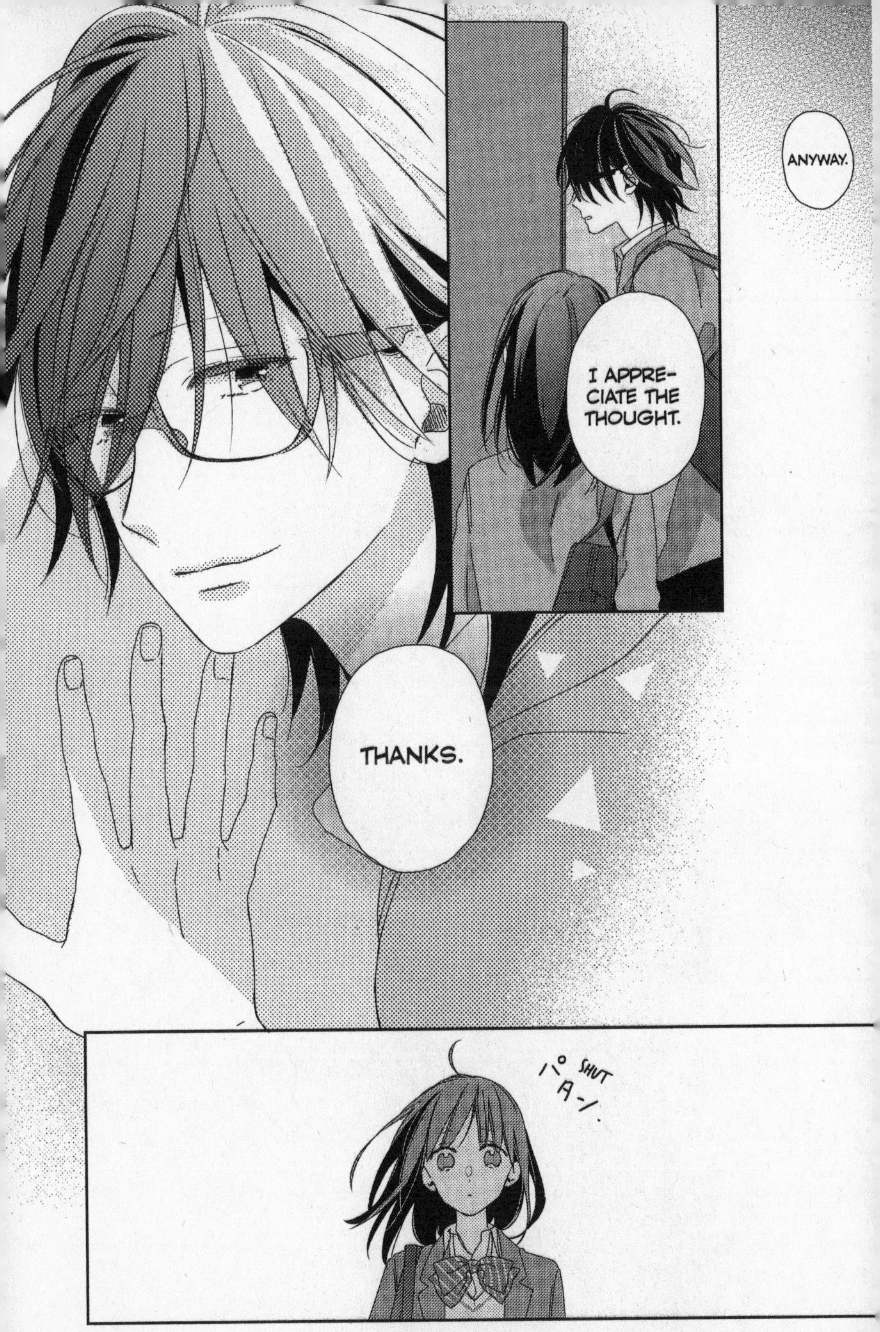
ANYWAY.
I APPRECIATE THE THOUGHT.
THANKS.
パターン
SHUT

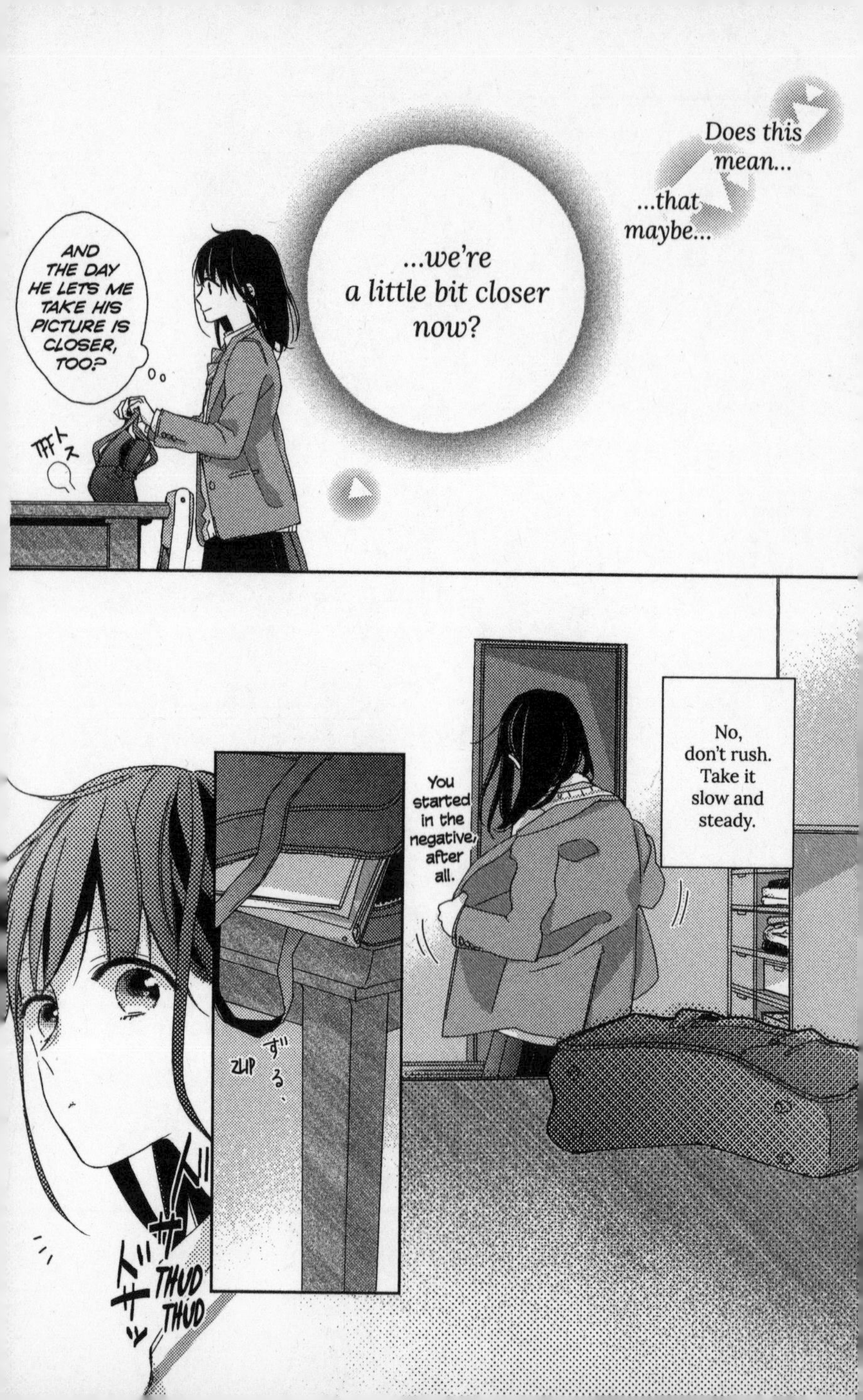
Does this mean...
...that maybe...
...we're a little bit closer now?
AND THE DAY HE LETS ME TAKE HIS PICTURE IS CLOSER, TOO?
TFF
No, don't rush. Take it slow and steady.
You started in the negative, after all.
ZIP
THUD THUD

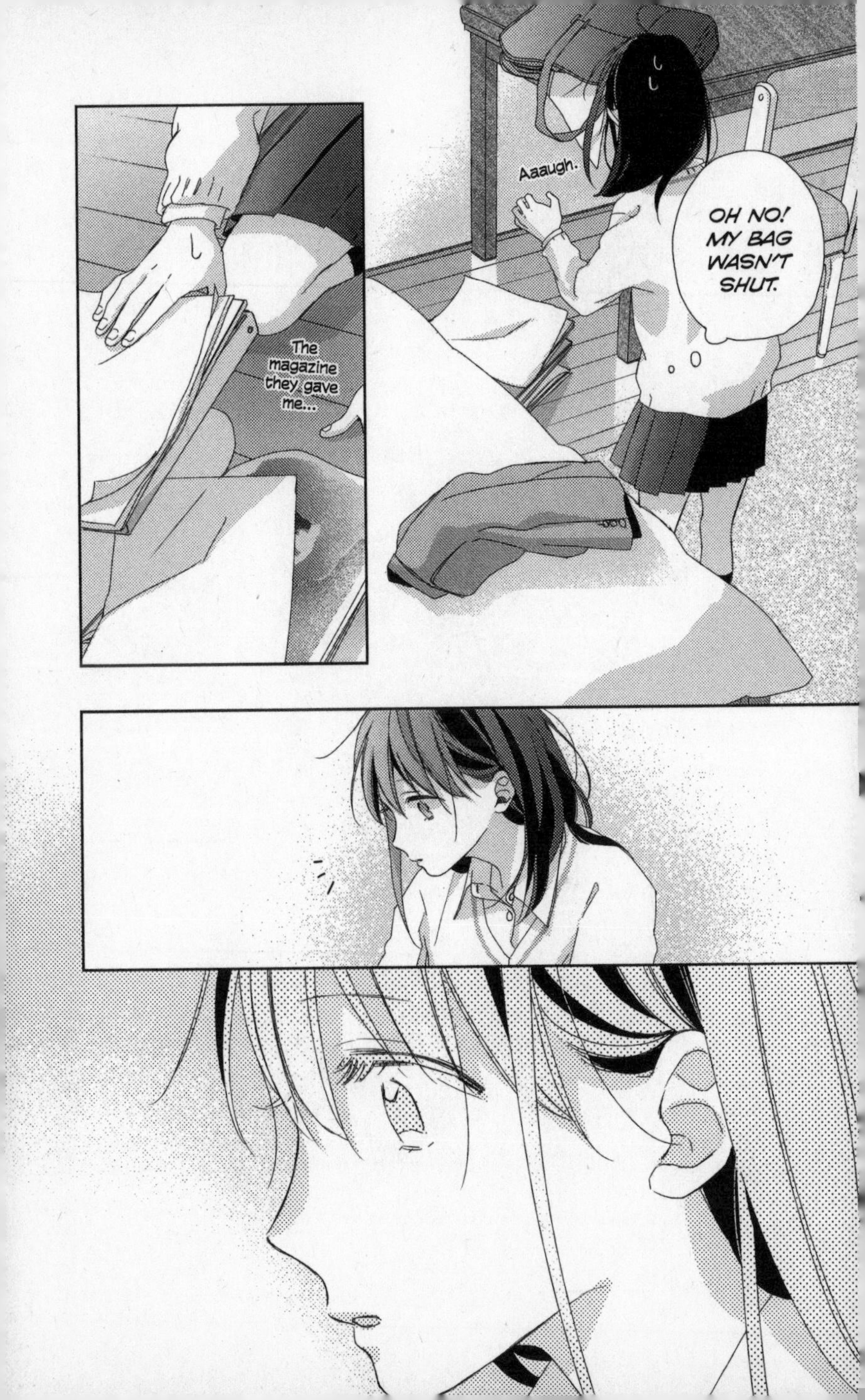
OH NO! MY BAG WASN'T SHUT.
Aaaugh.
The magazine they gave me...

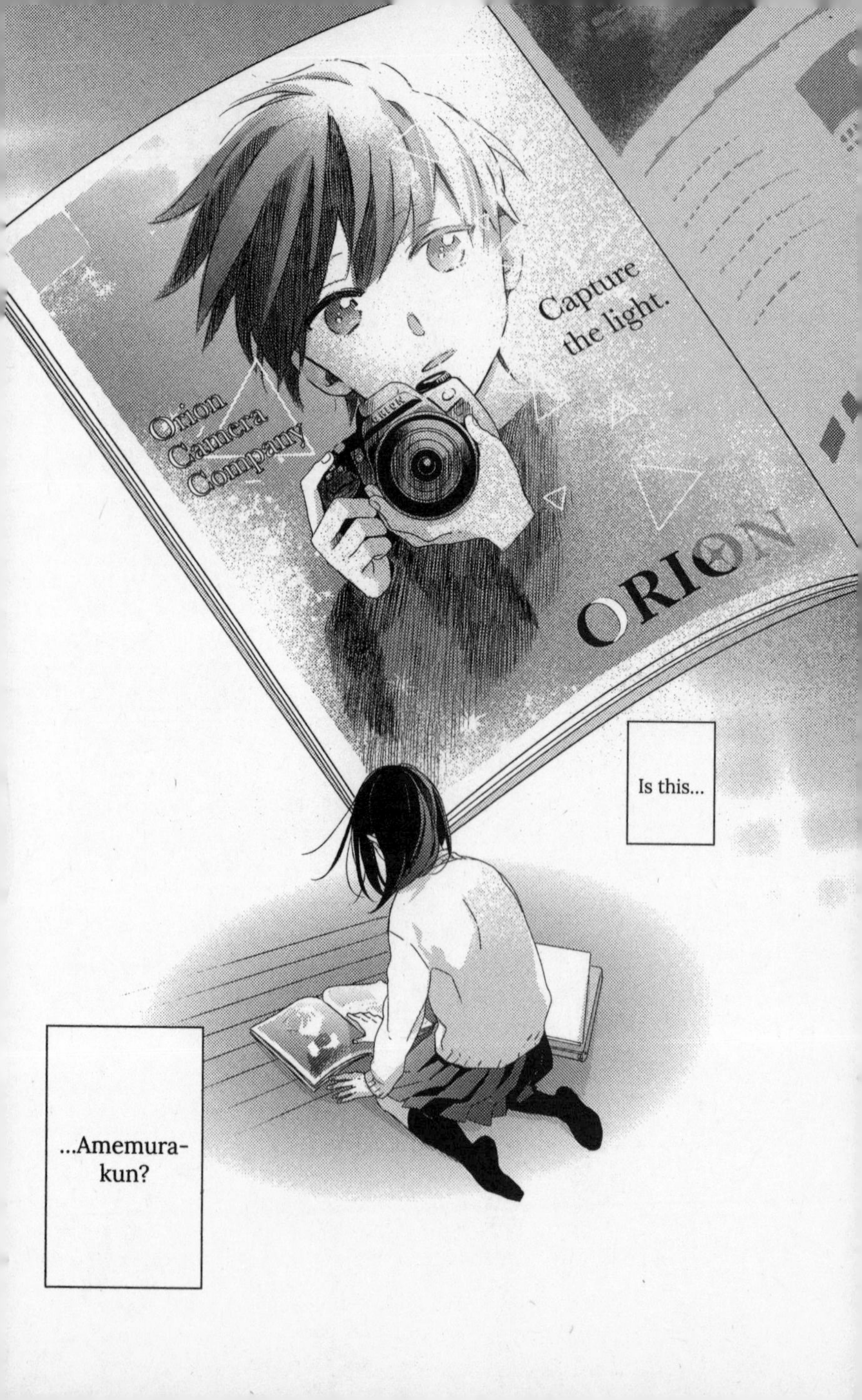
Capture the light.
Orion Camera Company
ORION
Is this...
...Amemura-kun?

FILM 3

The Secret Amemura-kun

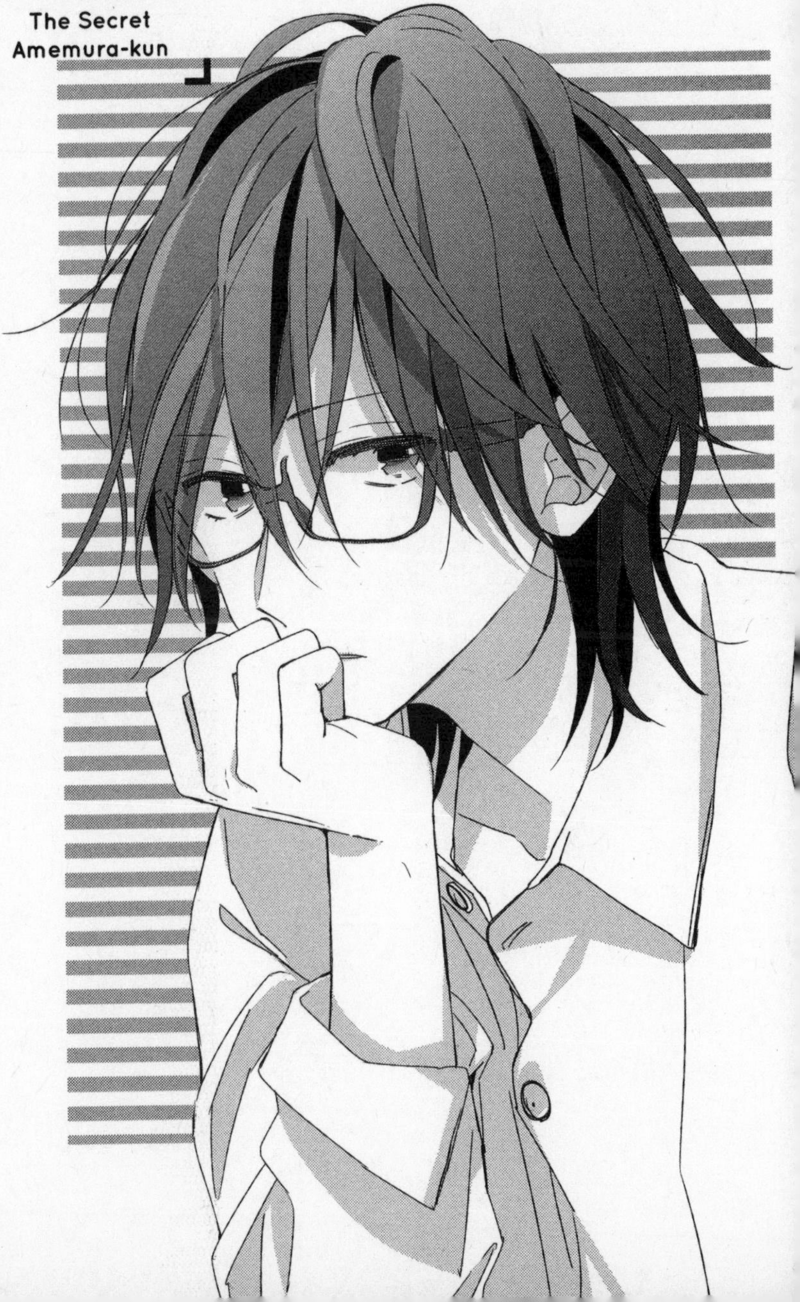

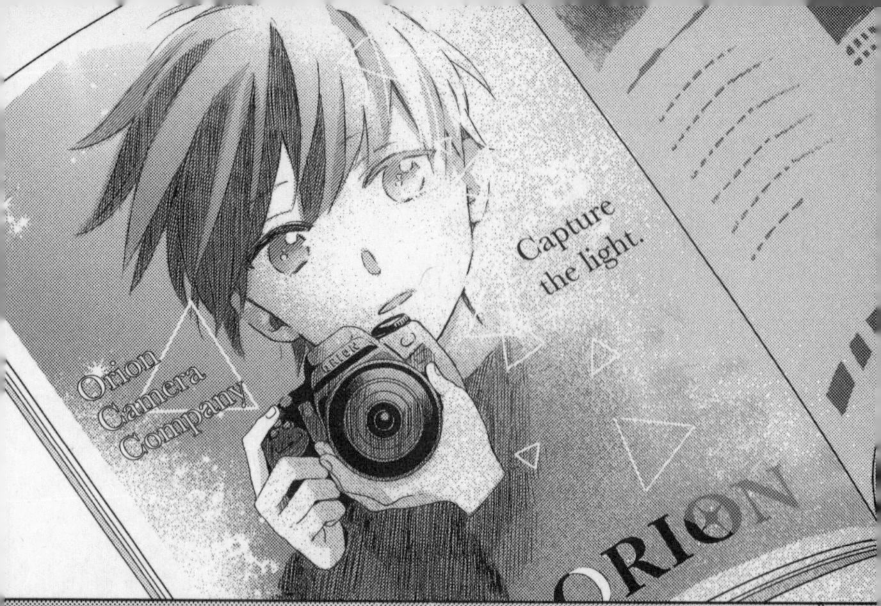
Capture the light.
Orion Camera Company
ORION

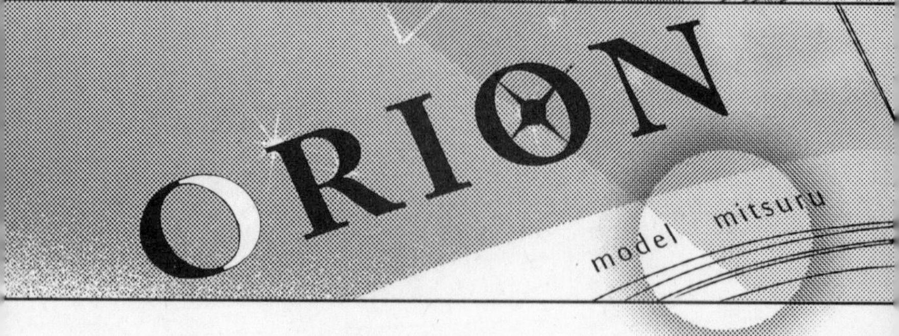
ORION
model mitsuru

LOVE IN FOCUS

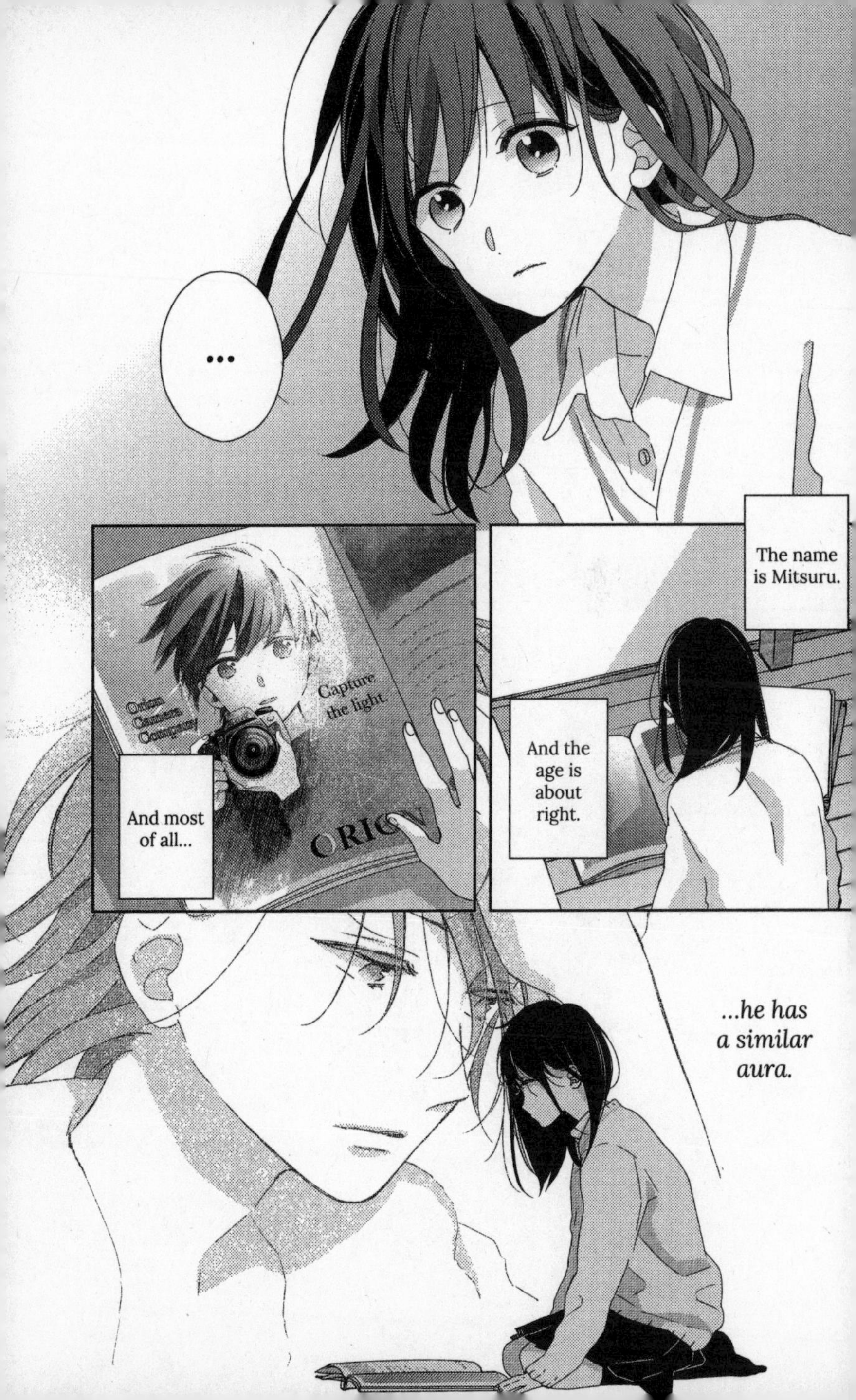
...
The name is Mitsuru.
And the age is about right.
Capture the light.
Orion Camera Company
And most of all...
...he has a similar aura.

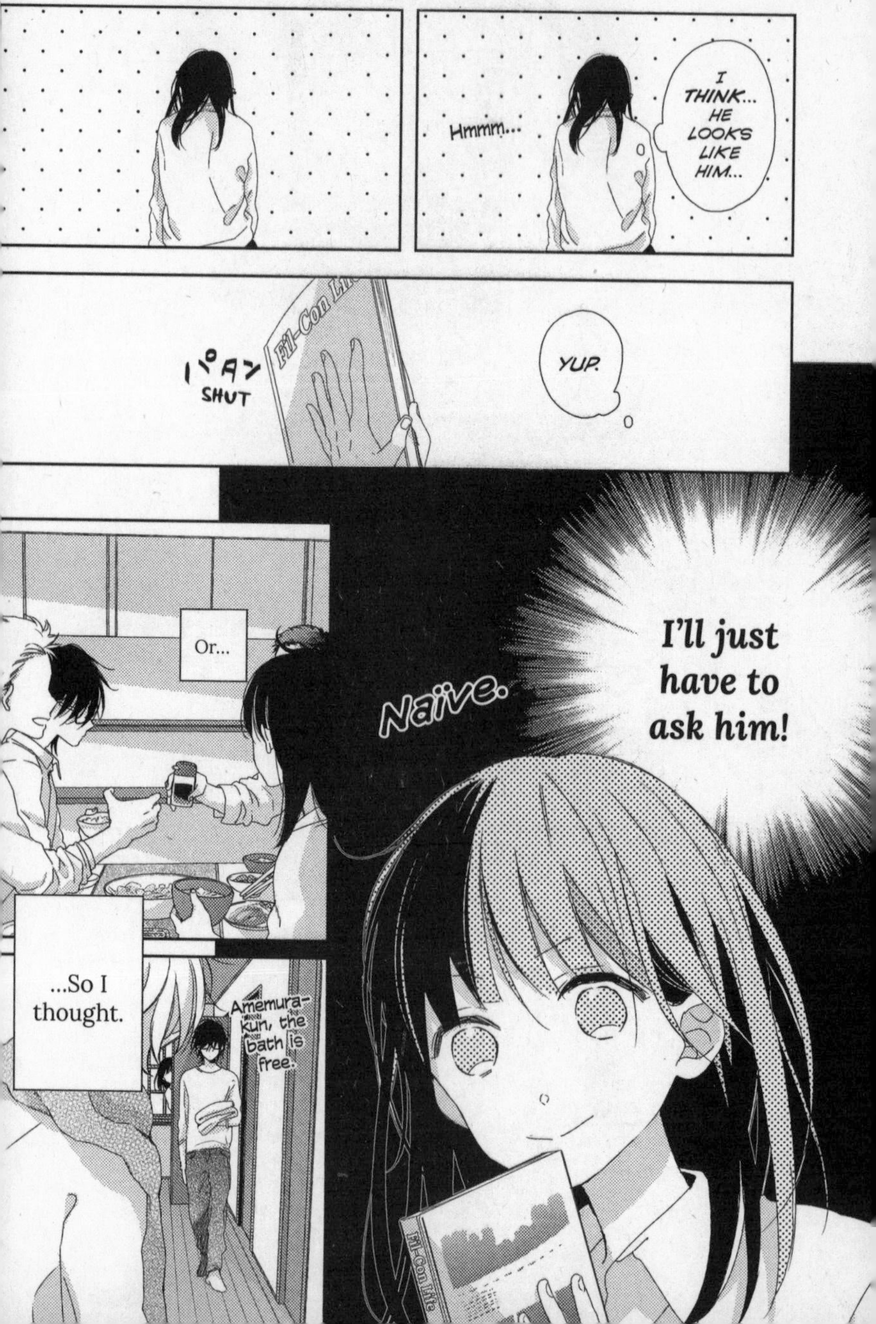

I THINK... HE LOOKS LIKE HIM...
Hmmm...
YUP.
パタン
SHUT
I'll just have to ask him!
Naïve.
Or...
...So I thought.
Amemura-kun, the bath is free.

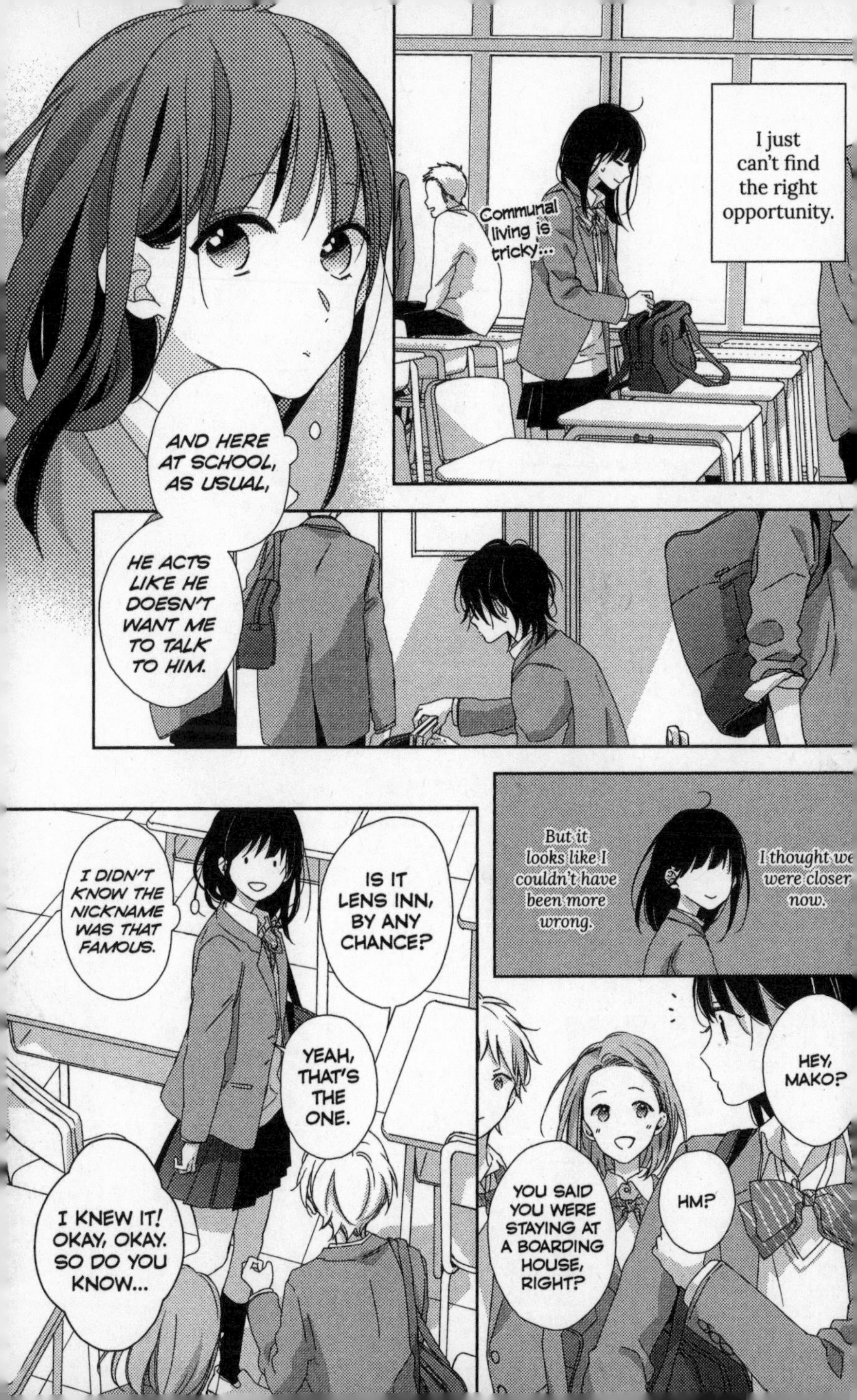
I just can't find the right opportunity.
Communal living is tricky...
AND HERE AT SCHOOL, AS USUAL,
HE ACTS LIKE HE DOESN'T WANT ME TO TALK TO HIM.
I thought we were closer now.
But it looks like I couldn't have been more wrong.
HEY, MAKO?
HM?
YOU SAID YOU WERE STAYING AT A BOARDING HOUSE, RIGHT?
IS IT LENS INN, BY ANY CHANCE?
I DIDN'T KNOW THE NICKNAME WAS THAT FAMOUS.
YEAH, THAT'S THE ONE.
I KNEW IT! OKAY, OKAY. SO DO YOU KNOW...

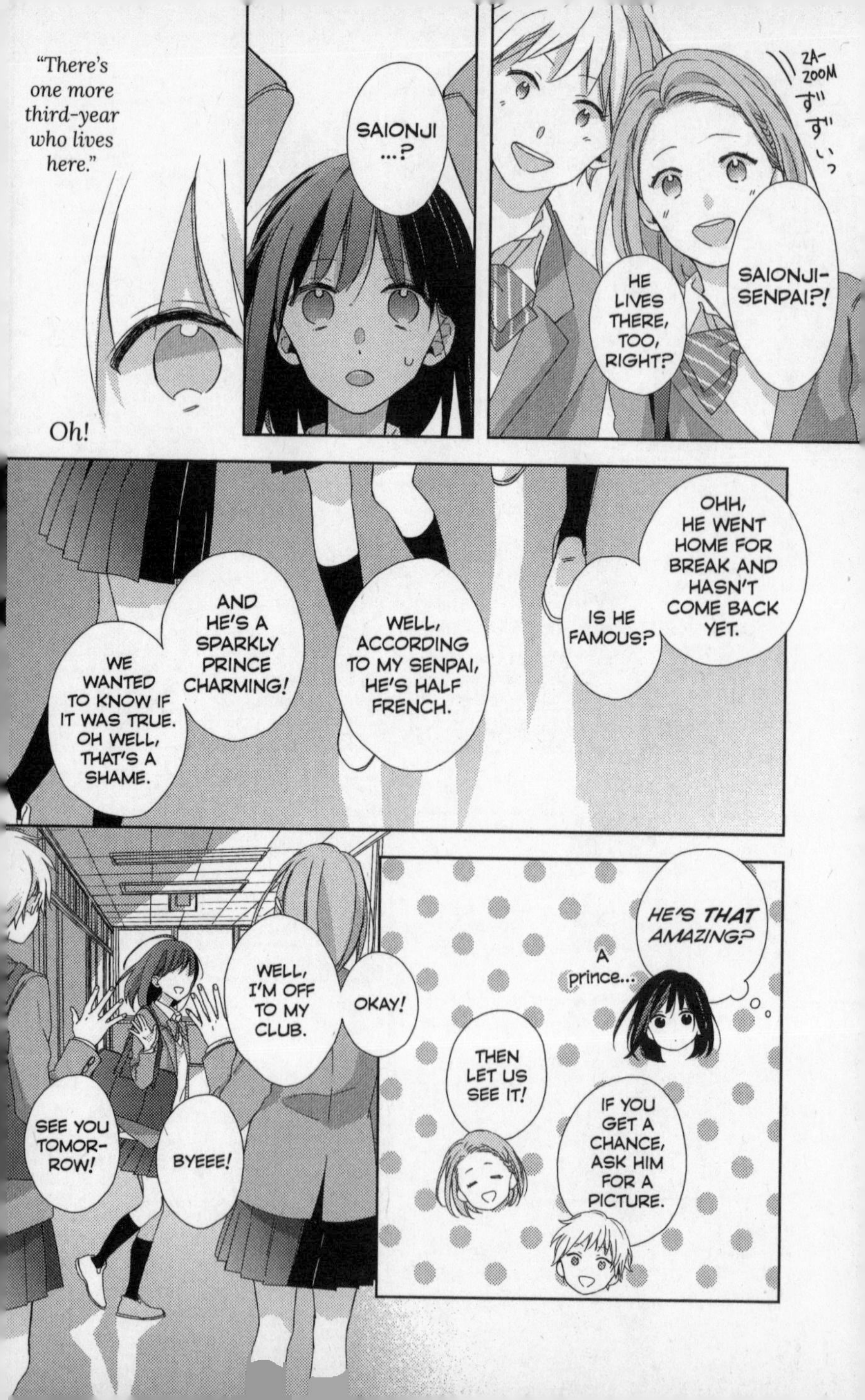
ZA-ZOOM
ずずいっ
SAIONJI-SENPAI?!
HE LIVES THERE, TOO, RIGHT?
SAIONJI ...?
"There's one more third-year who lives here."
Oh!
OHH, HE WENT HOME FOR BREAK AND HASN'T COME BACK YET.
IS HE FAMOUS?
WELL, ACCORDING TO MY SENPAI, HE'S HALF FRENCH.
AND HE'S A SPARKLY PRINCE CHARMING!
WE WANTED TO KNOW IF IT WAS TRUE. OH WELL, THAT'S A SHAME.
HE'S THAT AMAZING?
A prince...
IF YOU GET A CHANCE, ASK HIM FOR A PICTURE.
THEN LET US SEE IT!
WELL, I'M OFF TO MY CLUB.
OKAY!
BYEEE!
SEE YOU TOMORROW!

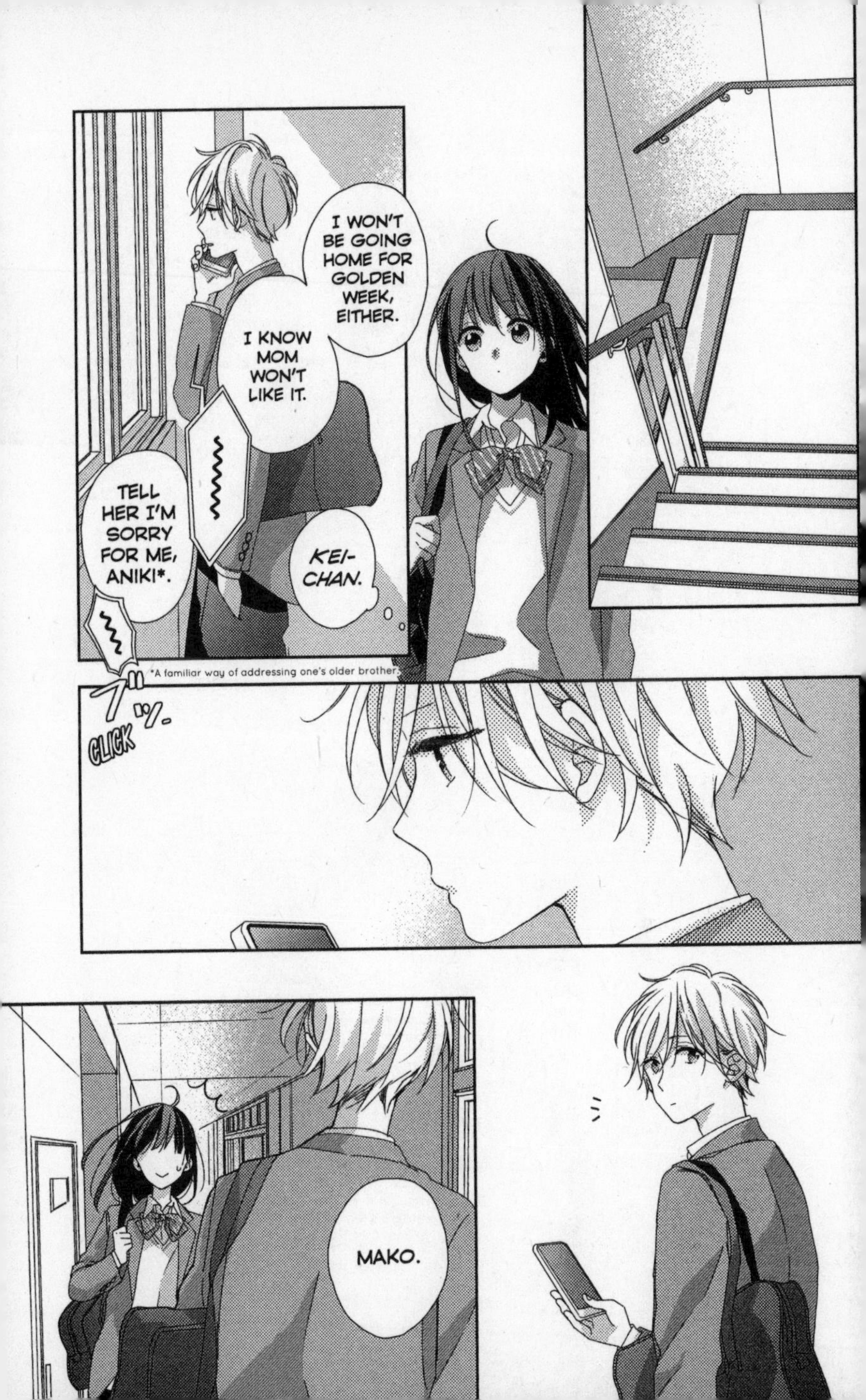
I WON'T BE GOING HOME FOR GOLDEN WEEK, EITHER.
I KNOW MOM WON'T LIKE IT.
KEI-CHAN.
TELL HER I'M SORRY FOR ME, ANIKI*.
CLICK
MAKO.
*A familiar way of addressing one's older brother.

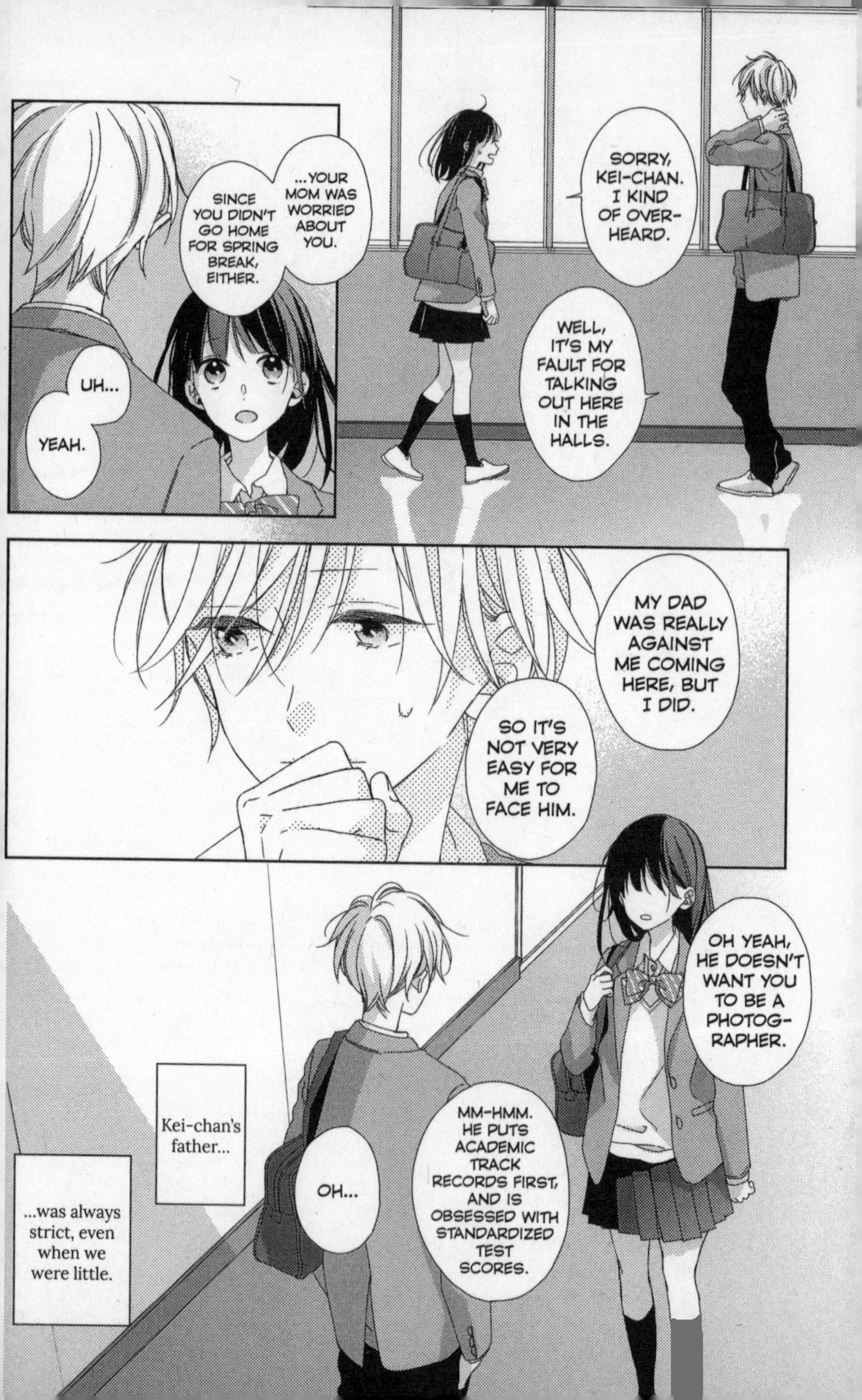
SORRY, KEI-CHAN. I KIND OF OVER-HEARD.
WELL, IT'S MY FAULT FOR TALKING OUT HERE IN THE HALLS.
...YOUR MOM WAS WORRIED ABOUT YOU.
SINCE YOU DIDN'T GO HOME FOR SPRING BREAK, EITHER.
UH...
YEAH.
MY DAD WAS REALLY AGAINST ME COMING HERE, BUT I DID.
SO IT'S NOT VERY EASY FOR ME TO FACE HIM.
OH YEAH, HE DOESN'T WANT YOU TO BE A PHOTOG-RAPHER.
MM-HMM. HE PUTS ACADEMIC TRACK RECORDS FIRST, AND IS OBSESSED WITH STANDARDIZED TEST SCORES.
OH...
Kei-chan's father...
...was always strict, even when we were little.

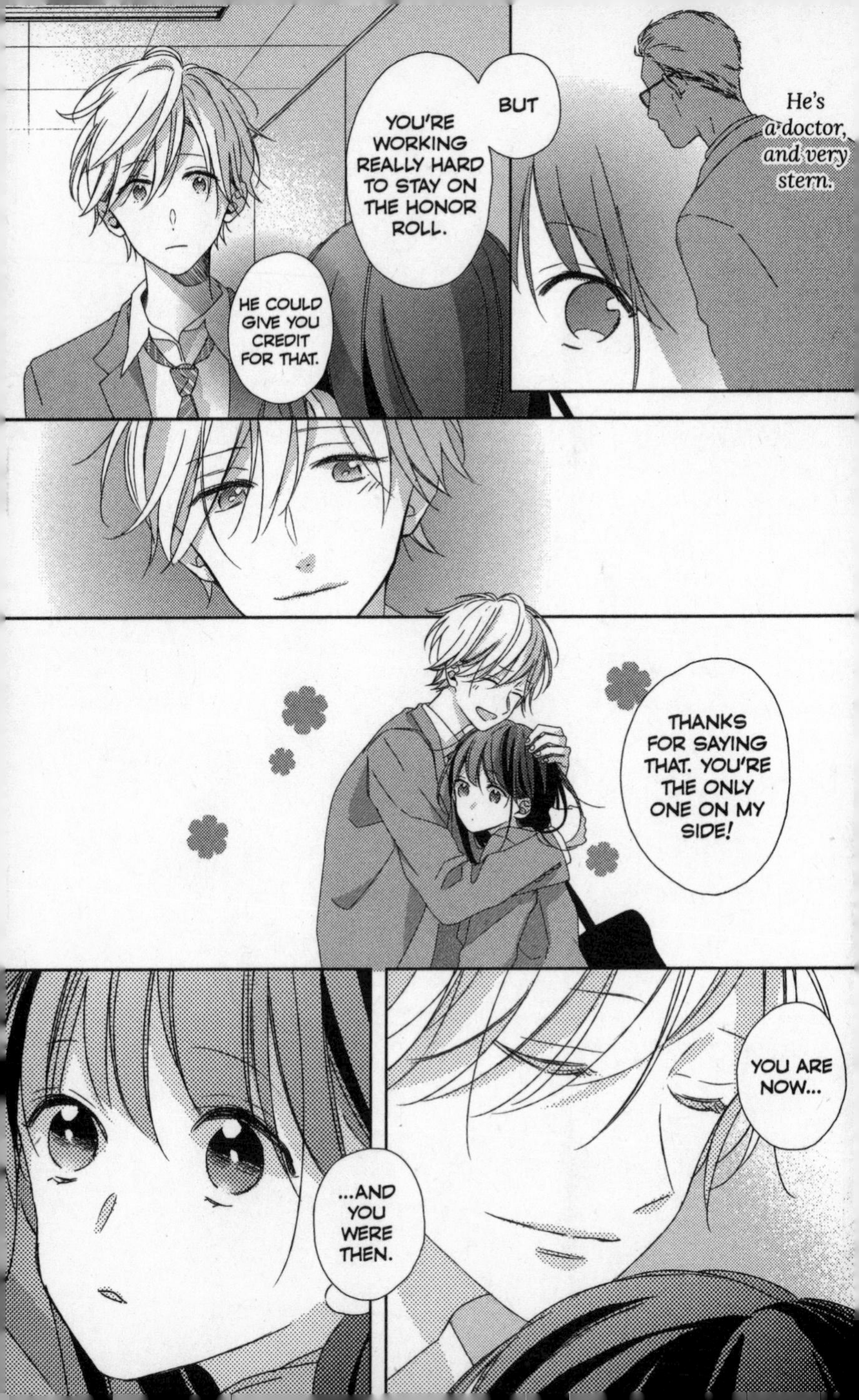
He's a doctor, and very stern.
BUT
YOU'RE WORKING REALLY HARD TO STAY ON THE HONOR ROLL.
HE COULD GIVE YOU CREDIT FOR THAT.
THANKS FOR SAYING THAT. YOU'RE THE ONLY ONE ON MY SIDE!
YOU ARE NOW...
...AND YOU WERE THEN.

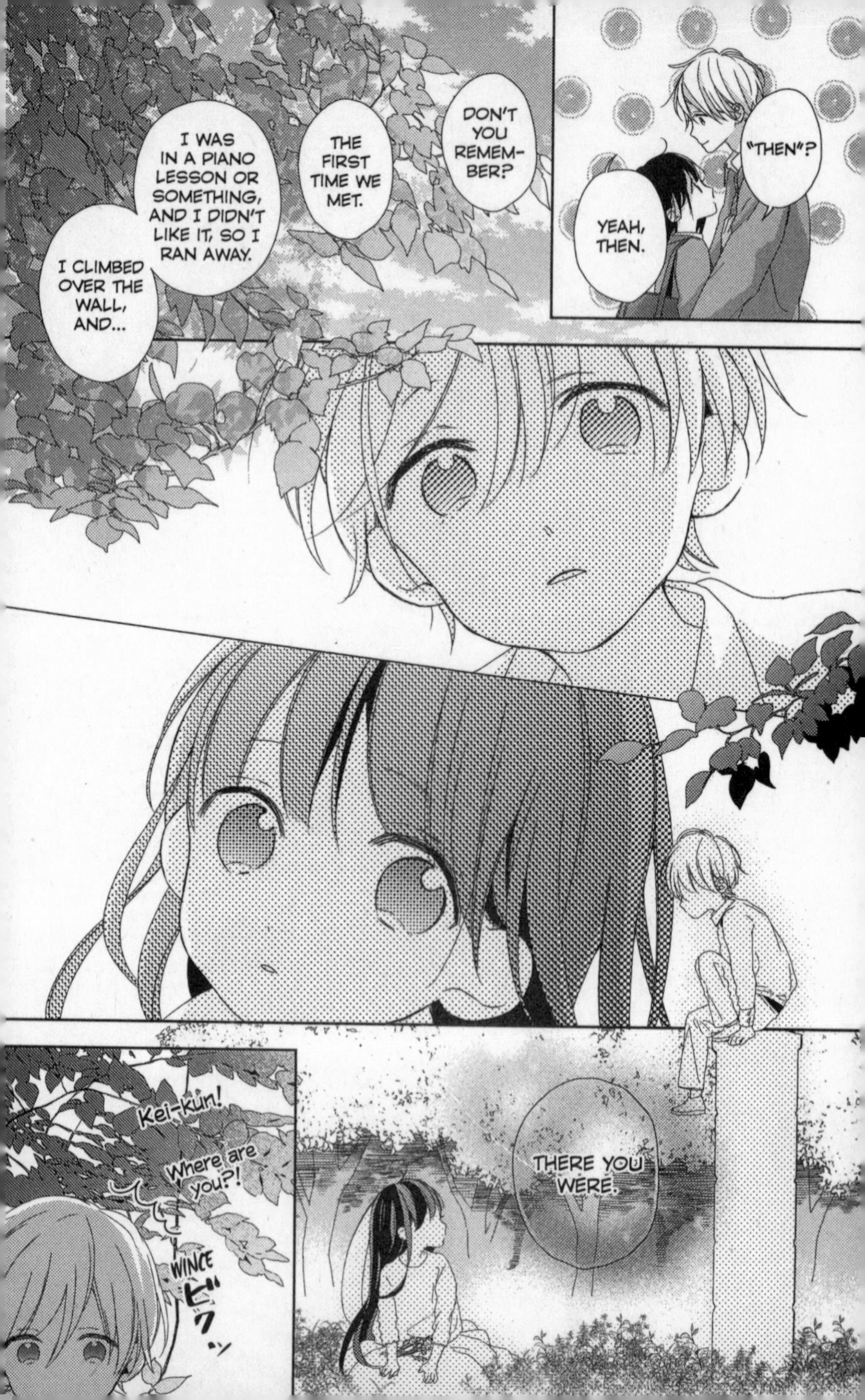
"THEN"?
YEAH, THEN.
DON'T YOU REMEMBER?
THE FIRST TIME WE MET.
I WAS IN A PIANO LESSON OR SOMETHING, AND I DIDN'T LIKE IT, SO I RAN AWAY.
I CLIMBED OVER THE WALL, AND...
THERE YOU WERE.
Kei-kun!
Where are you?!
WINCE
ビクッ

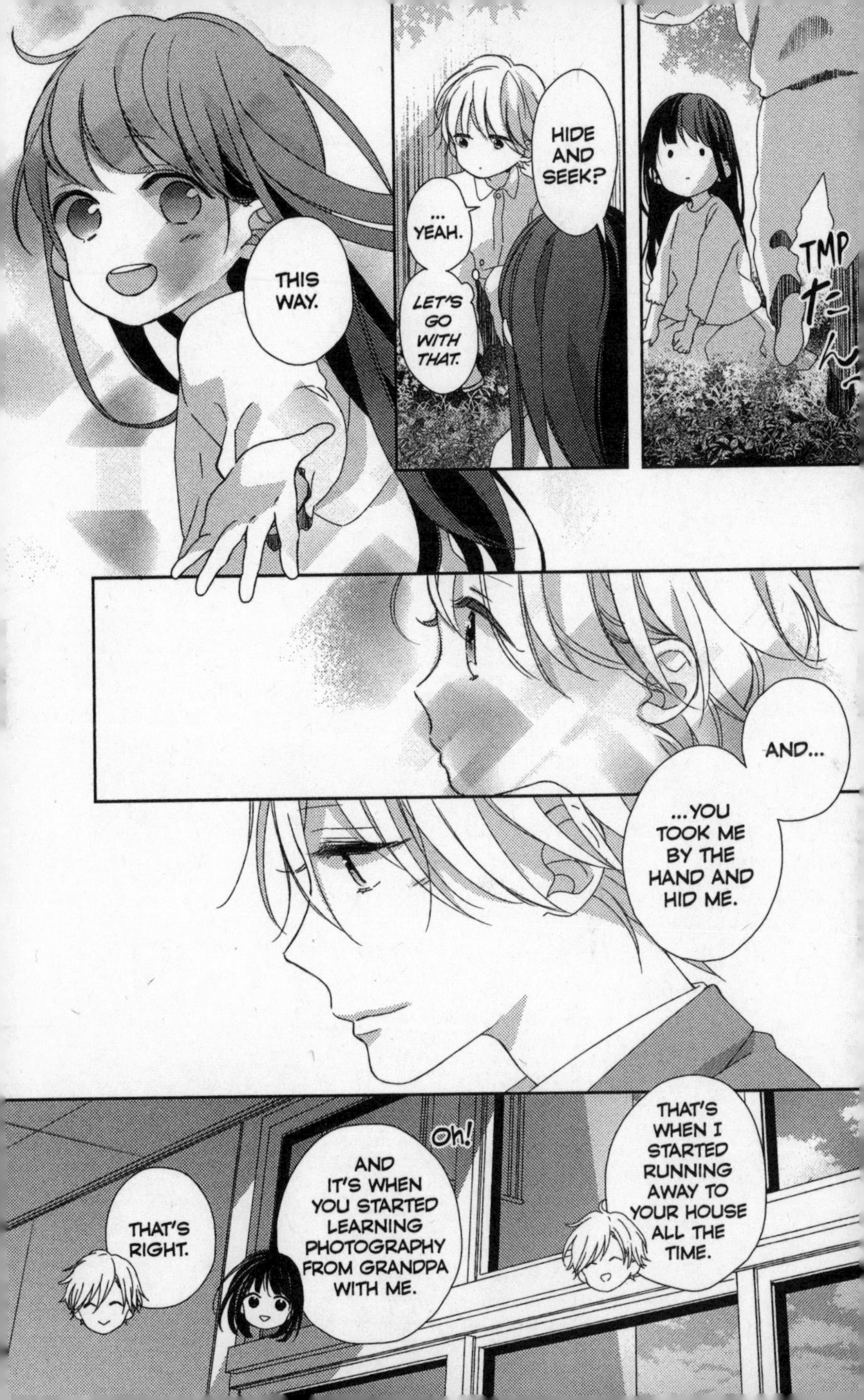
TMP
たん
HIDE AND SEEK?
...YEAH.
LET'S GO WITH THAT.
THIS WAY.
AND...
...YOU TOOK ME BY THE HAND AND HID ME.
THAT'S WHEN I STARTED RUNNING AWAY TO YOUR HOUSE ALL THE TIME.
Oh!
AND IT'S WHEN YOU STARTED LEARNING PHOTOGRAPHY FROM GRANDPA WITH ME.
THAT'S RIGHT.

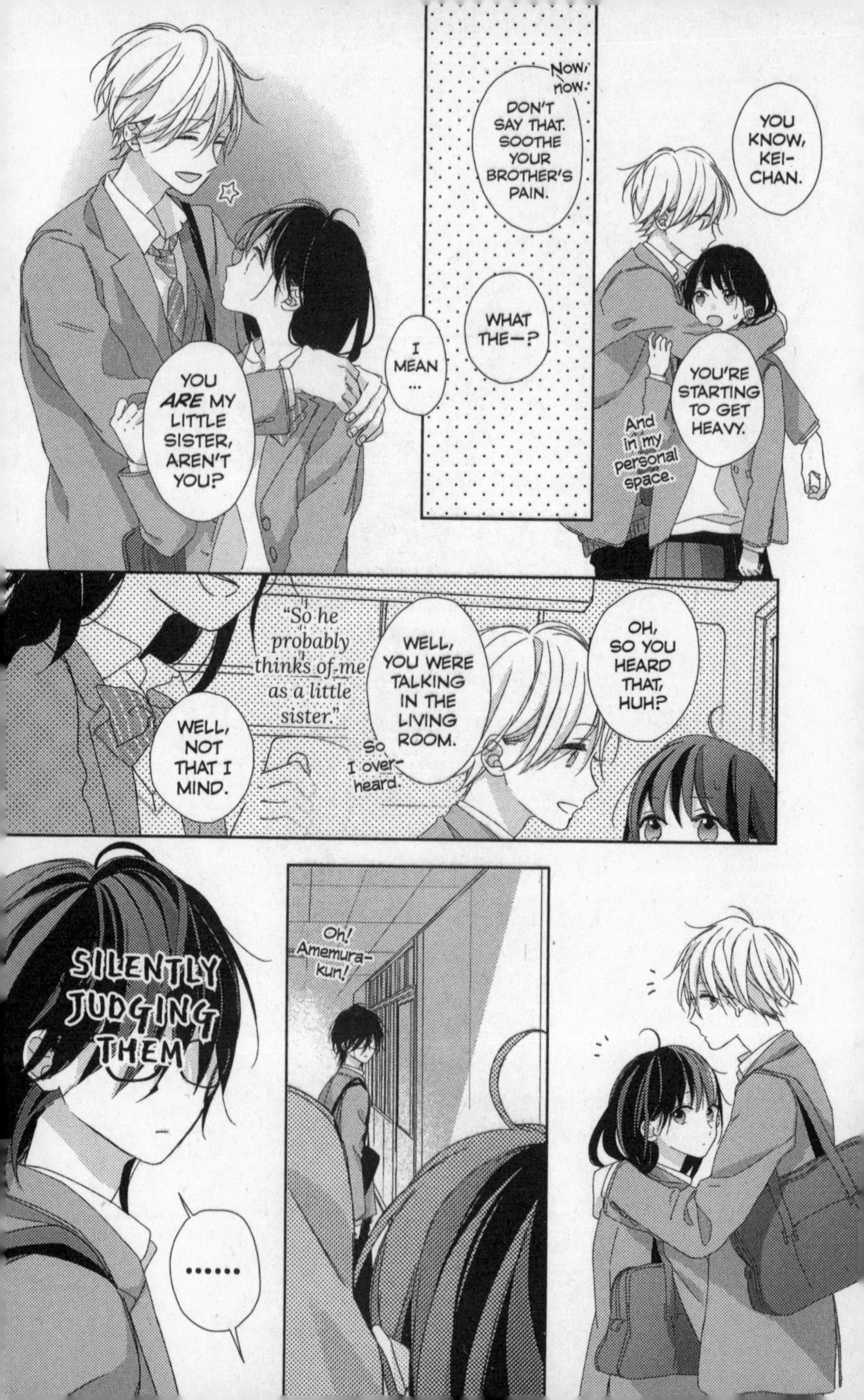

YOU KNOW, KEI-CHAN.
YOU'RE STARTING TO GET HEAVY.
And in my personal space.
Now, now.
DON'T SAY THAT. SOOTHE YOUR BROTHER'S PAIN.
WHAT THE—?
I MEAN ...
YOU *ARE* MY LITTLE SISTER, AREN'T YOU?
OH, SO YOU HEARD THAT, HUH?
WELL, YOU WERE TALKING IN THE LIVING ROOM.
So I over-heard.
"So he probably thinks of me as a little sister."
WELL, NOT THAT I MIND.
Oh! Amemura-kun!
SILENTLY JUDGING THEM
......

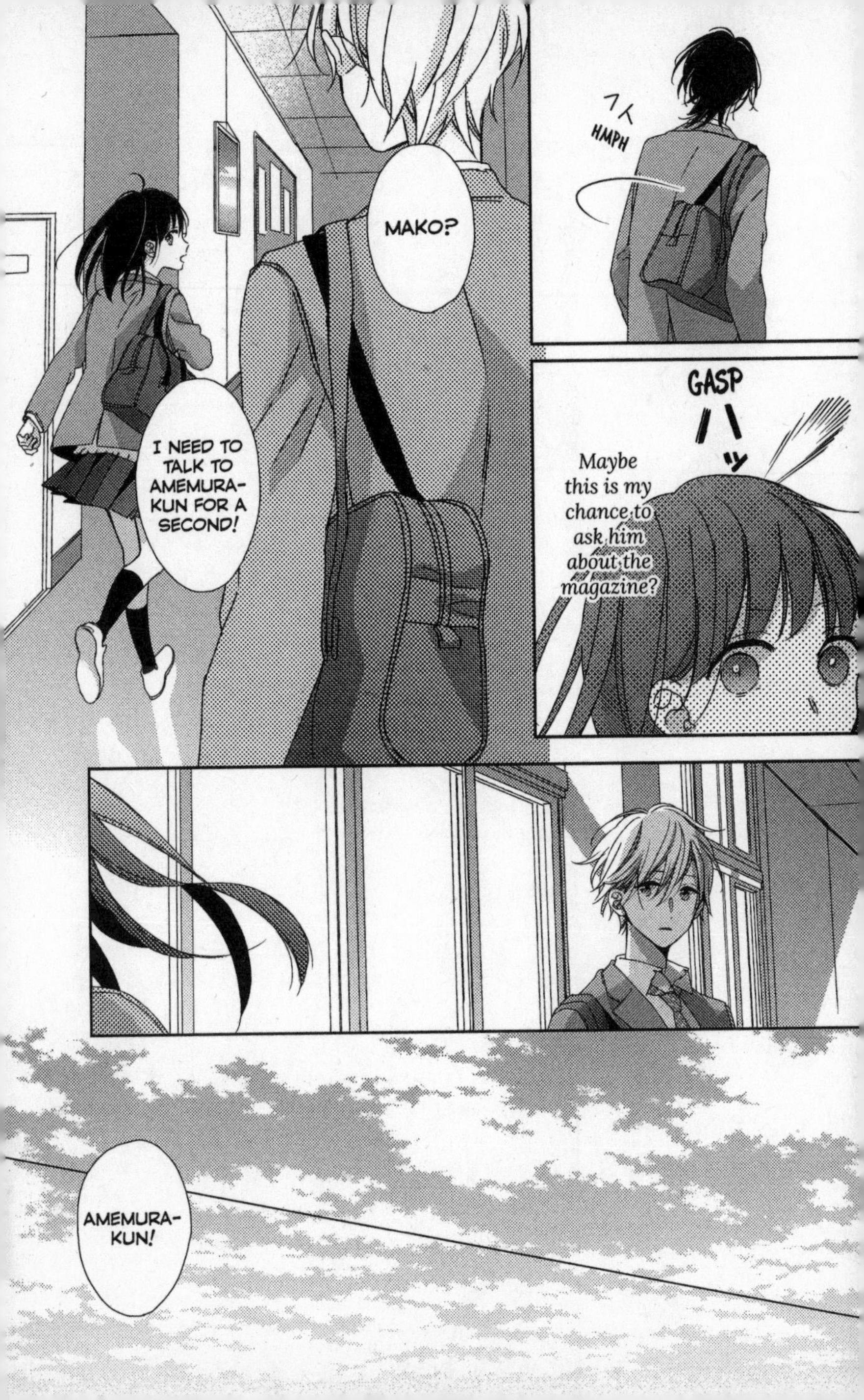

へ人
HMPH
GASP
ハッ
Maybe this is my chance to ask him about the magazine?
MAKO?
I NEED TO TALK TO AMEMURA-KUN FOR A SECOND!
AMEMURA-KUN!

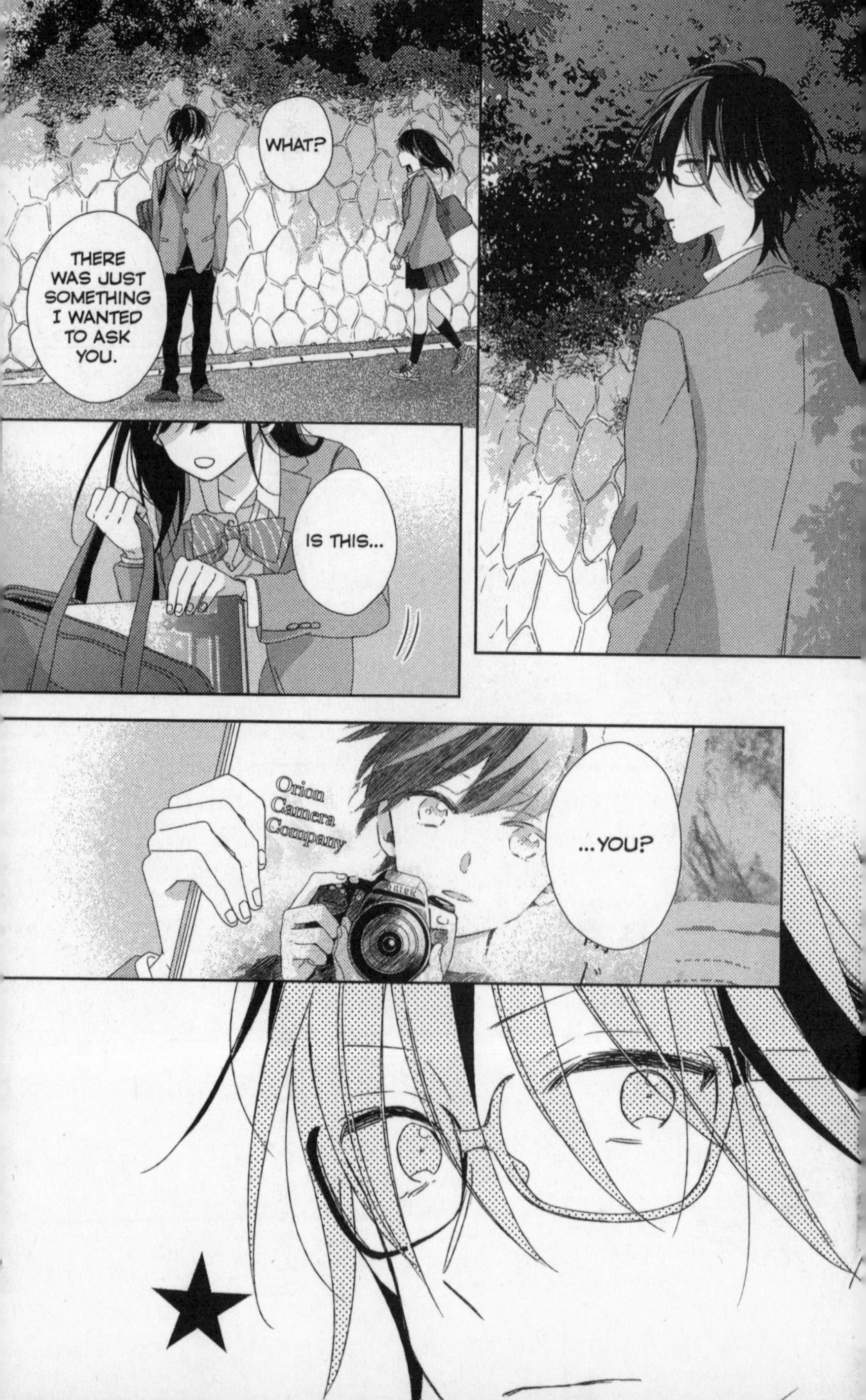
WHAT?
THERE WAS JUST SOMETHING I WANTED TO ASK YOU.
IS THIS...
...YOU?
Orion Camera Company

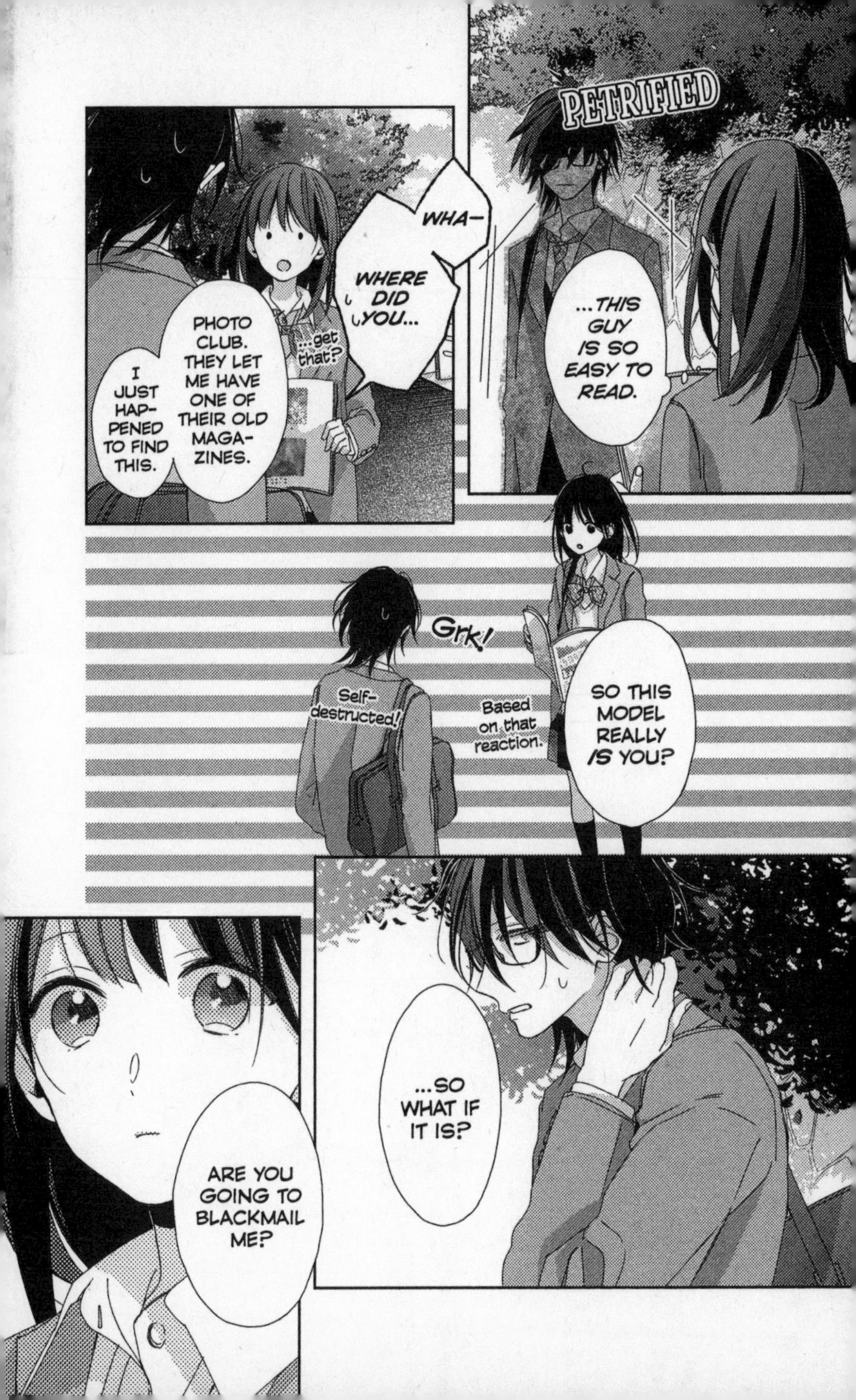
PETRIFIED
...THIS GUY IS SO EASY TO READ.
WHA—
WHERE DID YOU...
...get that?
PHOTO CLUB. THEY LET ME HAVE ONE OF THEIR OLD MAGA-ZINES.
I JUST HAP-PENED TO FIND THIS.
SO THIS MODEL REALLY IS YOU?
Grk!
Based on that reaction.
Self-destructed!
...SO WHAT IF IT IS?
ARE YOU GOING TO BLACKMAIL ME?

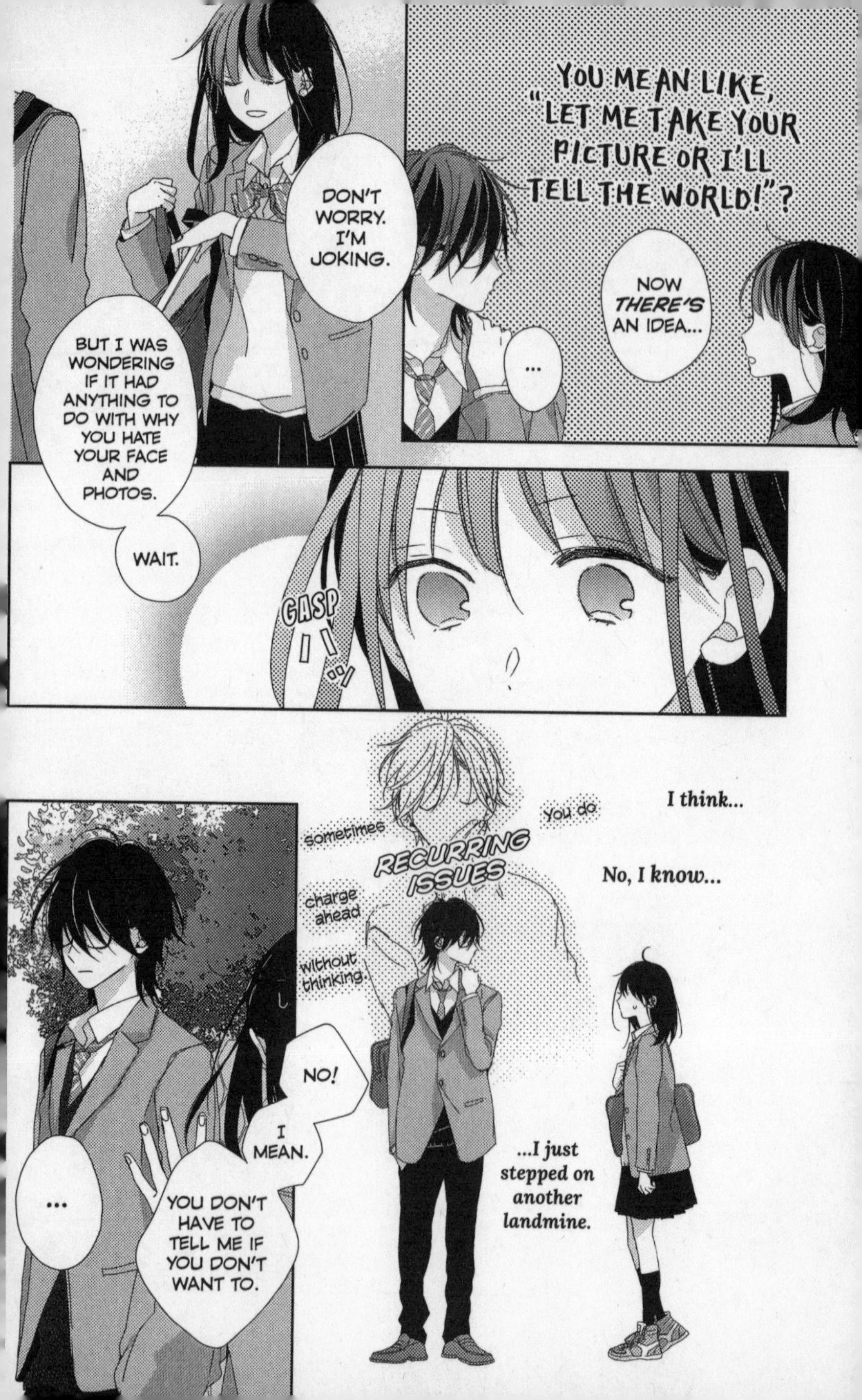
YOU MEAN LIKE, "LET ME TAKE YOUR PICTURE OR I'LL TELL THE WORLD!"?
NOW THERE'S AN IDEA...
...
DON'T WORRY. I'M JOKING.
BUT I WAS WONDERING IF IT HAD ANYTHING TO DO WITH WHY YOU HATE YOUR FACE AND PHOTOS.
WAIT.
GASP
I think...
No, I know...
You do
sometimes
charge ahead
without thinking.
RECURRING ISSUES
...I just stepped on another landmine.
NO!
I MEAN.
YOU DON'T HAVE TO TELL ME IF YOU DON'T WANT TO.
...

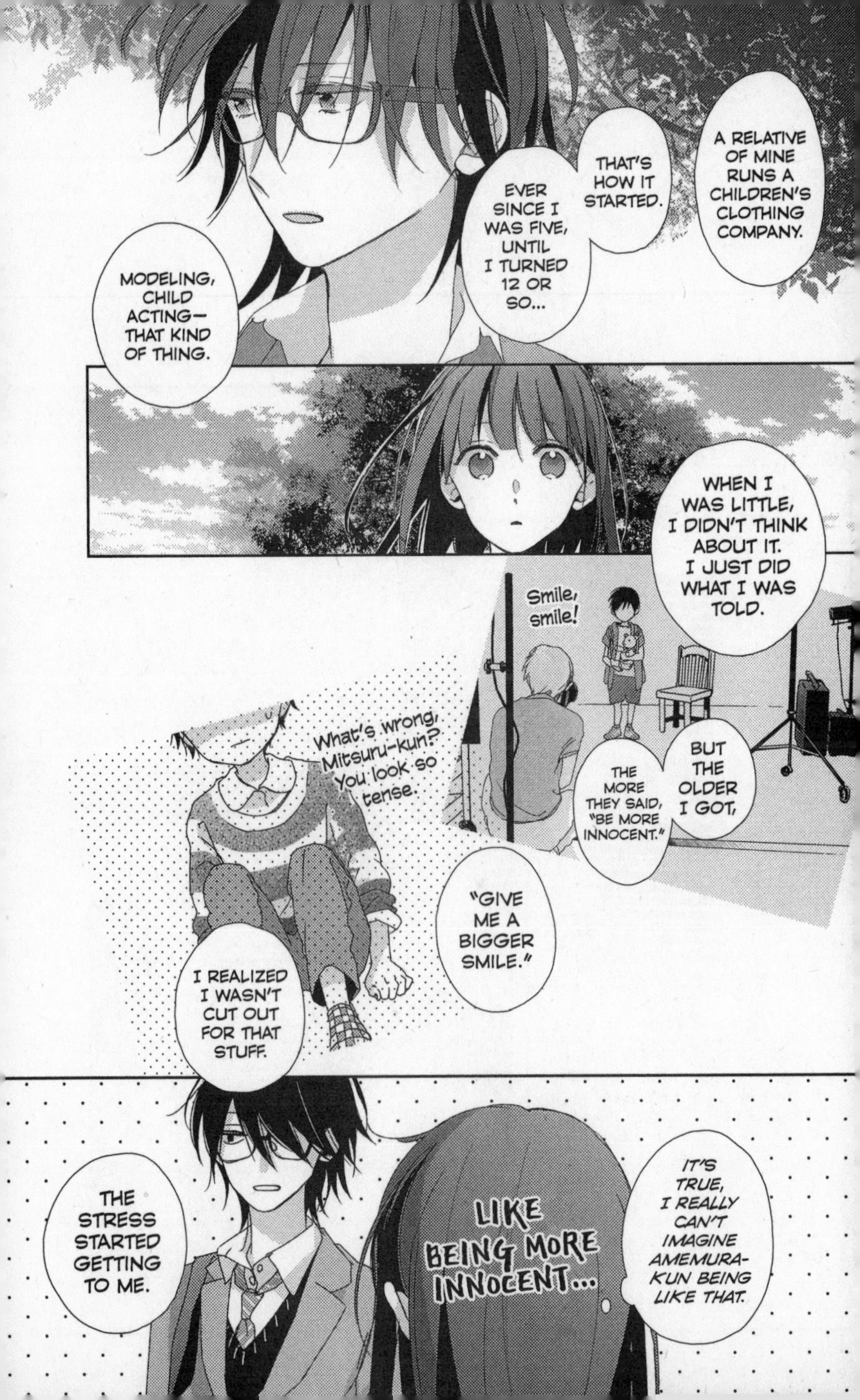
A RELATIVE OF MINE RUNS A CHILDREN'S CLOTHING COMPANY.
THAT'S HOW IT STARTED.
EVER SINCE I WAS FIVE, UNTIL I TURNED 12 OR SO...
MODELING, CHILD ACTING—THAT KIND OF THING.
WHEN I WAS LITTLE, I DIDN'T THINK ABOUT IT. I JUST DID WHAT I WAS TOLD.
Smile, smile!
BUT THE OLDER I GOT,
THE MORE THEY SAID, "BE MORE INNOCENT."
What's wrong, Mitsuru-kun? You look so tense.
"GIVE ME A BIGGER SMILE."
I REALIZED I WASN'T CUT OUT FOR THAT STUFF.
IT'S TRUE, I REALLY CAN'T IMAGINE AMEMURA-KUN BEING LIKE THAT.
LIKE BEING MORE INNOCENT...
THE STRESS STARTED GETTING TO ME.

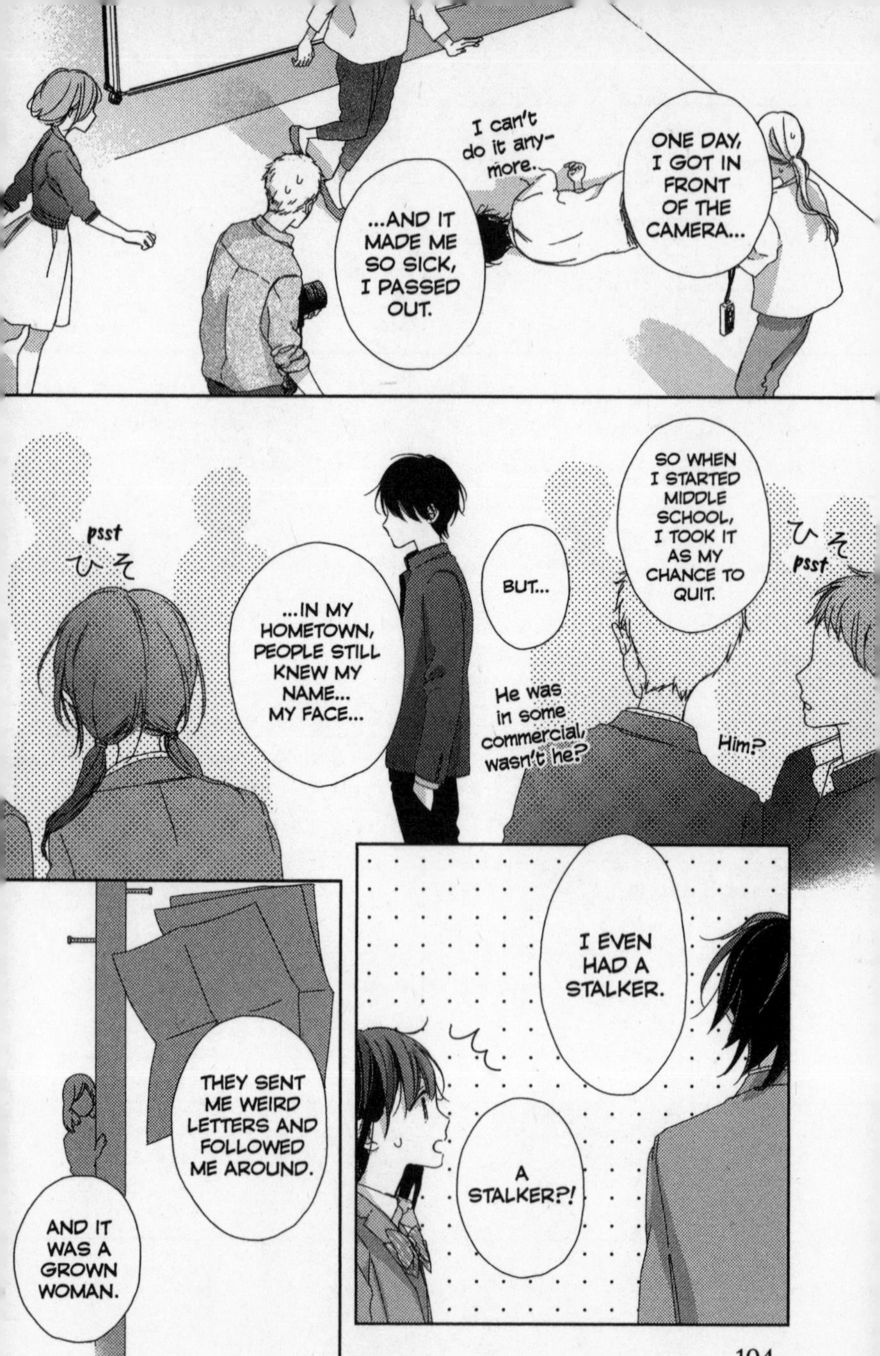
ONE DAY, I GOT IN FRONT OF THE CAMERA...
I can't do it any-more.
...AND IT MADE ME SO SICK, I PASSED OUT.
SO WHEN I STARTED MIDDLE SCHOOL, I TOOK IT AS MY CHANCE TO QUIT.
ひそ psst
Him?
He was in some commercial, wasn't he?
BUT...
...IN MY HOMETOWN, PEOPLE STILL KNEW MY NAME... MY FACE...
psst ひそ
I EVEN HAD A STALKER.
A STALKER?!
THEY SENT ME WEIRD LETTERS AND FOLLOWED ME AROUND.
AND IT WAS A GROWN WOMAN.

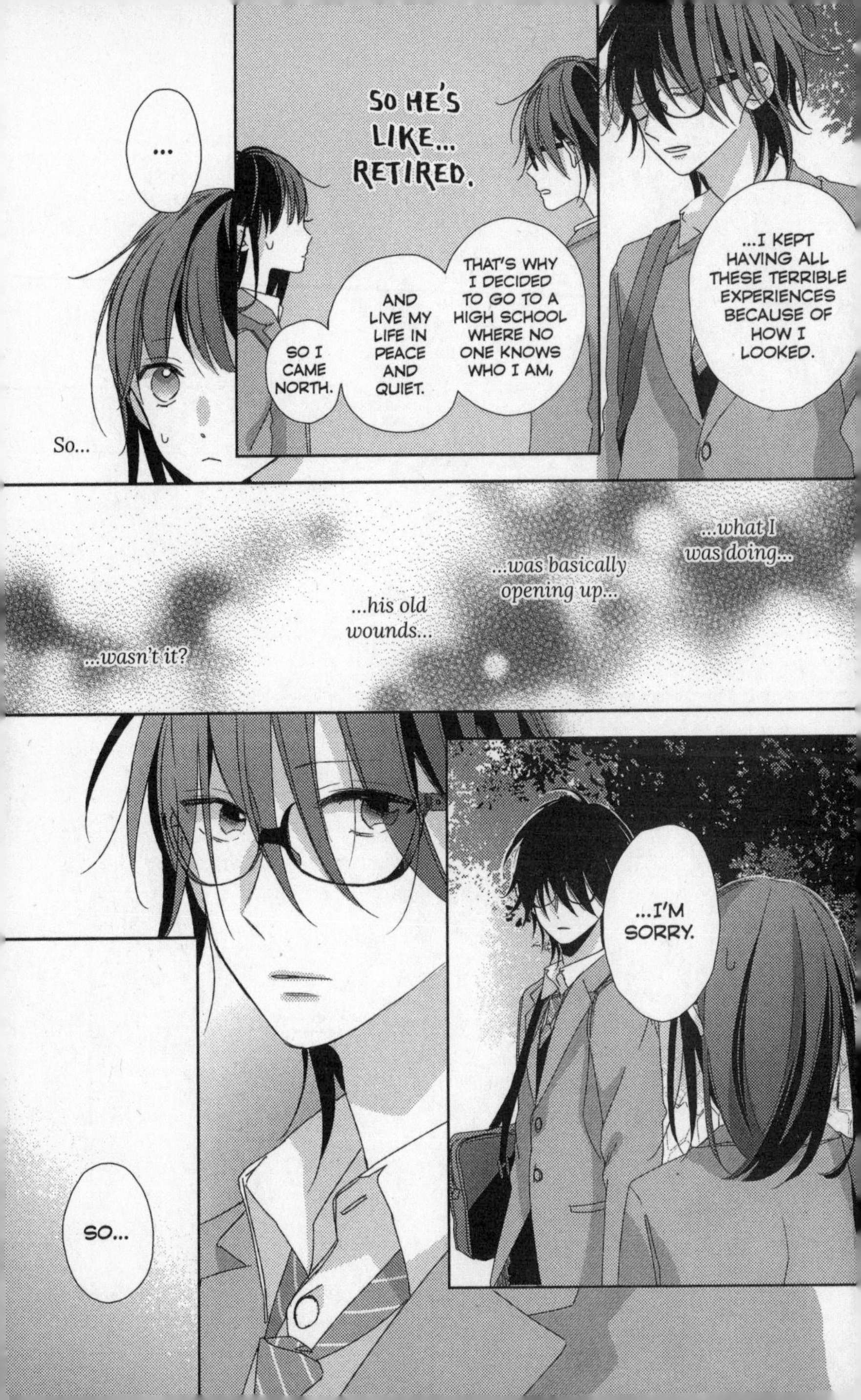

...I KEPT HAVING ALL THESE TERRIBLE EXPERIENCES BECAUSE OF HOW I LOOKED.
THAT'S WHY I DECIDED TO GO TO A HIGH SCHOOL WHERE NO ONE KNOWS WHO I AM,
AND LIVE MY LIFE IN PEACE AND QUIET.
SO I CAME NORTH.
SO HE'S LIKE... RETIRED.
...
So...
...what I was doing...
...was basically opening up...
...his old wounds...
...wasn't it?
...I'M SORRY.
SO...

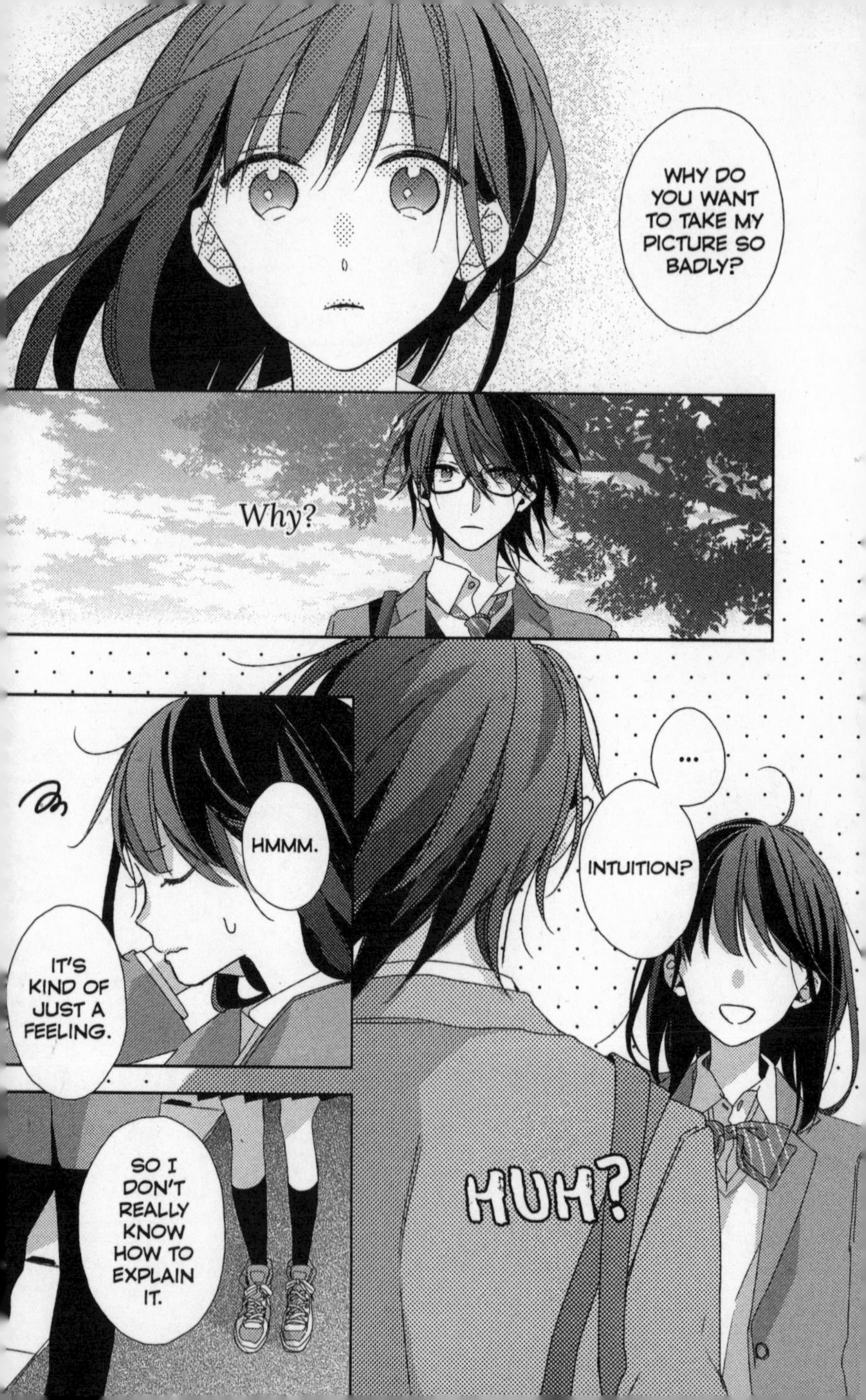
WHY DO YOU WANT TO TAKE MY PICTURE SO BADLY?
Why?
...
INTUITION?
HUH?
HMMM.
IT'S KIND OF JUST A FEELING.
SO I DON'T REALLY KNOW HOW TO EXPLAIN IT.

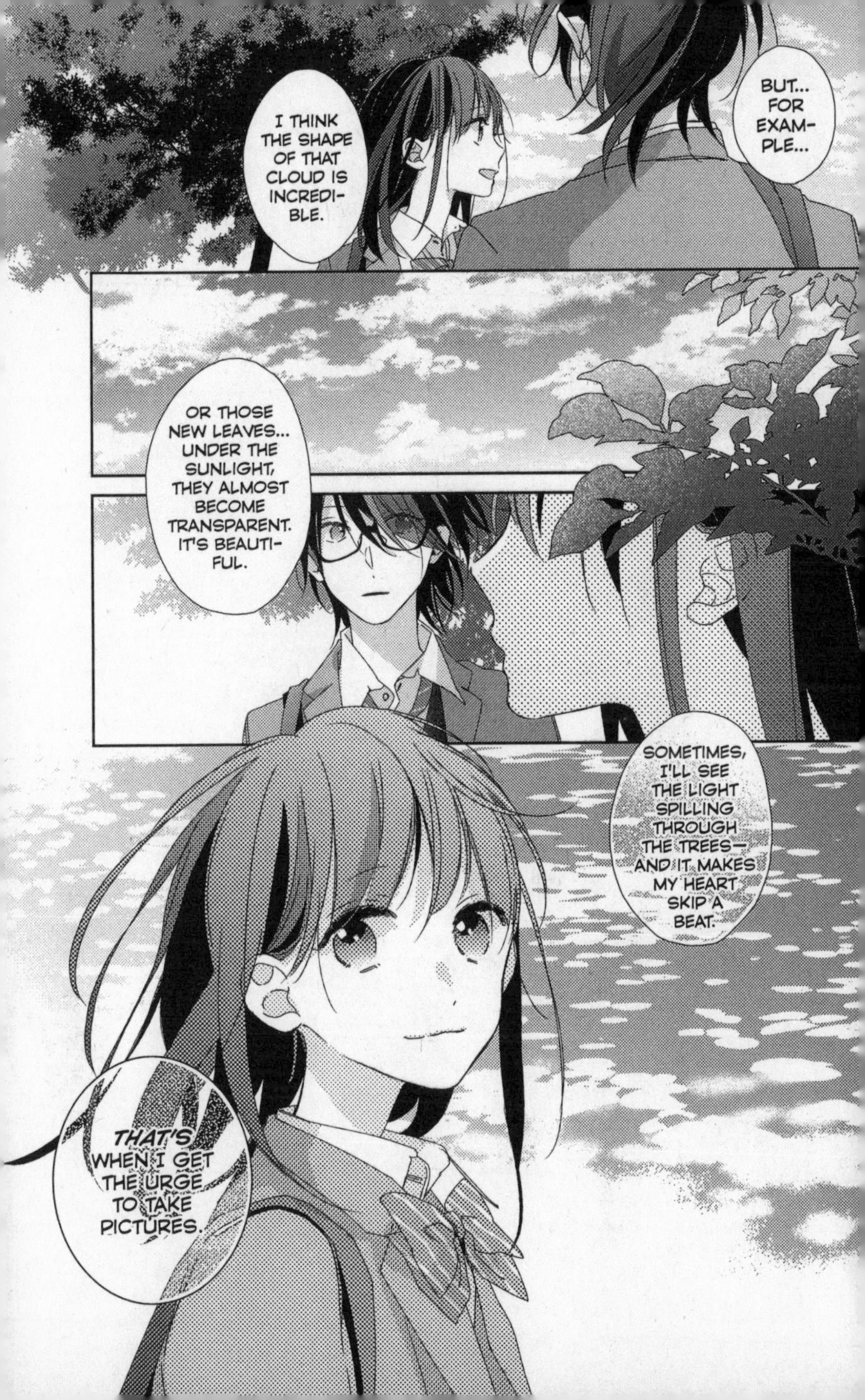
BUT... FOR EXAMPLE...
I THINK THE SHAPE OF THAT CLOUD IS INCREDIBLE.
OR THOSE NEW LEAVES... UNDER THE SUNLIGHT, THEY ALMOST BECOME TRANSPARENT. IT'S BEAUTIFUL.
SOMETIMES, I'LL SEE THE LIGHT SPILLING THROUGH THE TREES—AND IT MAKES MY HEART SKIP A BEAT.
THAT'S WHEN I GET THE URGE TO TAKE PICTURES.

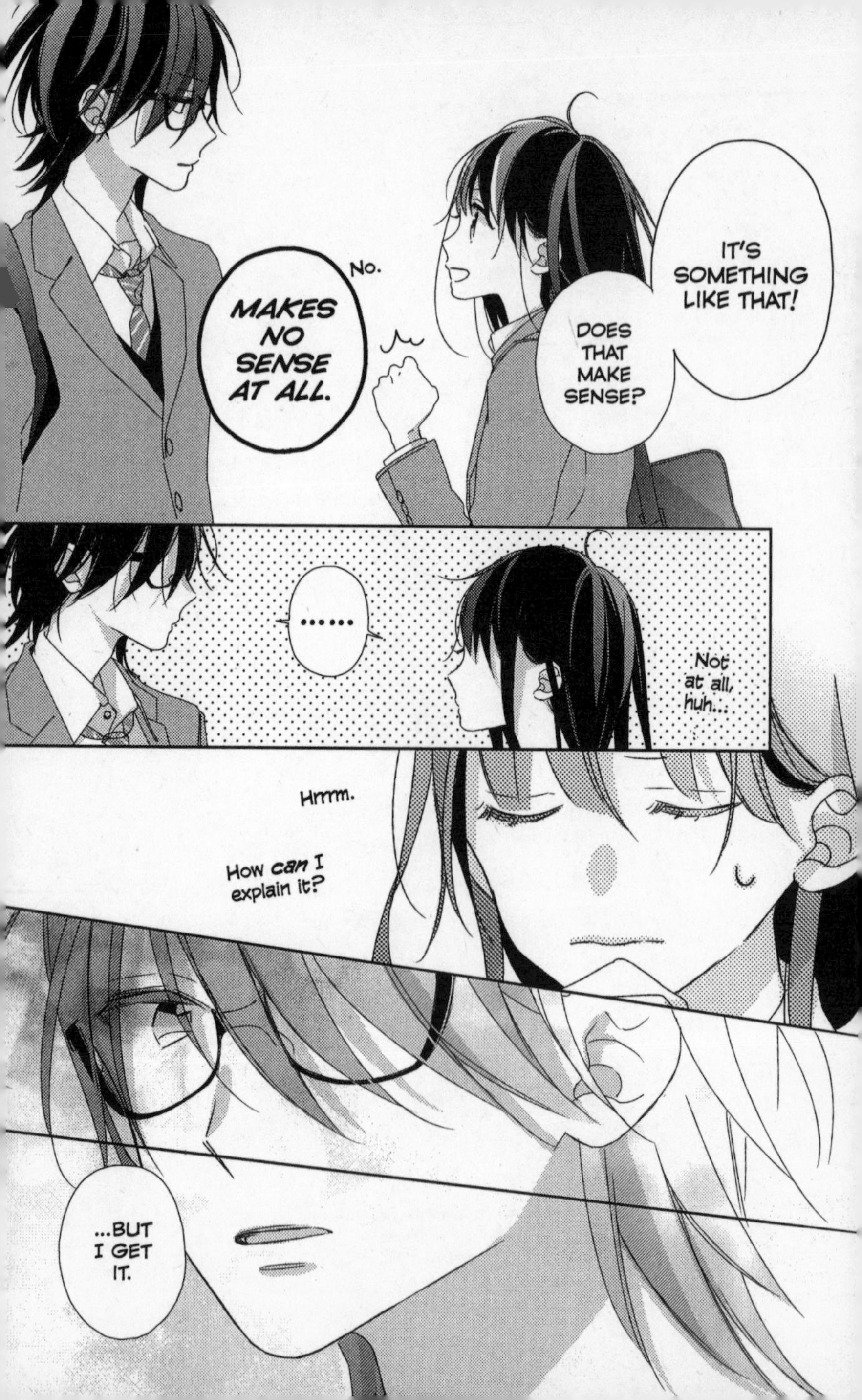
IT'S SOMETHING LIKE THAT!
DOES THAT MAKE SENSE?
No.
MAKES NO SENSE AT ALL.
Not at all, huh...
......
Hrrm.
How can I explain it?
...BUT I GET IT.

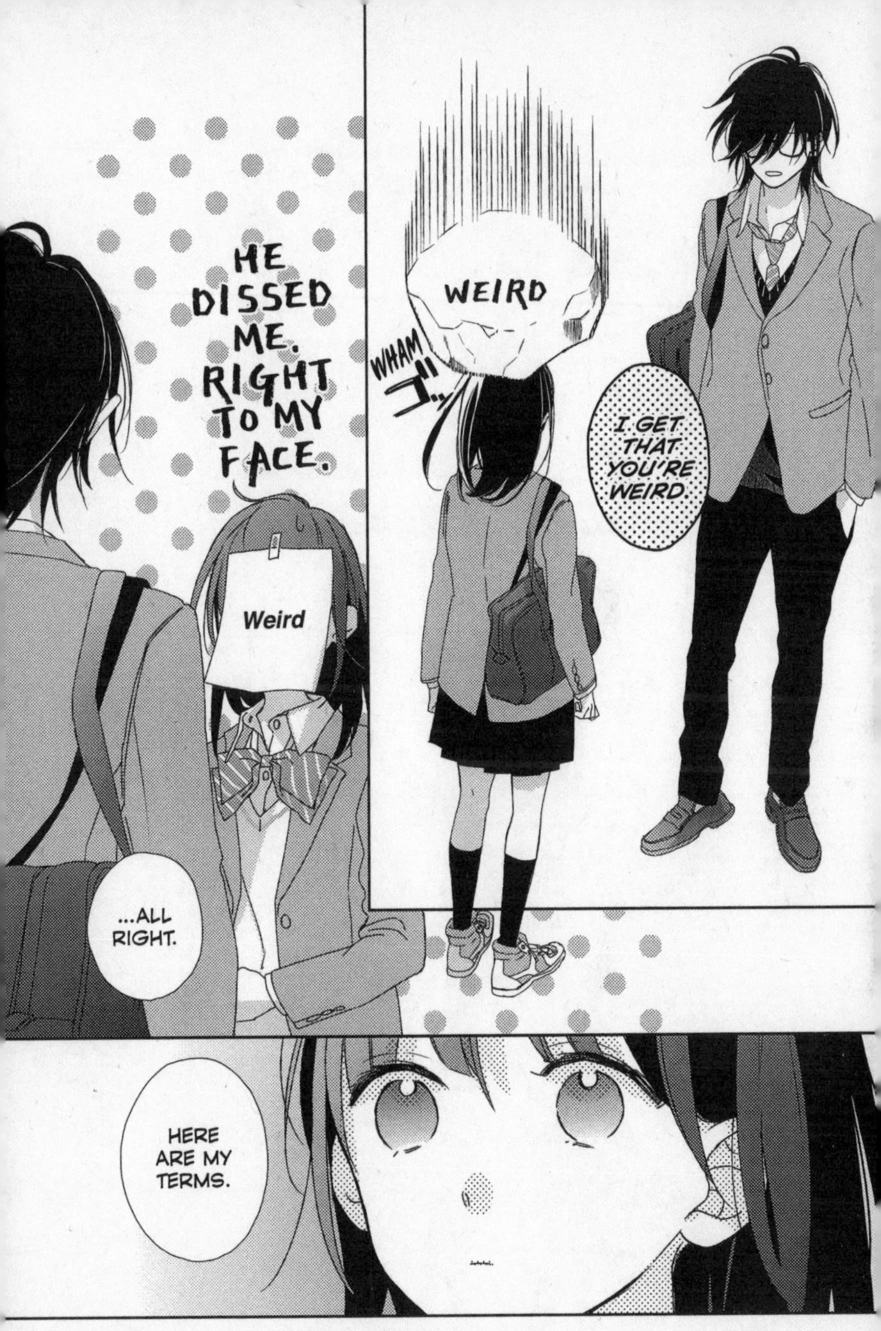
I GET THAT YOU'RE WEIRD.
WHAM
WEIRD
HE DISSED ME. RIGHT TO MY FACE.
Weird
...ALL RIGHT.
HERE ARE MY TERMS.

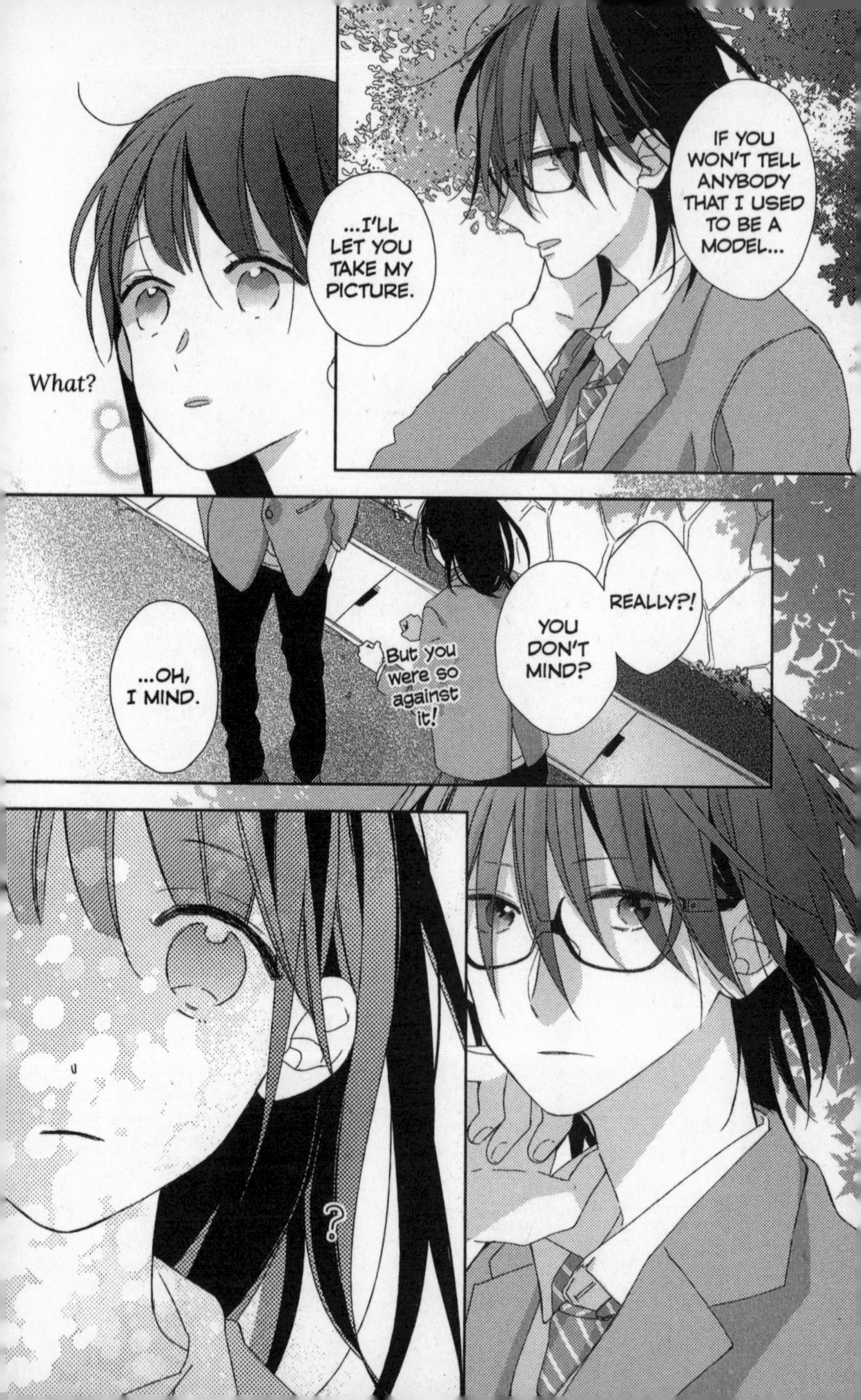
IF YOU WON'T TELL ANYBODY THAT I USED TO BE A MODEL...
...I'LL LET YOU TAKE MY PICTURE.
What?
REALLY?!
YOU DON'T MIND?
But you were so against it!
...OH, I MIND.

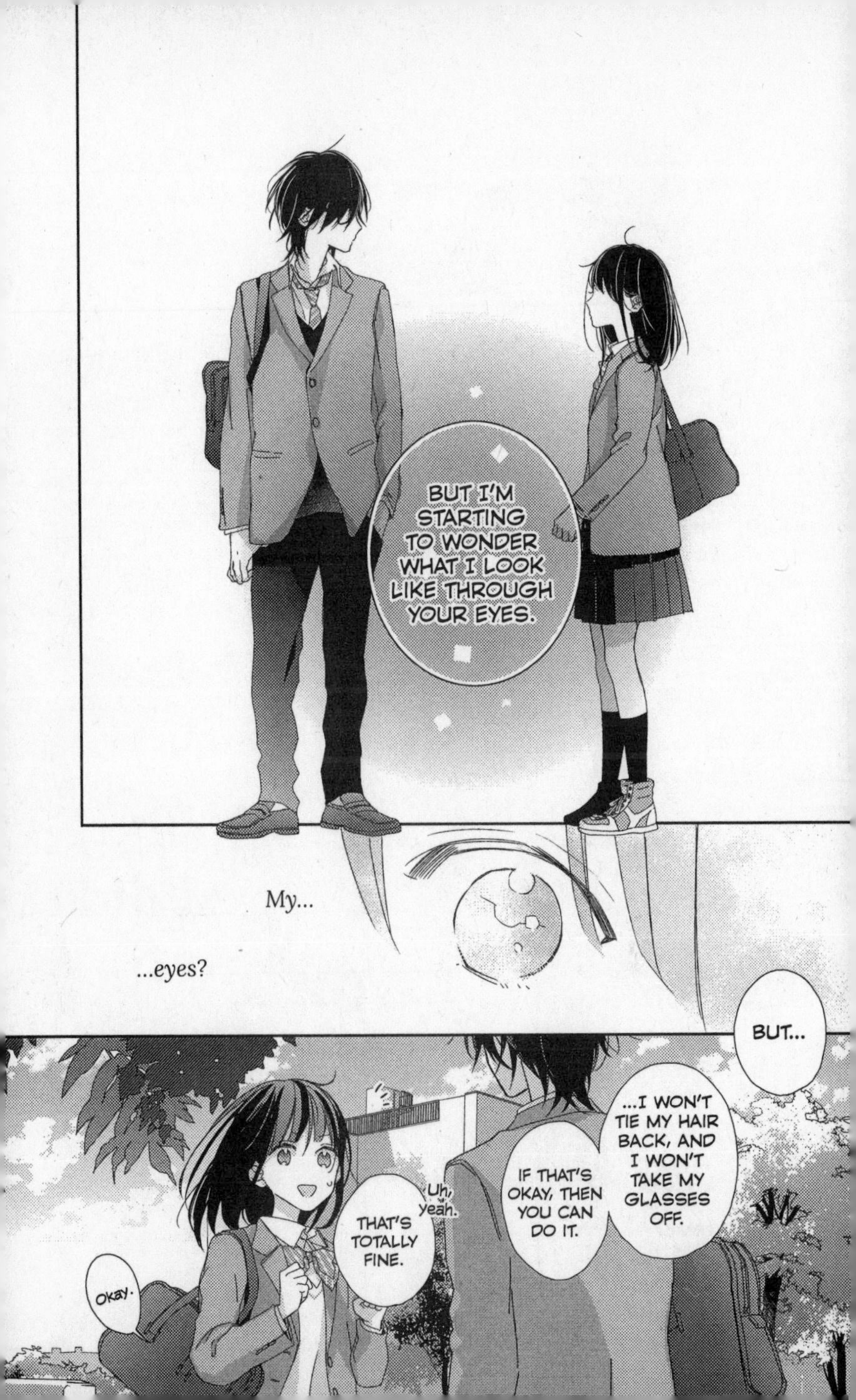
BUT I'M STARTING TO WONDER WHAT I LOOK LIKE THROUGH YOUR EYES.
My...
...eyes?
BUT...
...I WON'T TIE MY HAIR BACK, AND I WON'T TAKE MY GLASSES OFF.
IF THAT'S OKAY, THEN YOU CAN DO IT.
Uh, yeah.
THAT'S TOTALLY FINE.
Okay.

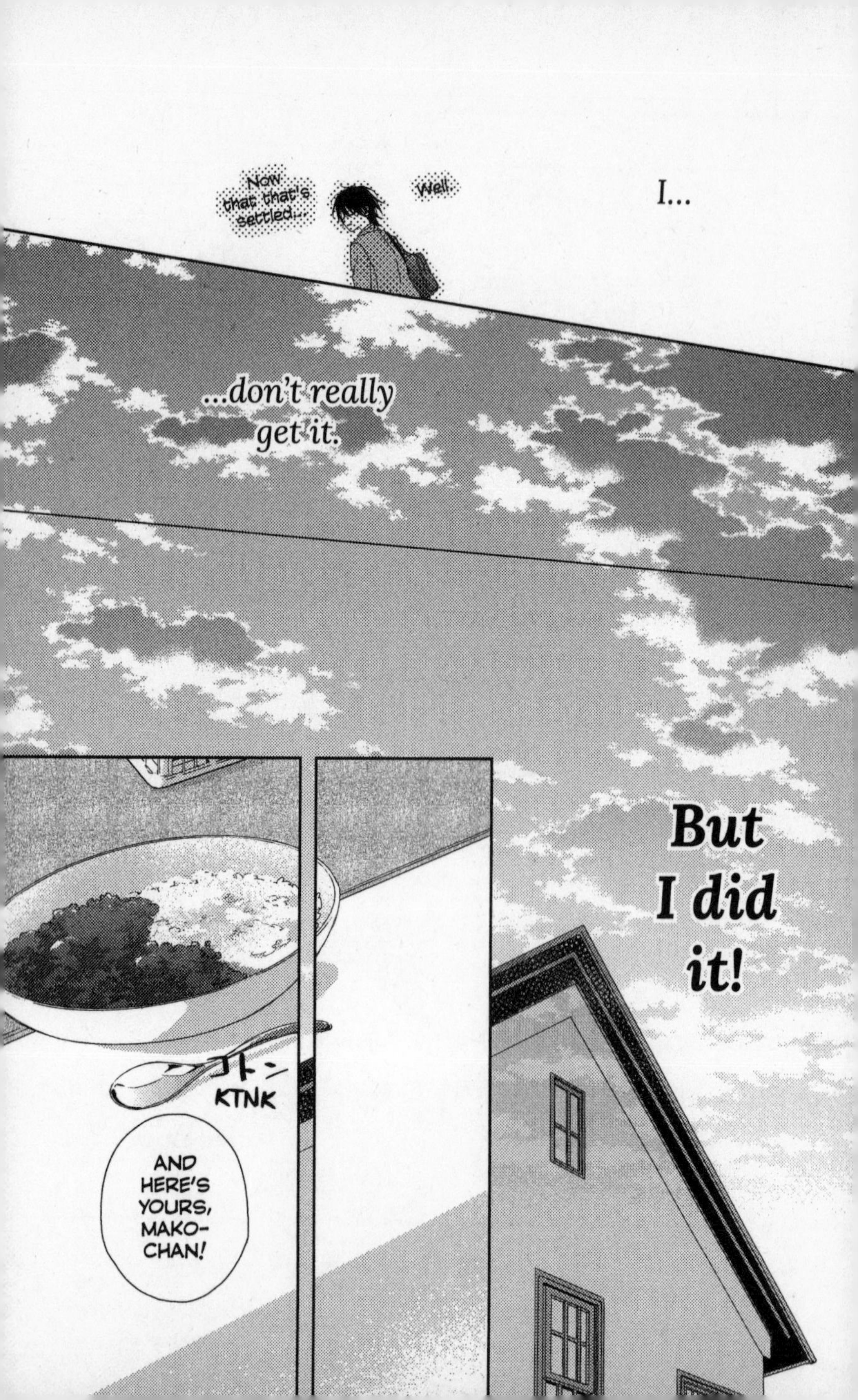
I...
Well.
Now that that's settled...
...don't really get it.
But I did it!
コトン
KTNK
AND HERE'S YOURS, MAKO-CHAN!

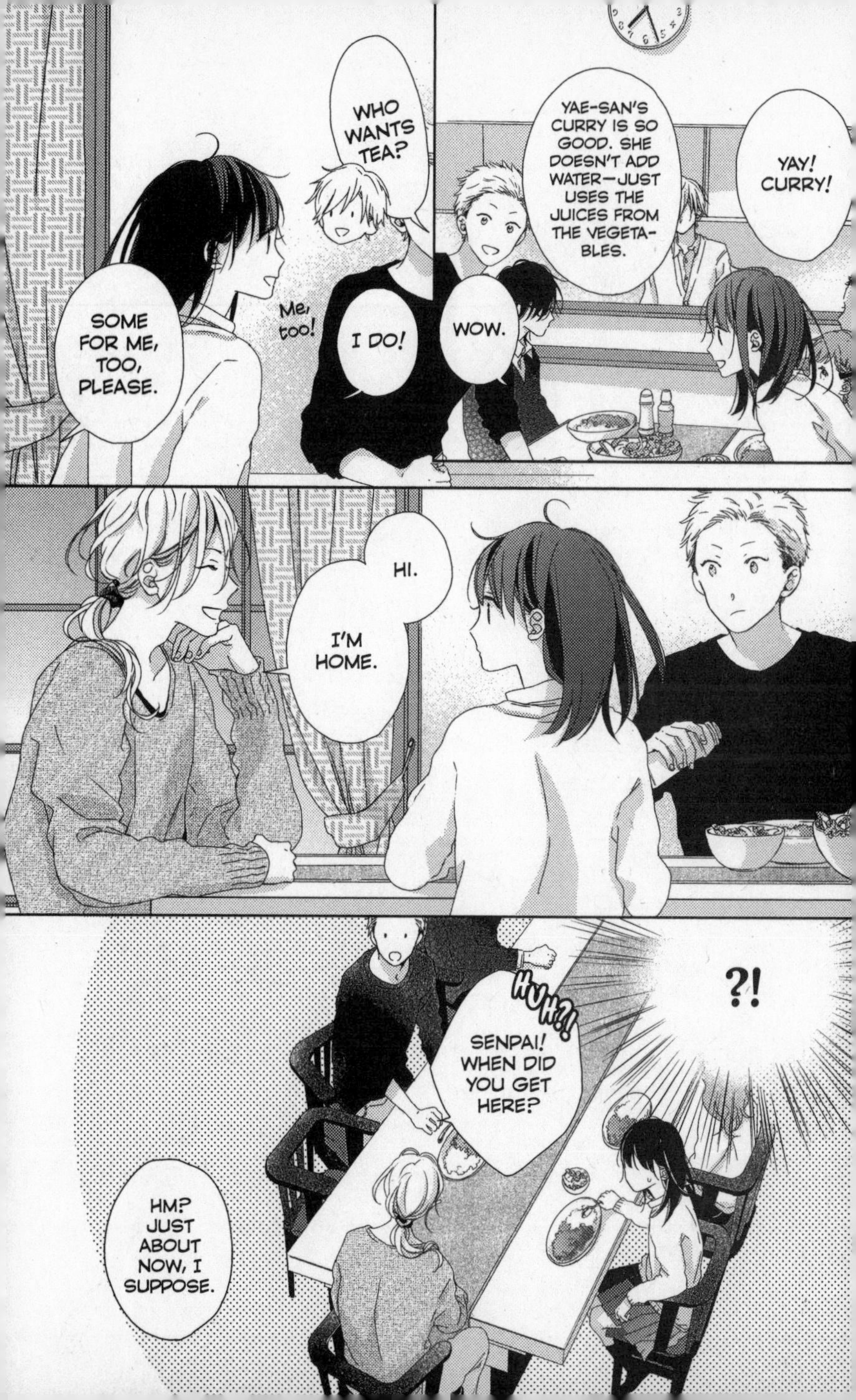
YAY! CURRY!
YAE-SAN'S CURRY IS SO GOOD. SHE DOESN'T ADD WATER—JUST USES THE JUICES FROM THE VEGETA-BLES.
WOW.
WHO WANTS TEA?
I DO!
Me, too!
SOME FOR ME, TOO, PLEASE.
HI.
I'M HOME.
?!
HUH?!
SENPAI! WHEN DID YOU GET HERE?
HM? JUST ABOUT NOW, I SUPPOSE.

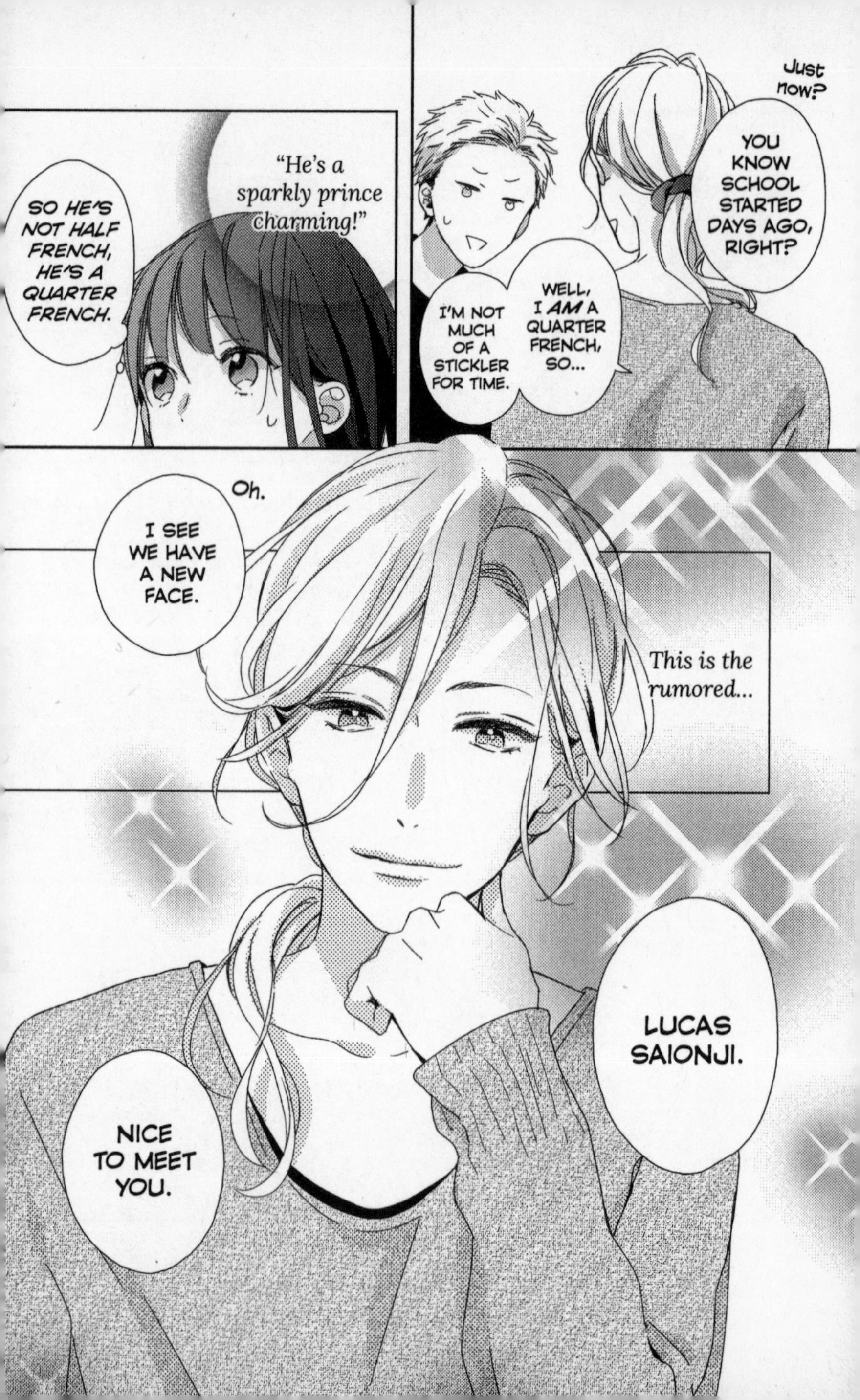
Just now?
YOU KNOW SCHOOL STARTED DAYS AGO, RIGHT?
WELL, I *AM* A QUARTER FRENCH, SO...
I'M NOT MUCH OF A STICKLER FOR TIME.
"He's a sparkly prince charming!"
SO HE'S NOT HALF FRENCH, HE'S A QUARTER FRENCH.
Oh.
I SEE WE HAVE A NEW FACE.
This is the rumored...
LUCAS SAIONJI.
NICE TO MEET YOU.

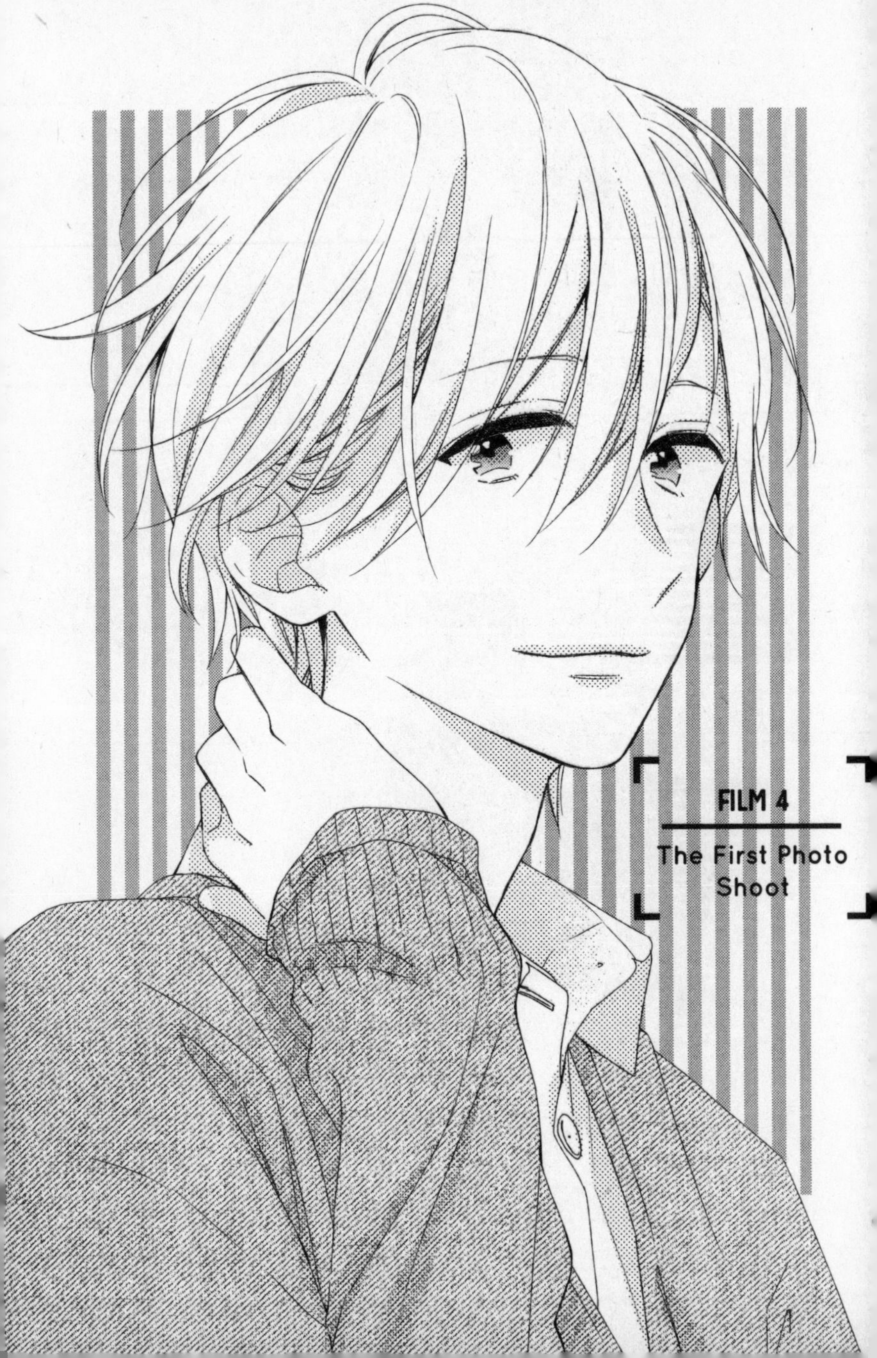
FILM 4
The First Photo Shoot

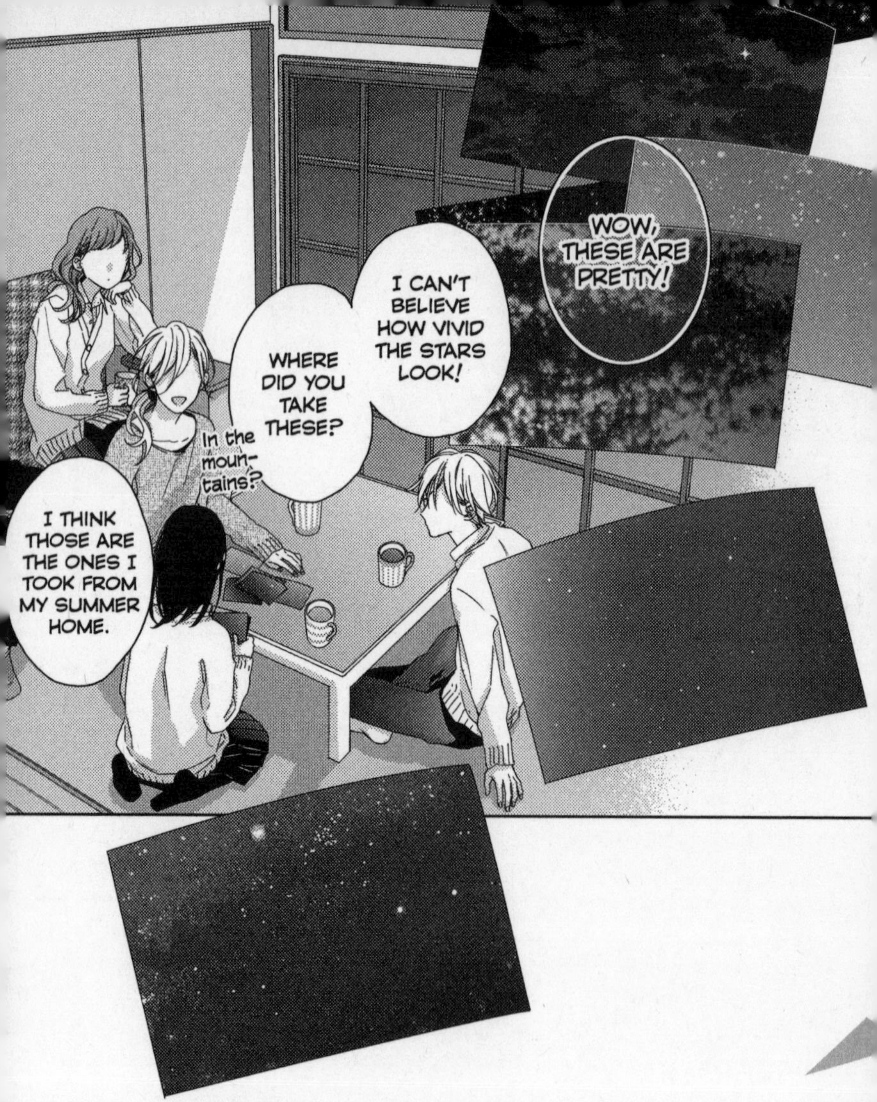
WOW, THESE ARE PRETTY!
I CAN'T BELIEVE HOW VIVID THE STARS LOOK!
WHERE DID YOU TAKE THESE?
In the moun-tains?
I THINK THOSE ARE THE ONES I TOOK FROM MY SUMMER HOME.

LOVE IN FOCUS

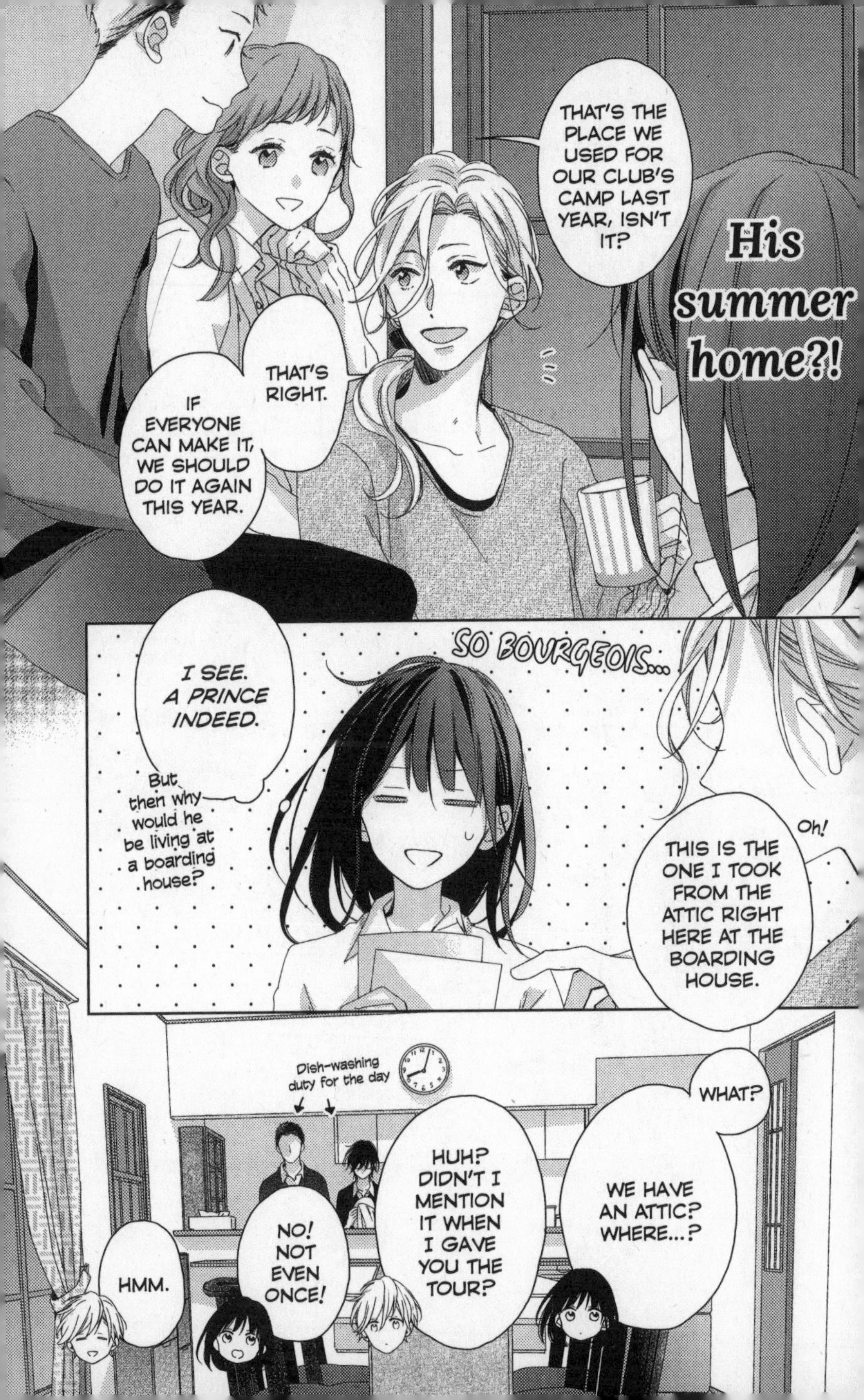
THAT'S THE PLACE WE USED FOR OUR CLUB'S CAMP LAST YEAR, ISN'T IT?
His summer home?!
THAT'S RIGHT.
IF EVERYONE CAN MAKE IT, WE SHOULD DO IT AGAIN THIS YEAR.
SO BOURGEOIS...
I SEE. A PRINCE INDEED.
But then why would he be living at a boarding house?
Oh!
THIS IS THE ONE I TOOK FROM THE ATTIC RIGHT HERE AT THE BOARDING HOUSE.
Dish-washing duty for the day
WHAT?
WE HAVE AN ATTIC? WHERE...?
HUH? DIDN'T I MENTION IT WHEN I GAVE YOU THE TOUR?
NO! NOT EVEN ONCE!
HMM.

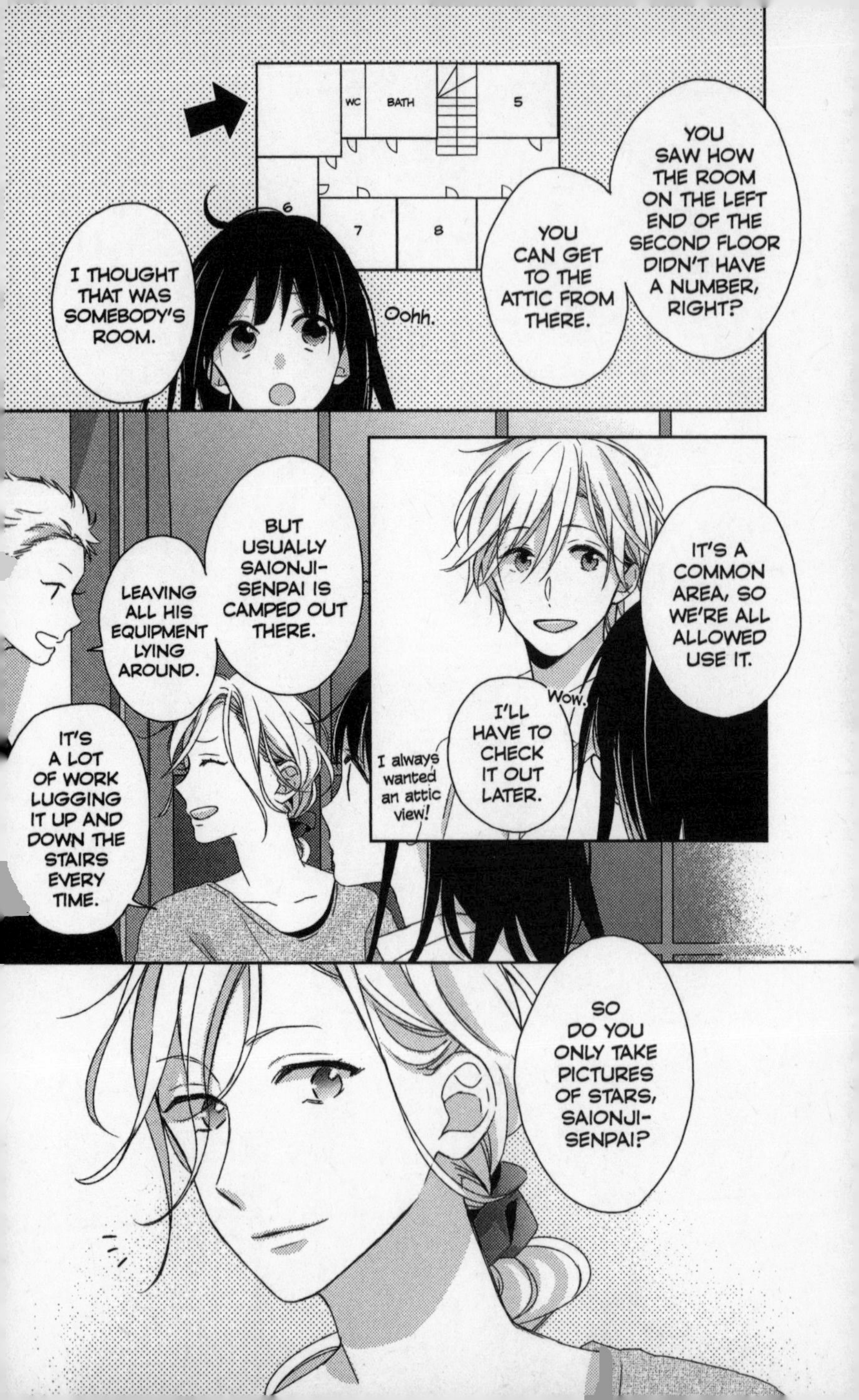
WC
BATH
5
6
7
8
YOU SAW HOW THE ROOM ON THE LEFT END OF THE SECOND FLOOR DIDN'T HAVE A NUMBER, RIGHT?
YOU CAN GET TO THE ATTIC FROM THERE.
Oohh.
I THOUGHT THAT WAS SOMEBODY'S ROOM.
IT'S A COMMON AREA, SO WE'RE ALL ALLOWED USE IT.
Wow.
I'LL HAVE TO CHECK IT OUT LATER.
I always wanted an attic view!
BUT USUALLY SAIONJI-SENPAI IS CAMPED OUT THERE.
LEAVING ALL HIS EQUIPMENT LYING AROUND.
IT'S A LOT OF WORK LUGGING IT UP AND DOWN THE STAIRS EVERY TIME.
SO DO YOU ONLY TAKE PICTURES OF STARS, SAIONJI-SENPAI?

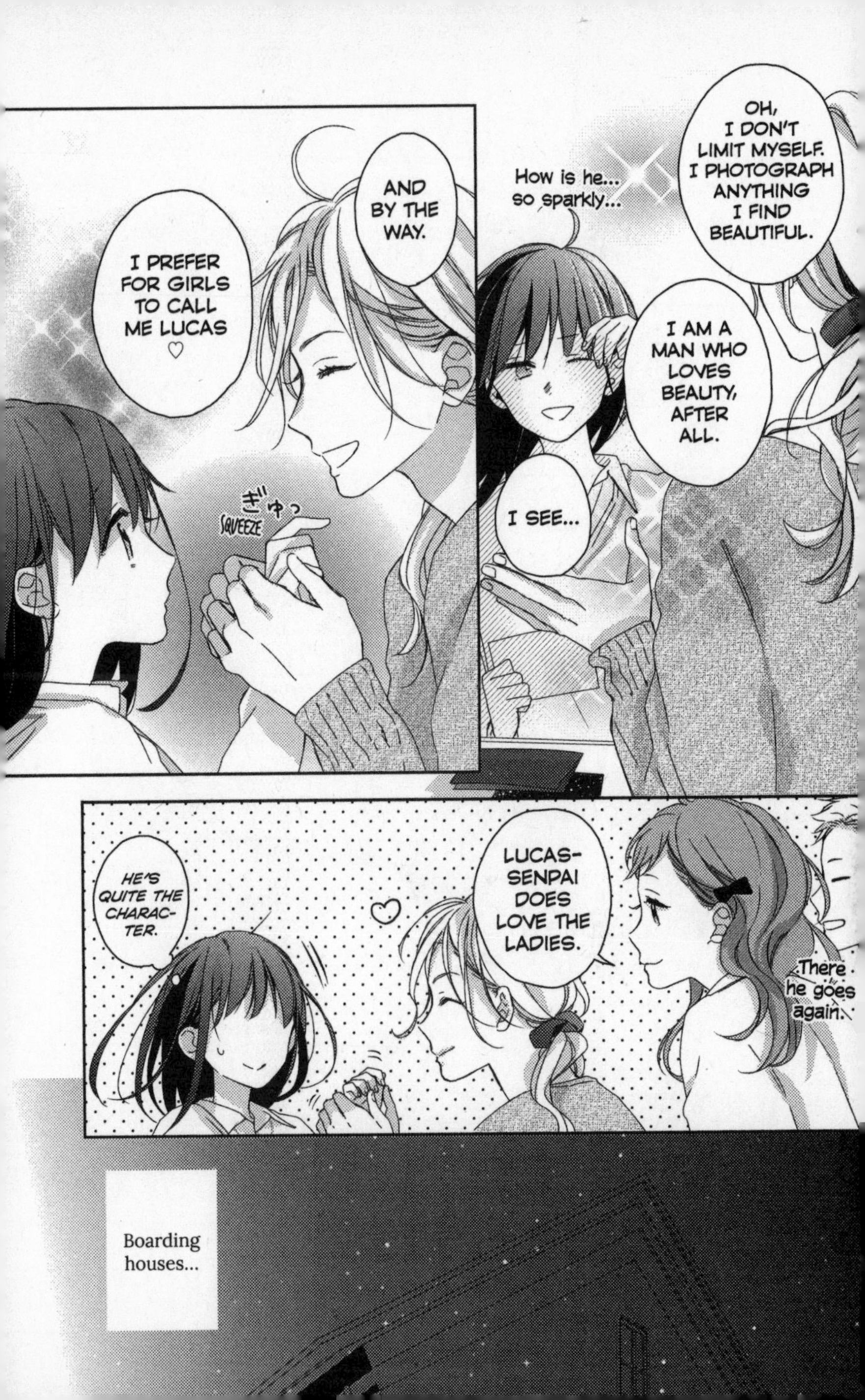
OH, I DON'T LIMIT MYSELF. I PHOTOGRAPH ANYTHING I FIND BEAUTIFUL.
How is he... so sparkly...
I AM A MAN WHO LOVES BEAUTY, AFTER ALL.
I SEE...
AND BY THE WAY.
I PREFER FOR GIRLS TO CALL ME LUCAS ♡
ぎゅっ
SQUEEZE
There he goes again.
LUCAS-SENPAI DOES LOVE THE LADIES.
HE'S QUITE THE CHARACTER.
Boarding houses...

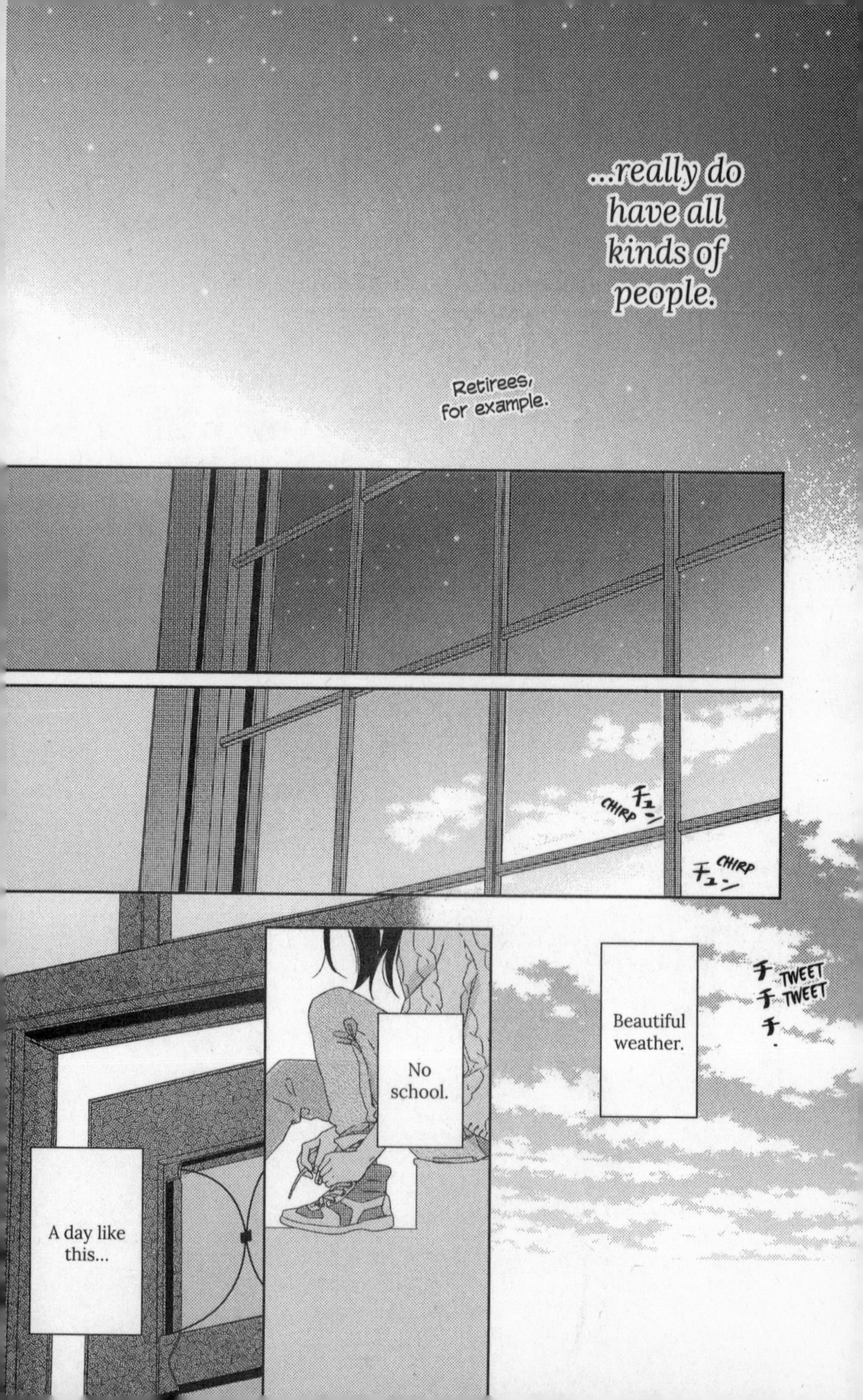
...really do have all kinds of people.
Retirees, for example.
チュン CHIRP
チュン CHIRP
チ TWEET チ TWEET チ.
Beautiful weather.
No school.
A day like this...

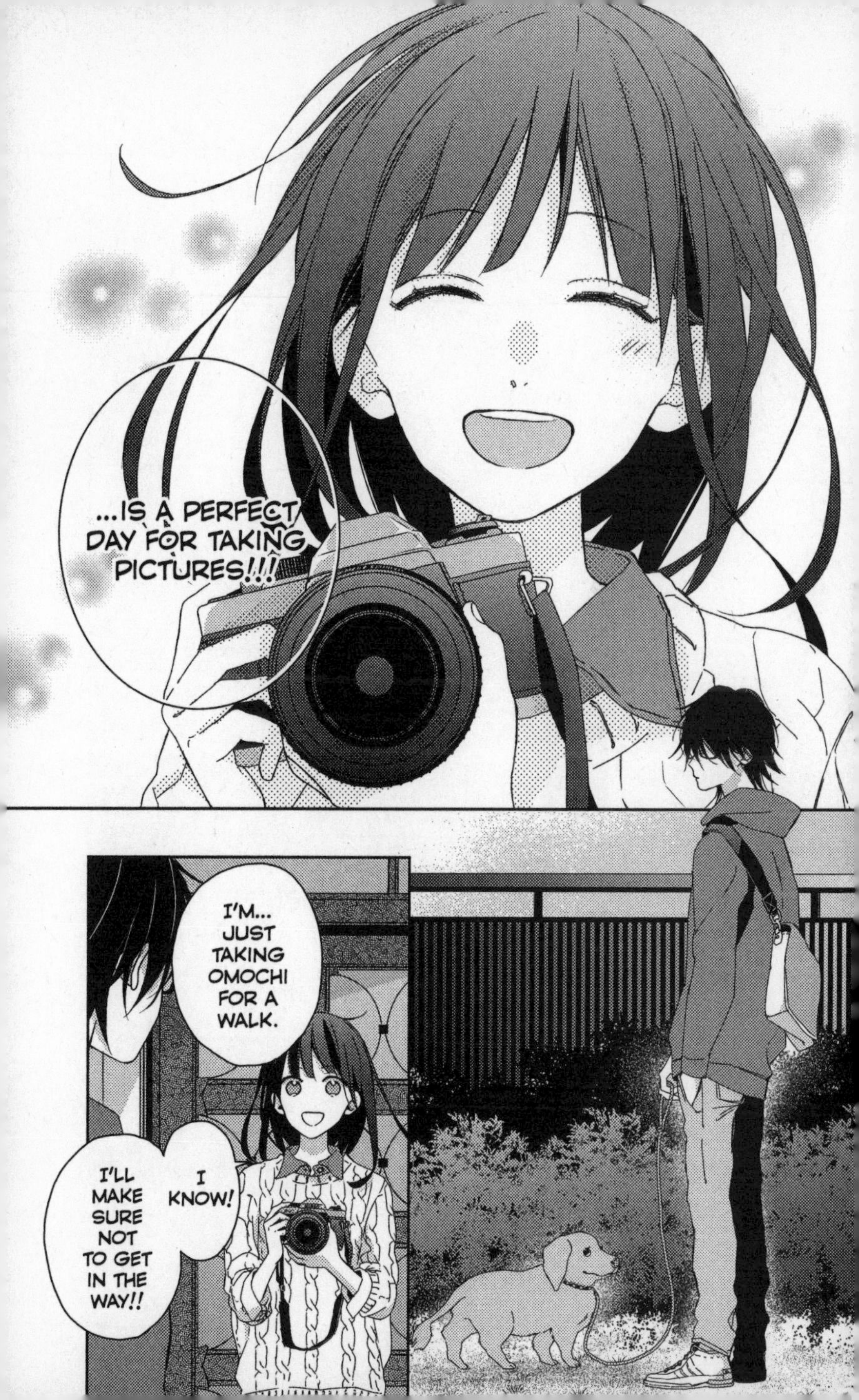
...IS A PERFECT DAY FOR TAKING PICTURES!!!
I'M... JUST TAKING OMOCHI FOR A WALK.
I KNOW!
I'LL MAKE SURE NOT TO GET IN THE WAY!!

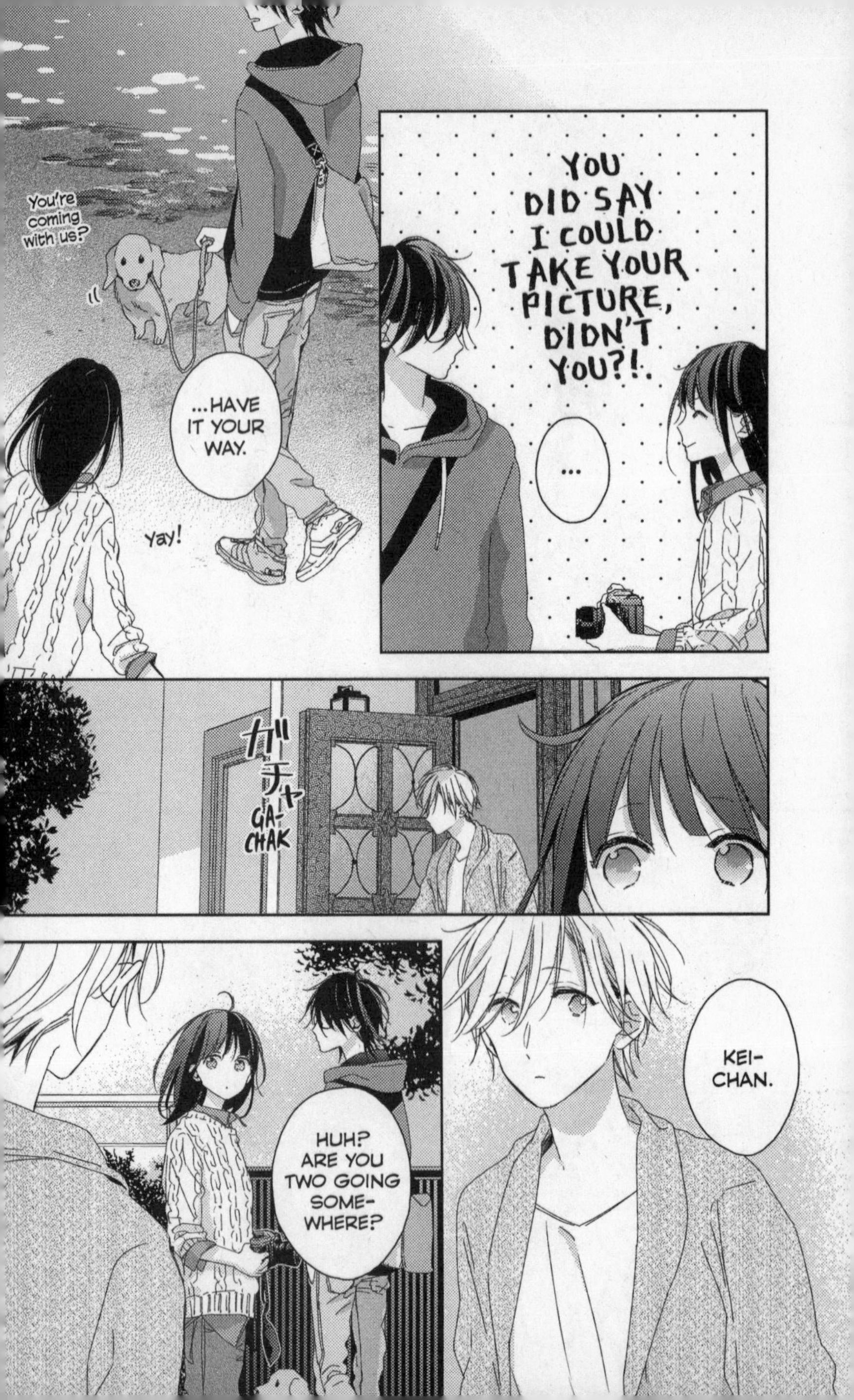
YOU DID SAY I COULD TAKE YOUR PICTURE, DIDN'T YOU?!
...
You're coming with us?
...HAVE IT YOUR WAY.
Yay!
ガチャ GA-CHAK
KEI-CHAN.
HUH? ARE YOU TWO GOING SOME-WHERE?

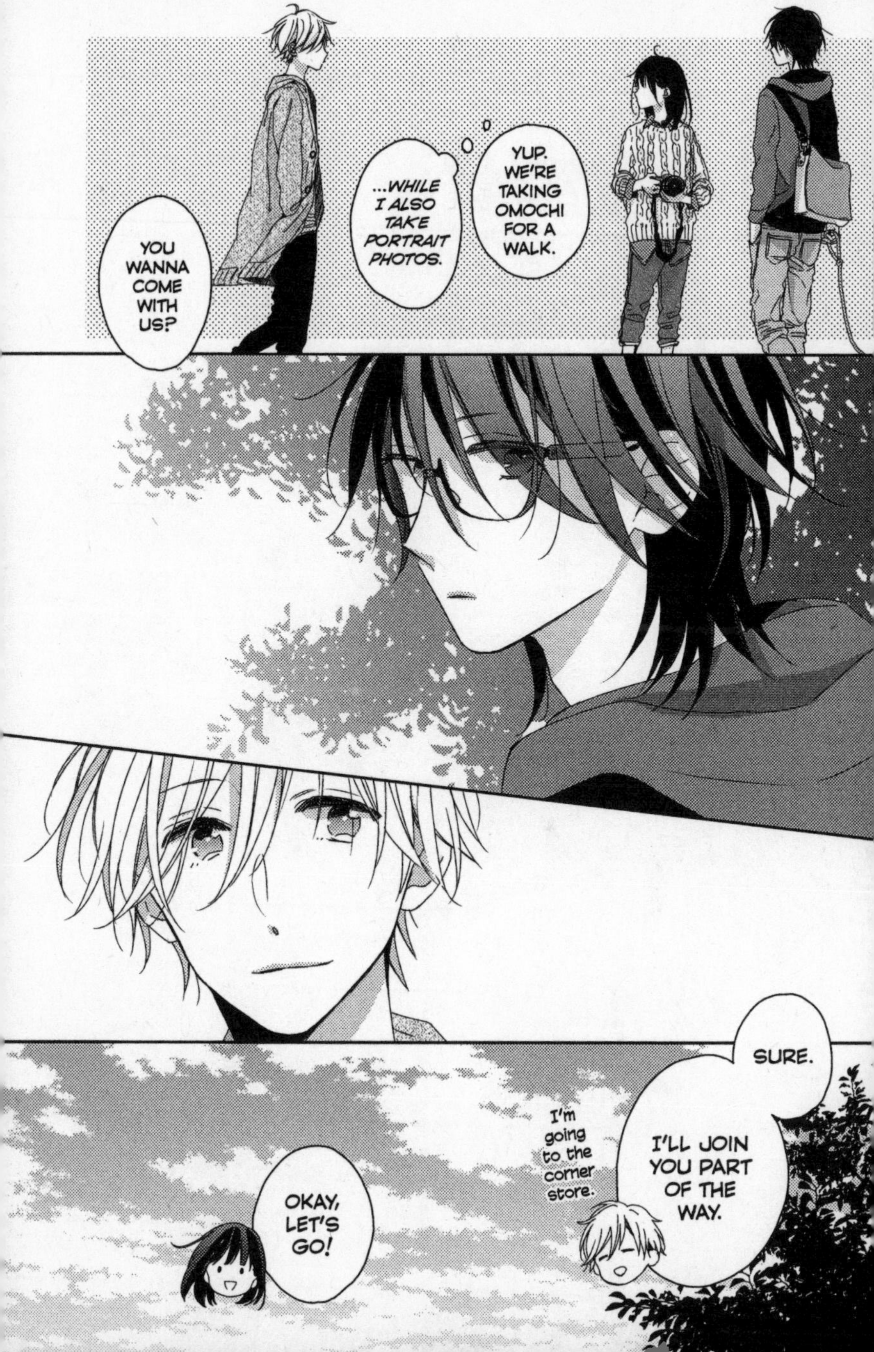
YUP. WE'RE TAKING OMOCHI FOR A WALK.
...WHILE I ALSO TAKE PORTRAIT PHOTOS.
YOU WANNA COME WITH US?
SURE.
I'LL JOIN YOU PART OF THE WAY.
I'm going to the corner store.
OKAY, LET'S GO!

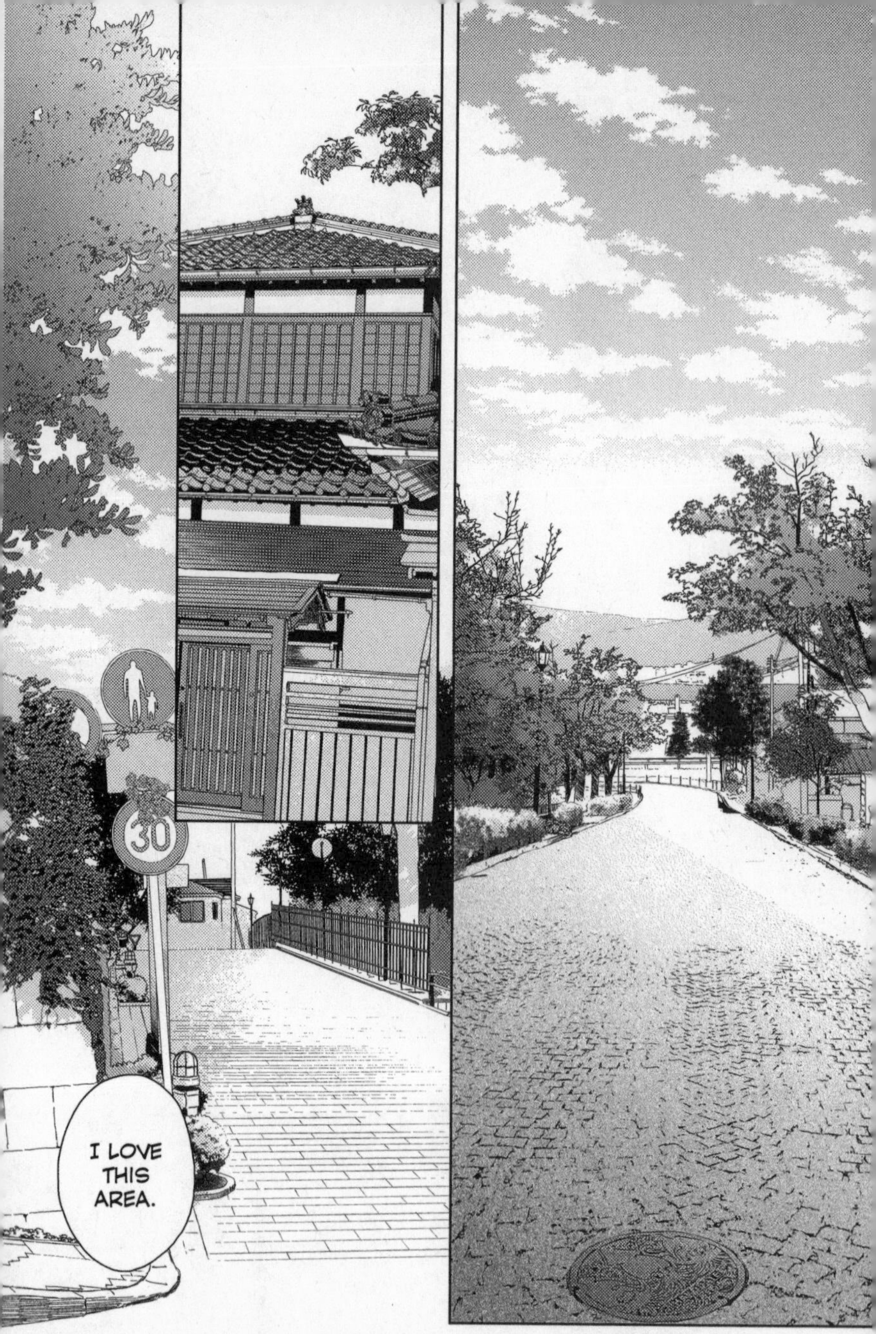
I LOVE THIS AREA.
30

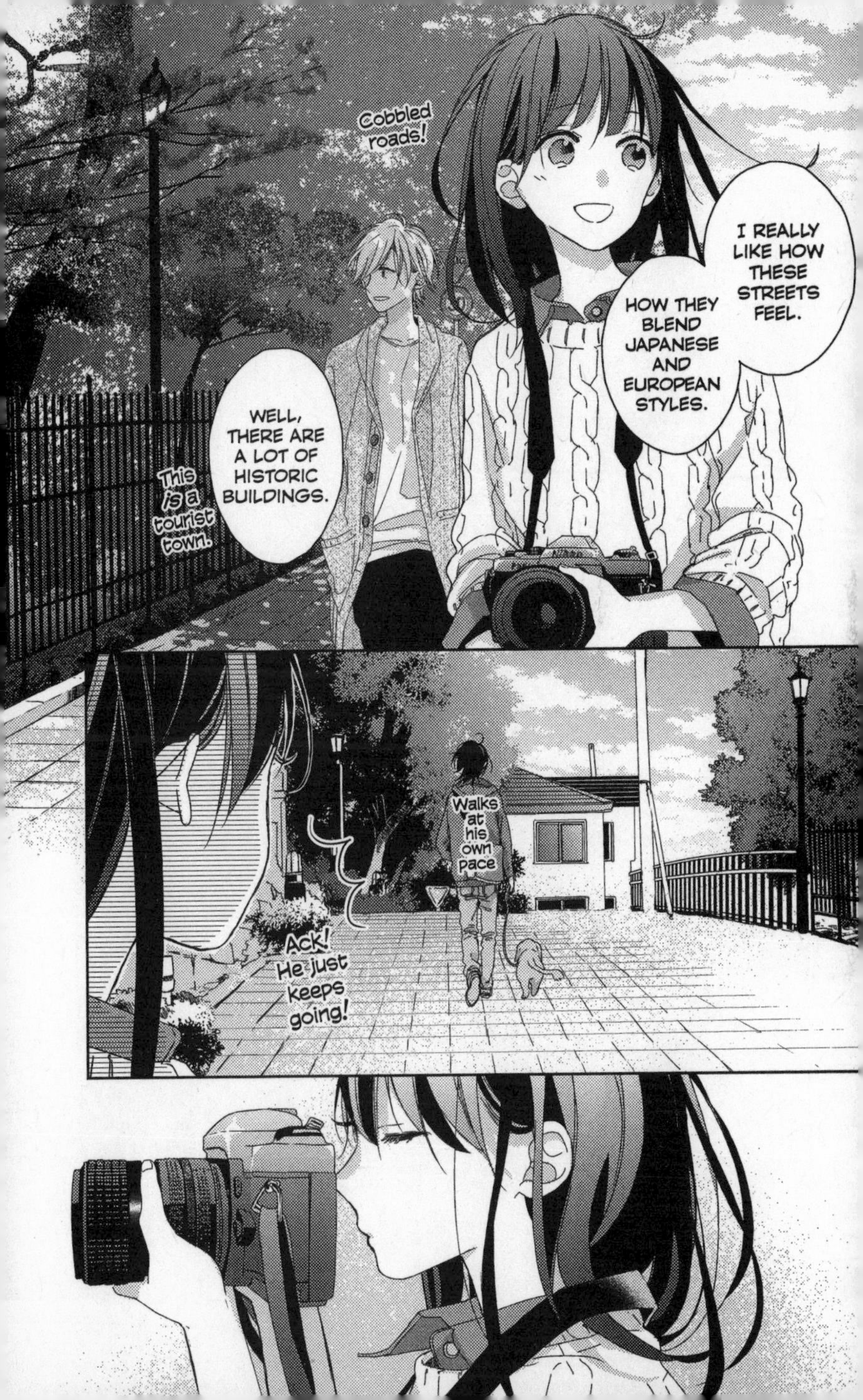
I REALLY LIKE HOW THESE STREETS FEEL.
HOW THEY BLEND JAPANESE AND EUROPEAN STYLES.
Cobbled roads!
WELL, THERE ARE A LOT OF HISTORIC BUILDINGS.
This is a tourist town.
Walks at his own pace
Ack! He just keeps going!

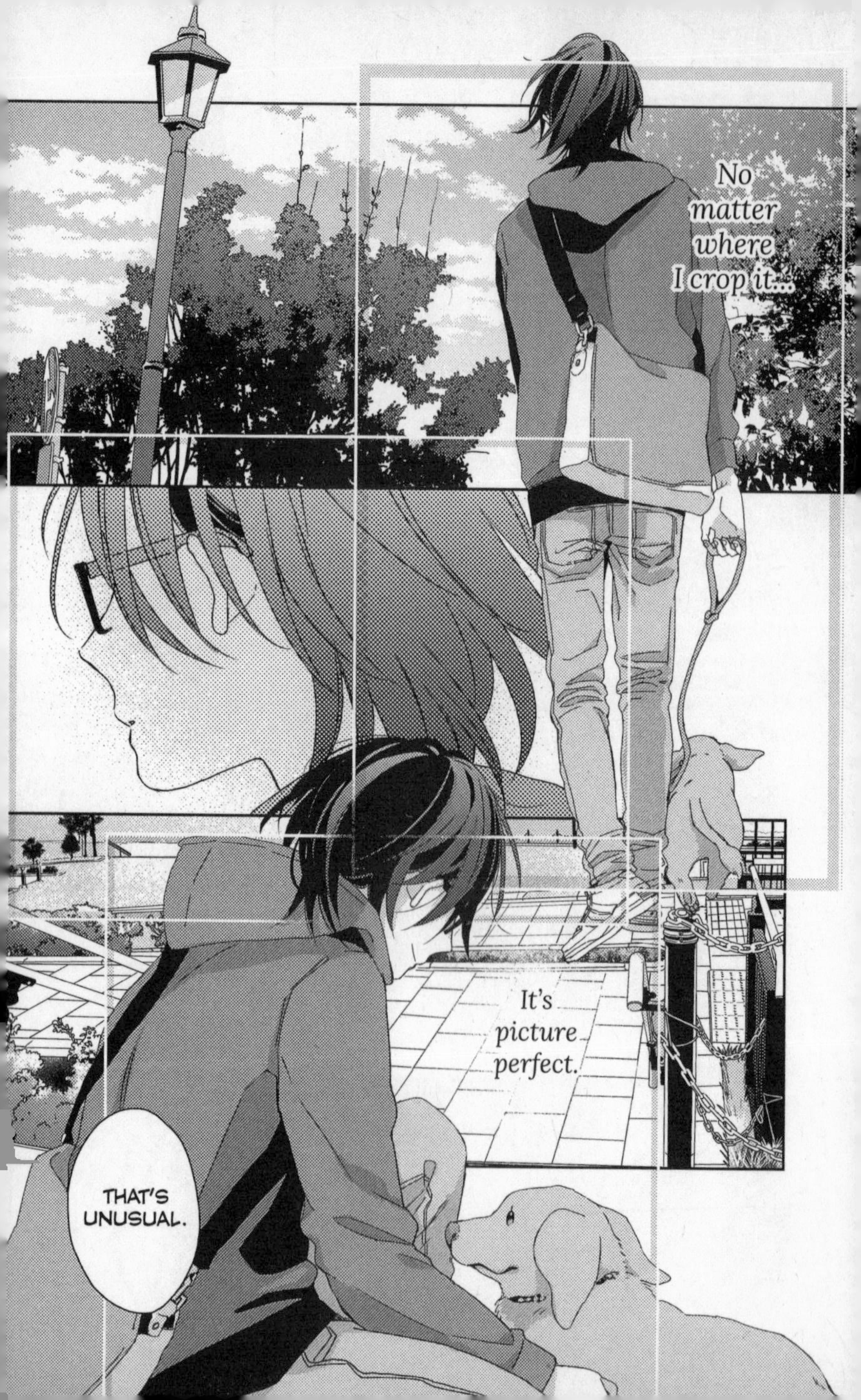
No matter where I crop it...
It's picture perfect.
THAT'S UNUSUAL.

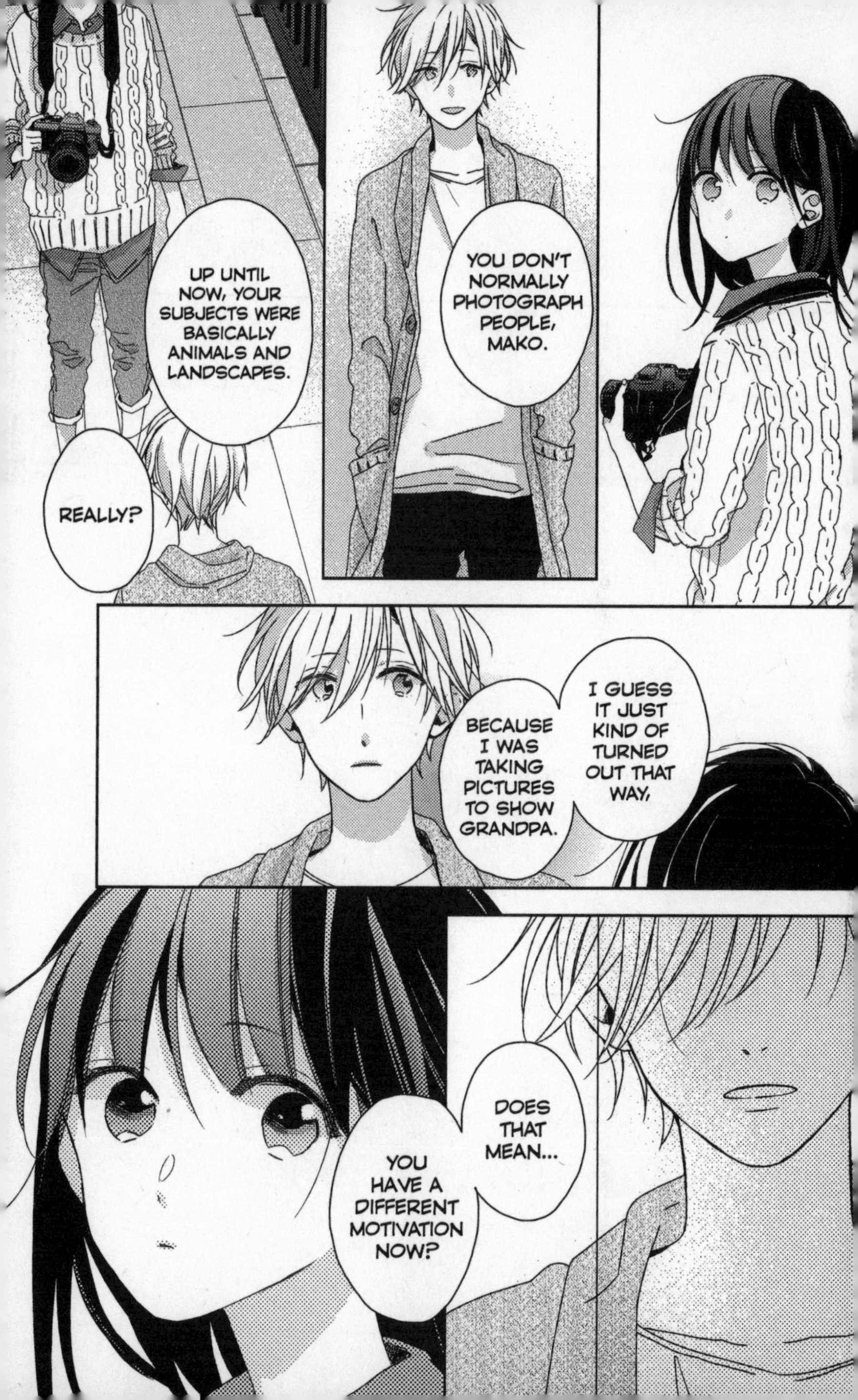
YOU DON'T NORMALLY PHOTOGRAPH PEOPLE, MAKO.
UP UNTIL NOW, YOUR SUBJECTS WERE BASICALLY ANIMALS AND LANDSCAPES.
REALLY?
I GUESS IT JUST KIND OF TURNED OUT THAT WAY,
BECAUSE I WAS TAKING PICTURES TO SHOW GRANDPA.
DOES THAT MEAN...
YOU HAVE A DIFFERENT MOTIVATION NOW?

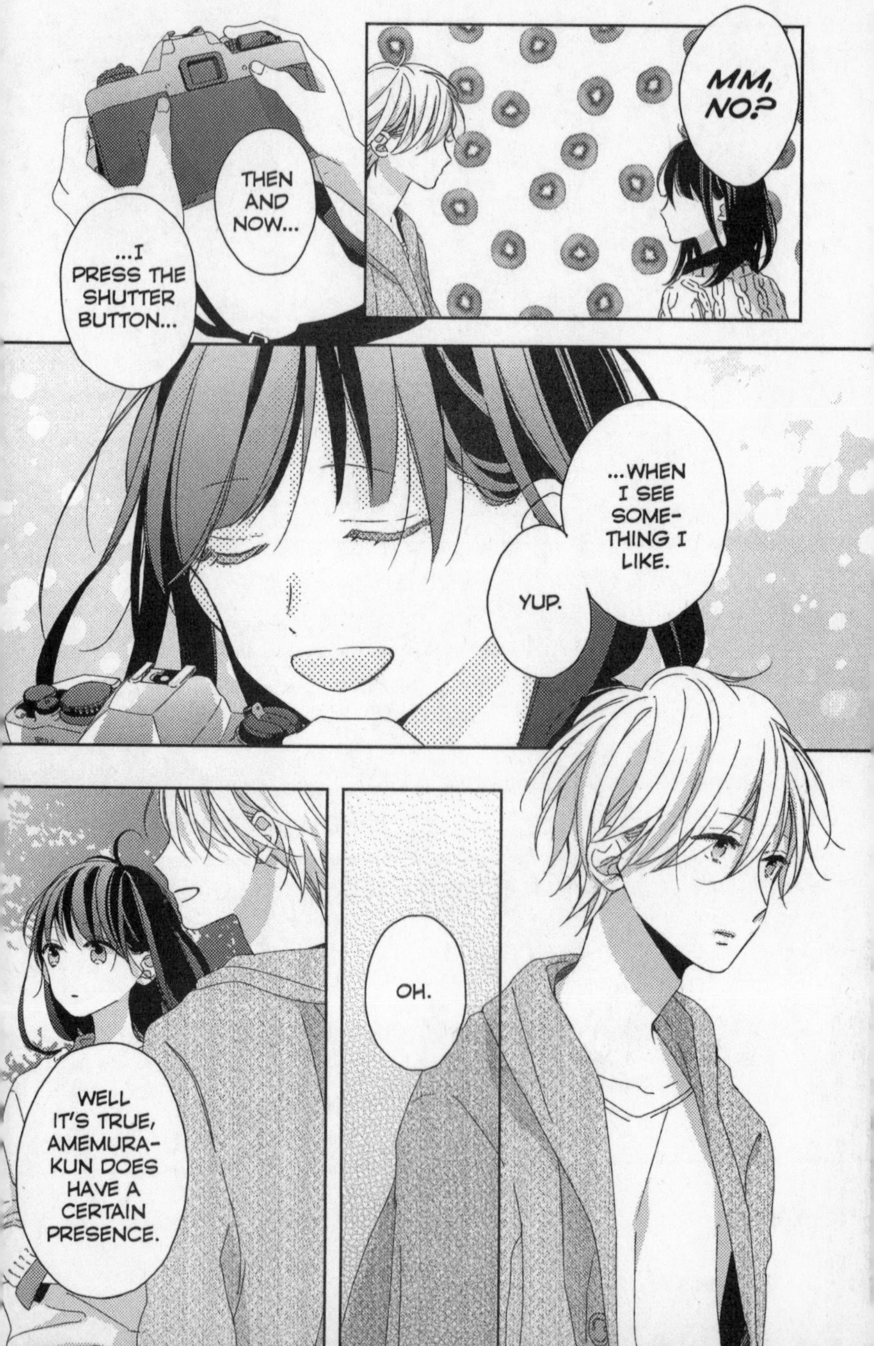
MM, NO?
THEN AND NOW...
...I PRESS THE SHUTTER BUTTON...
...WHEN I SEE SOMETHING I LIKE.
YUP.
OH.
WELL IT'S TRUE, AMEMURA-KUN DOES HAVE A CERTAIN PRESENCE.

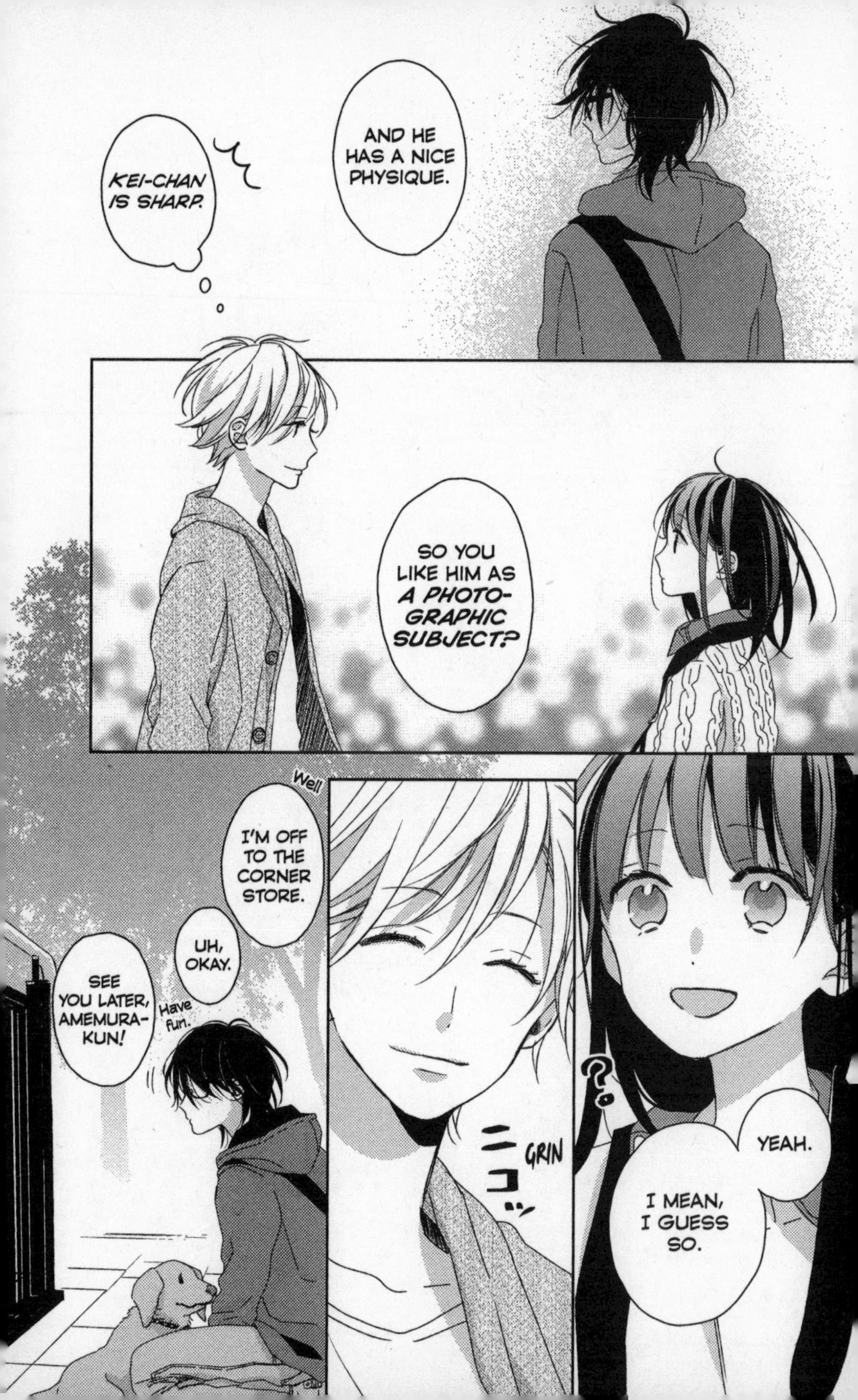
AND HE HAS A NICE PHYSIQUE.
KEI-CHAN IS SHARP.
SO YOU LIKE HIM AS A PHOTO-GRAPHIC SUBJECT?
?
YEAH.
I MEAN, I GUESS SO.
GRIN
Well
I'M OFF TO THE CORNER STORE.
UH, OKAY.
Have fun.
SEE YOU LATER, AMEMURA-KUN!

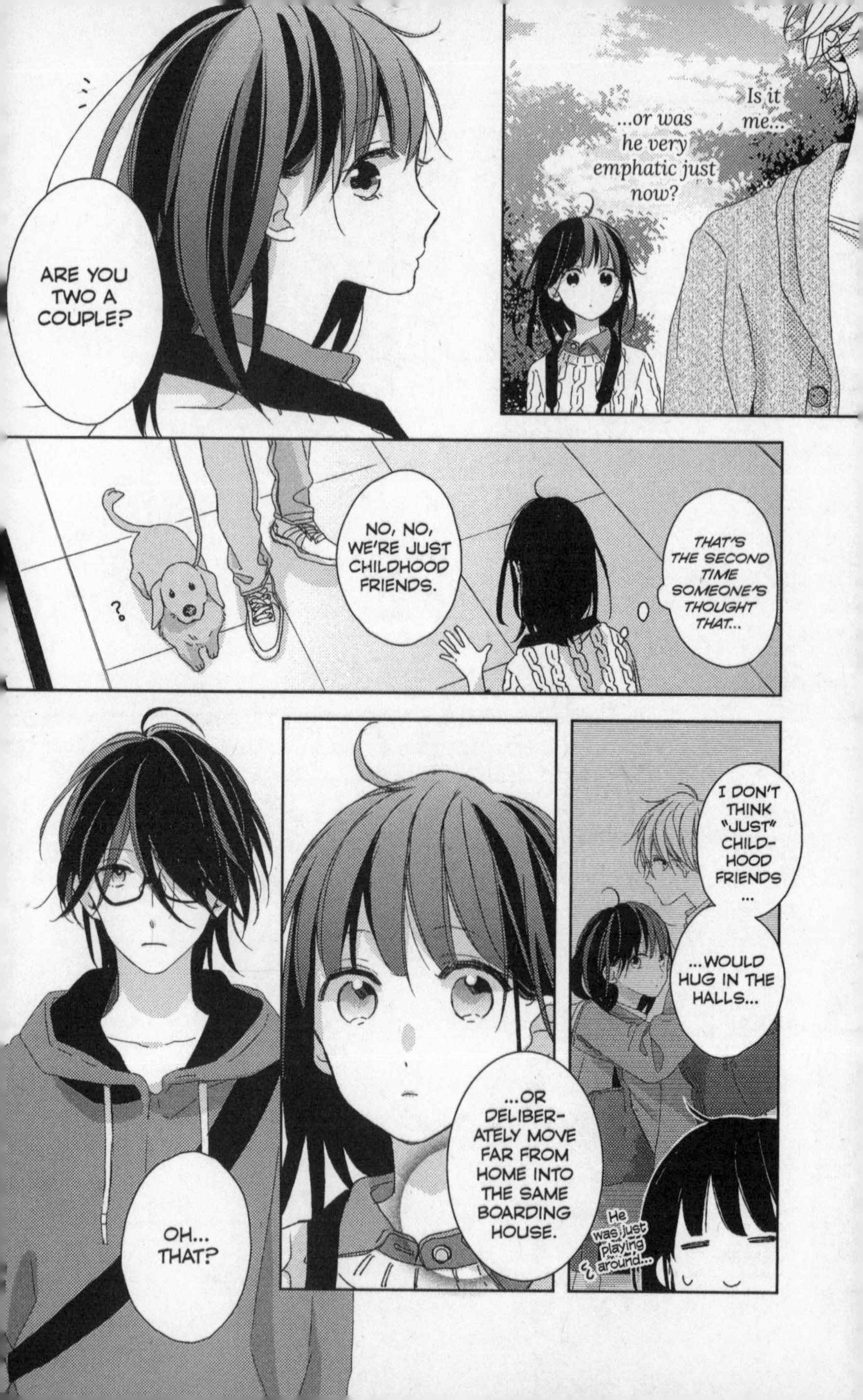
Is it me...
...or was he very emphatic just now?
ARE YOU TWO A COUPLE?
THAT'S THE SECOND TIME SOMEONE'S THOUGHT THAT...
NO, NO, WE'RE JUST CHILDHOOD FRIENDS.
?
I DON'T THINK "JUST" CHILDHOOD FRIENDS...
...WOULD HUG IN THE HALLS...
He was just playing around...
...OR DELIBERATELY MOVE FAR FROM HOME INTO THE SAME BOARDING HOUSE.
OH... THAT?

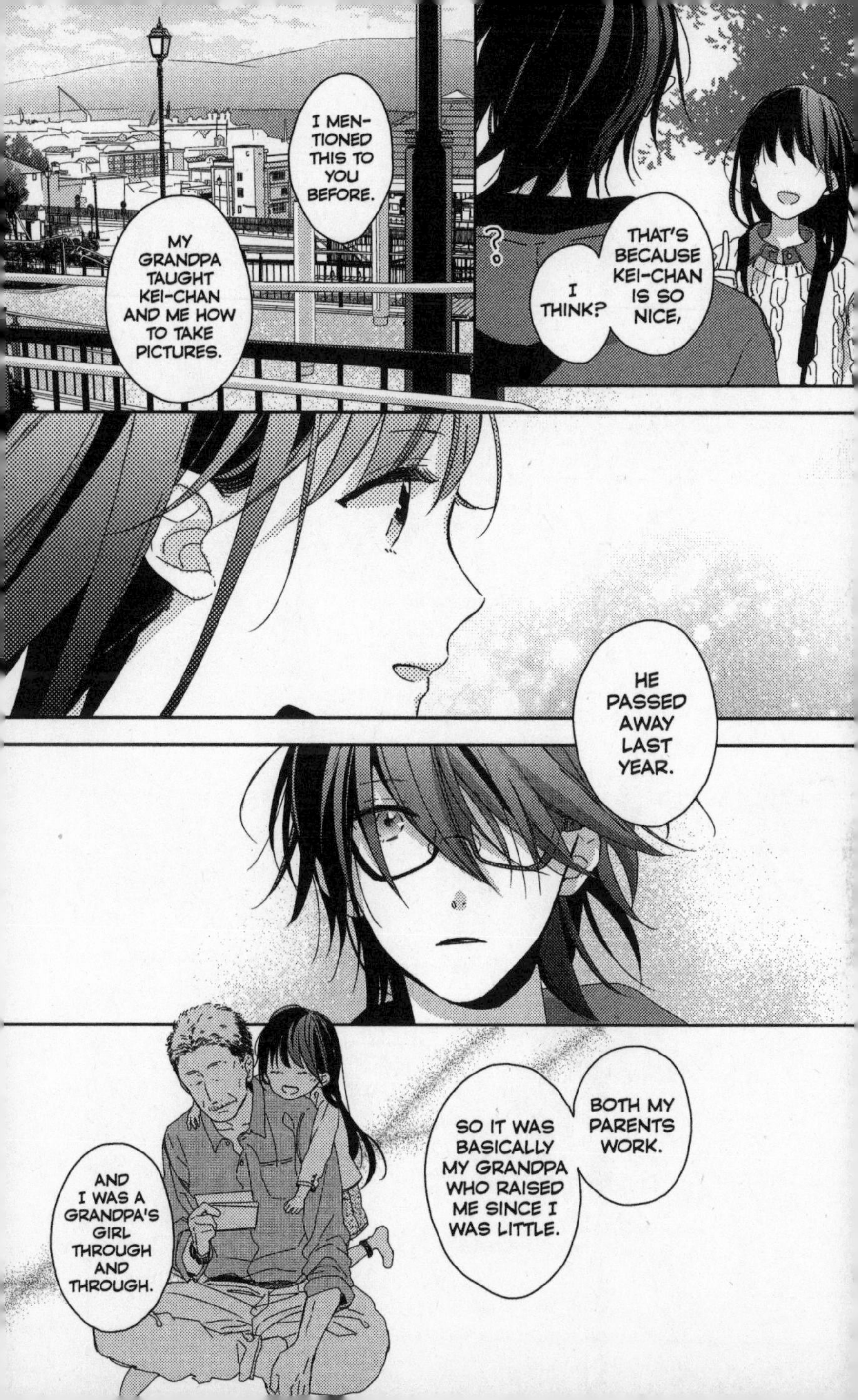
THAT'S BECAUSE KEI-CHAN IS SO NICE,
I THINK?
?
I MEN-TIONED THIS TO YOU BEFORE.
MY GRANDPA TAUGHT KEI-CHAN AND ME HOW TO TAKE PICTURES.
HE PASSED AWAY LAST YEAR.
BOTH MY PARENTS WORK.
SO IT WAS BASICALLY MY GRANDPA WHO RAISED ME SINCE I WAS LITTLE.
AND I WAS A GRANDPA'S GIRL THROUGH AND THROUGH.

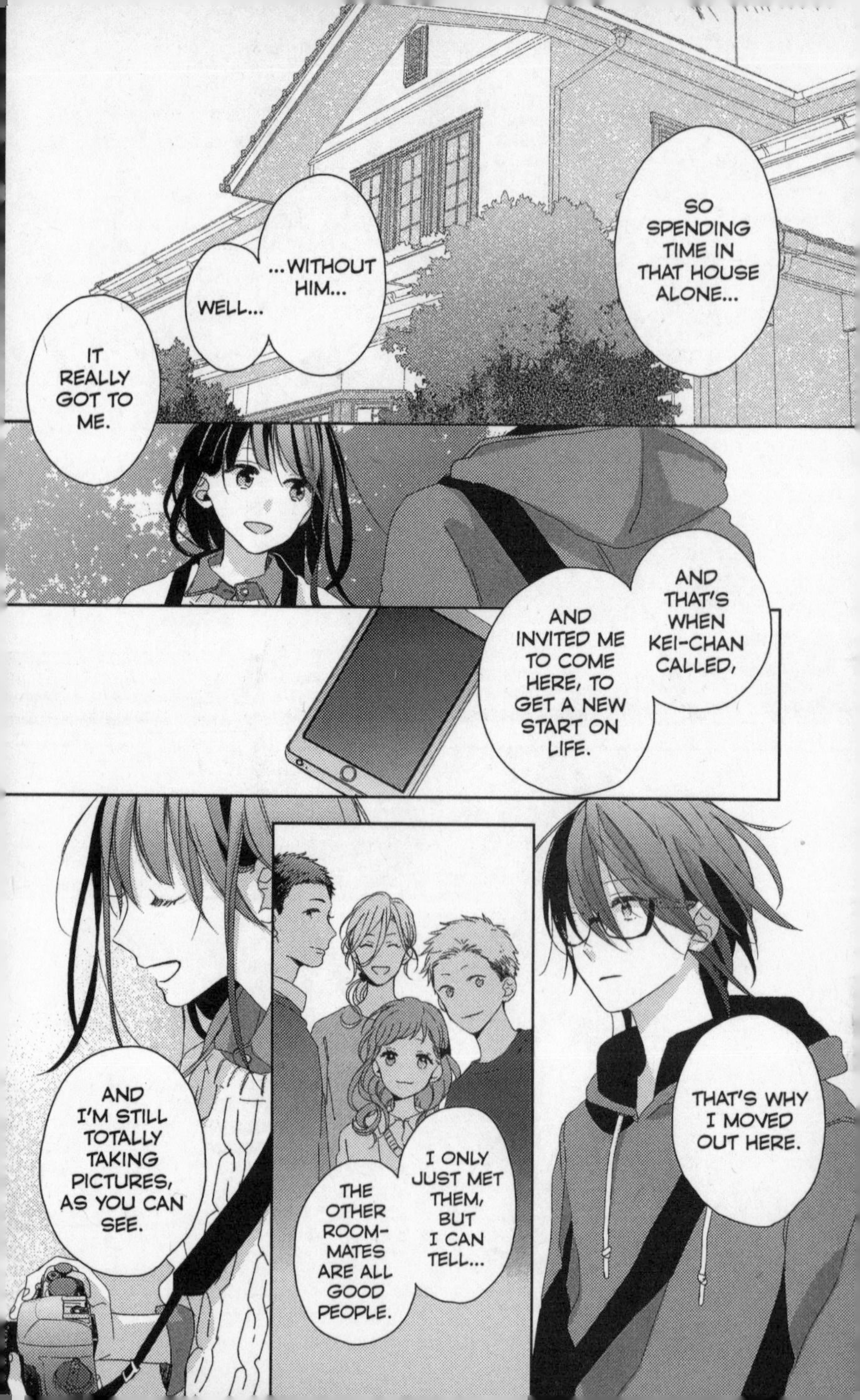
SO SPENDING TIME IN THAT HOUSE ALONE...
...WITHOUT HIM...
WELL...
IT REALLY GOT TO ME.
AND THAT'S WHEN KEI-CHAN CALLED,
AND INVITED ME TO COME HERE, TO GET A NEW START ON LIFE.
THAT'S WHY I MOVED OUT HERE.
I ONLY JUST MET THEM, BUT I CAN TELL...
THE OTHER ROOM-MATES ARE ALL GOOD PEOPLE.
AND I'M STILL TOTALLY TAKING PICTURES, AS YOU CAN SEE.

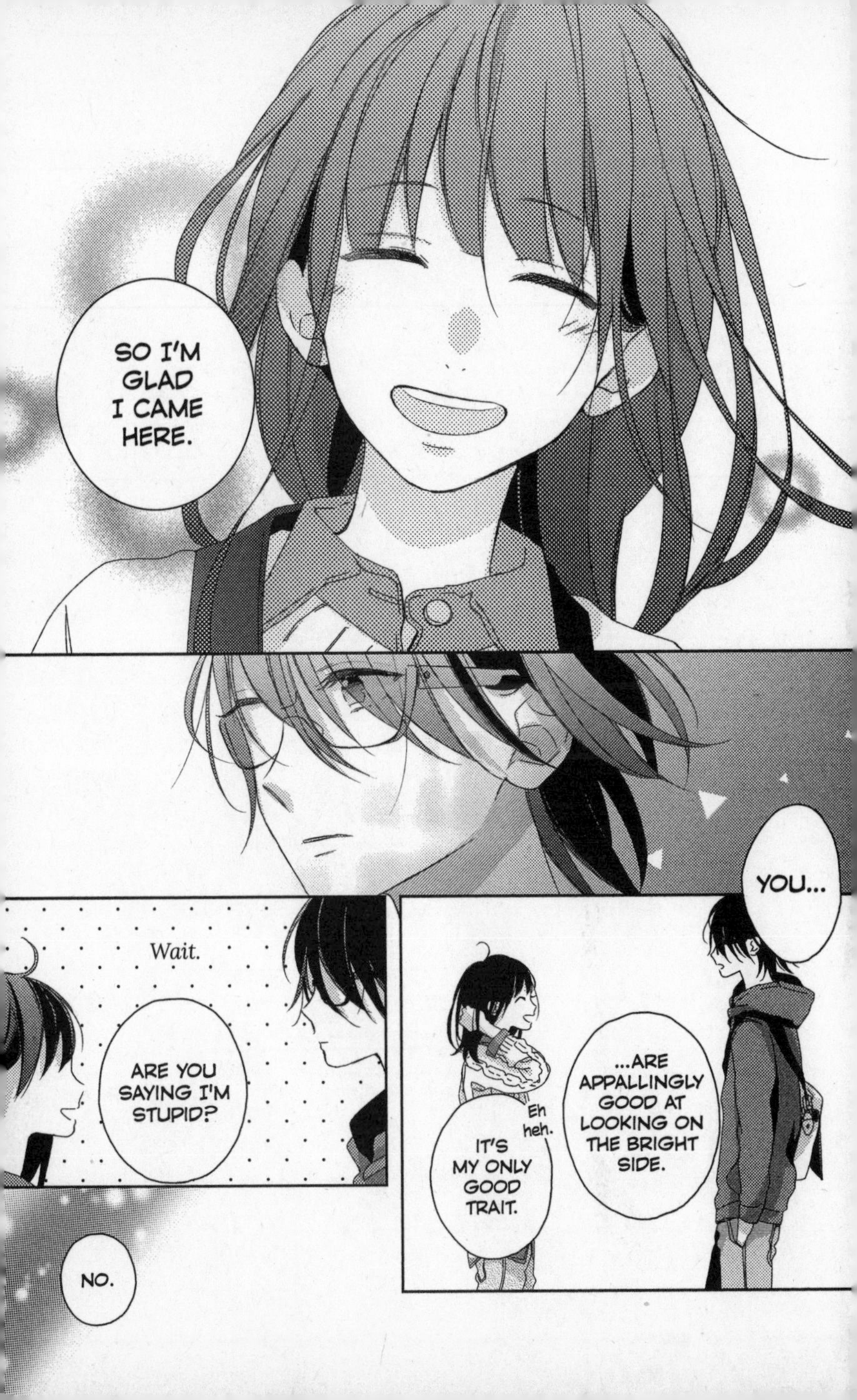
SO I'M GLAD I CAME HERE.
YOU...
...ARE APPALLINGLY GOOD AT LOOKING ON THE BRIGHT SIDE.
Eh heh.
IT'S MY ONLY GOOD TRAIT.
Wait.
ARE YOU SAYING I'M STUPID?
NO.

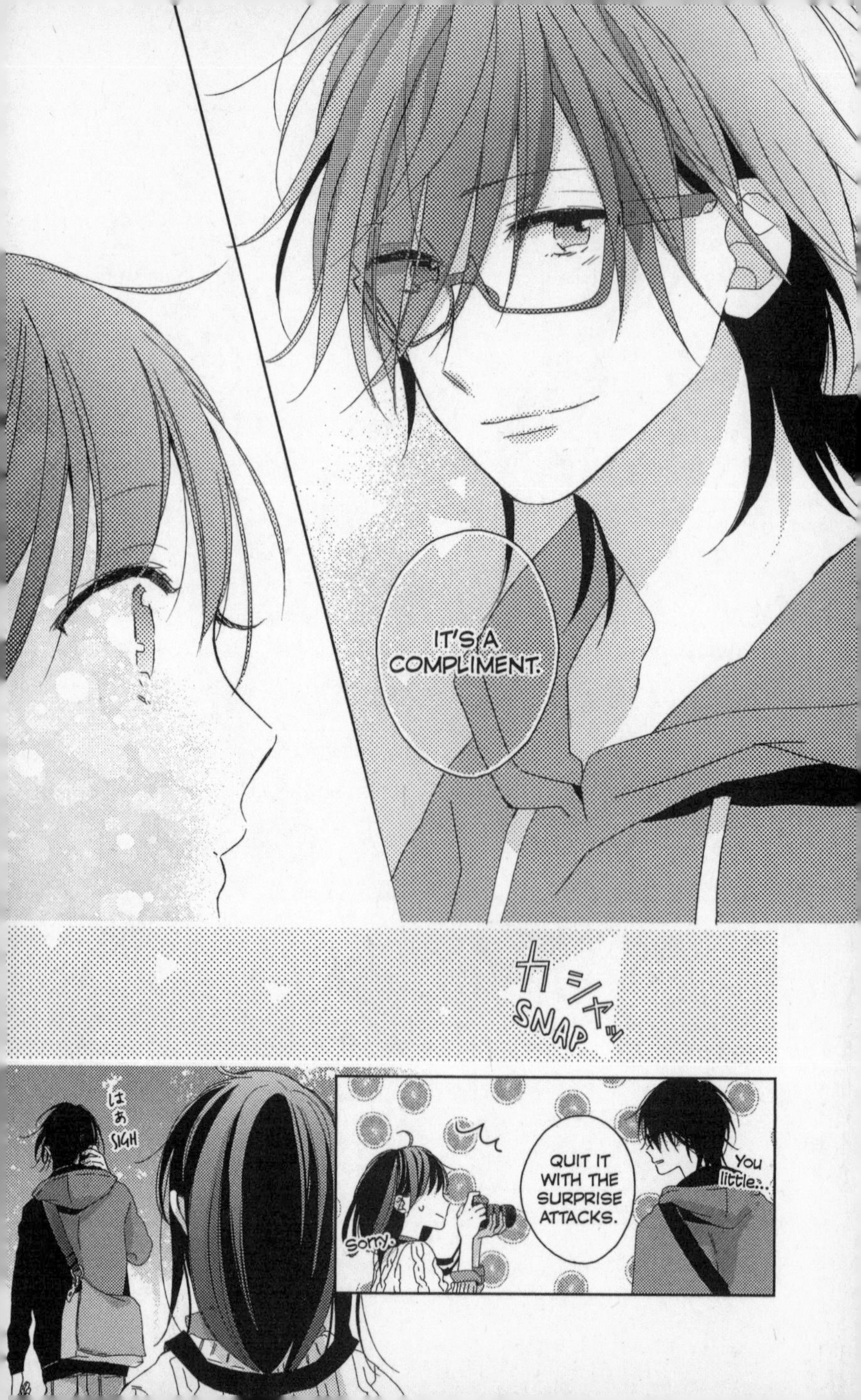
IT'S A COMPLIMENT.
カシャッ
SNAP
You little...
QUIT IT WITH THE SURPRISE ATTACKS.
Sorry.
はぁ
SIGH

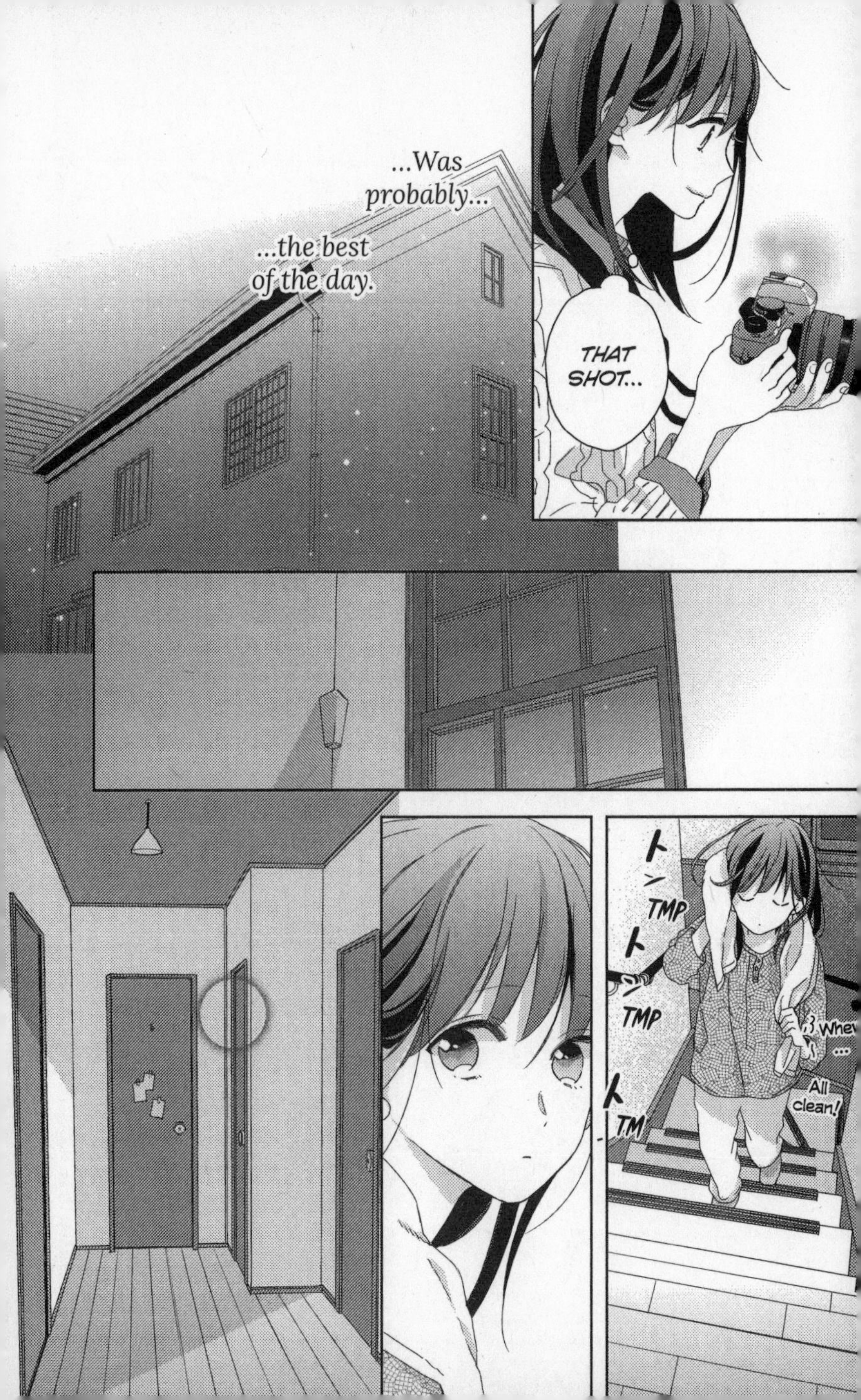
THAT SHOT...
...Was probably...
...the best of the day.
トン TMP
トン TMP
ト TM
Whew...
All clean!

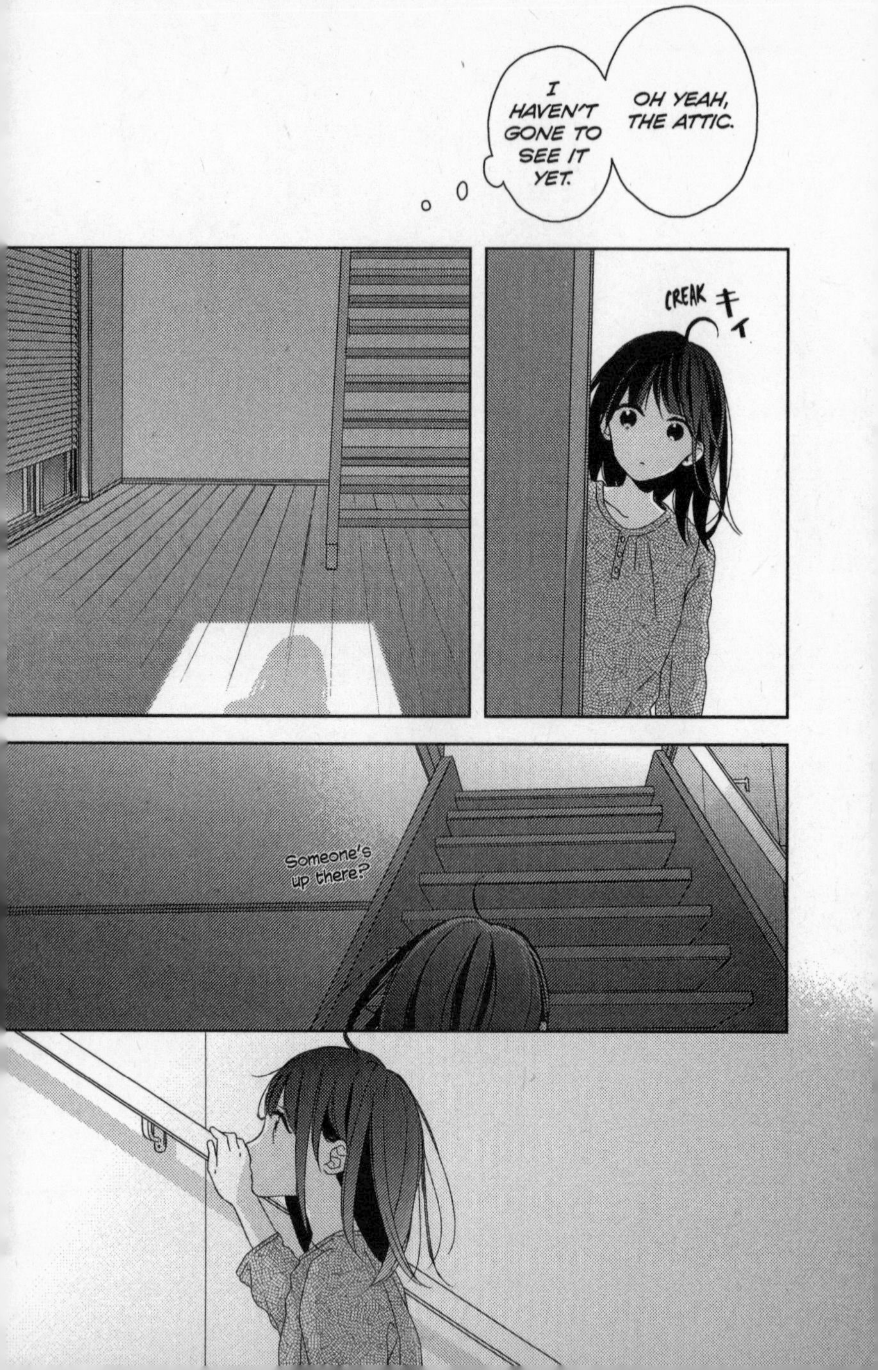
OH YEAH, THE ATTIC.
I HAVEN'T GONE TO SEE IT YET.
CREAK キィ
Someone's up there?

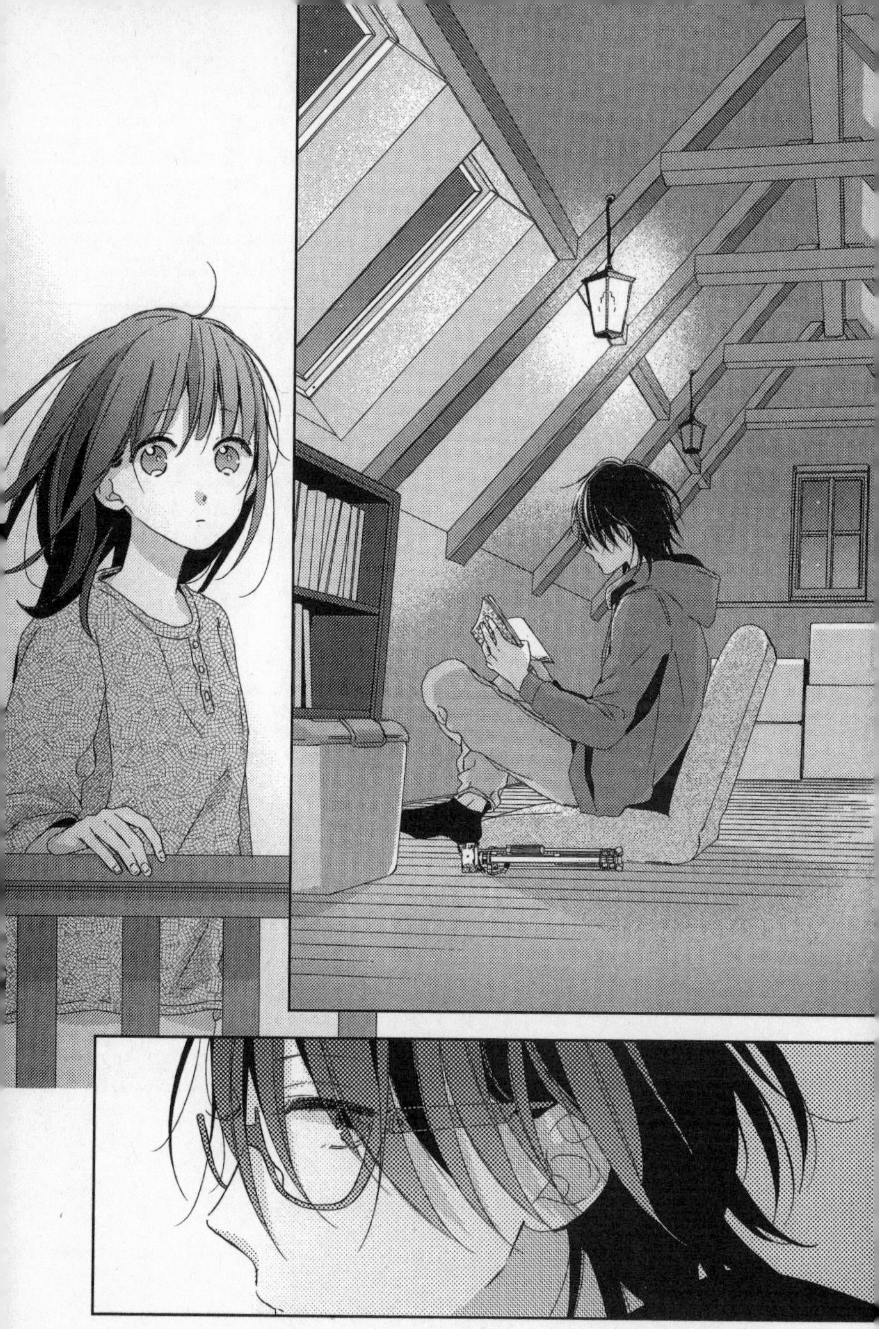

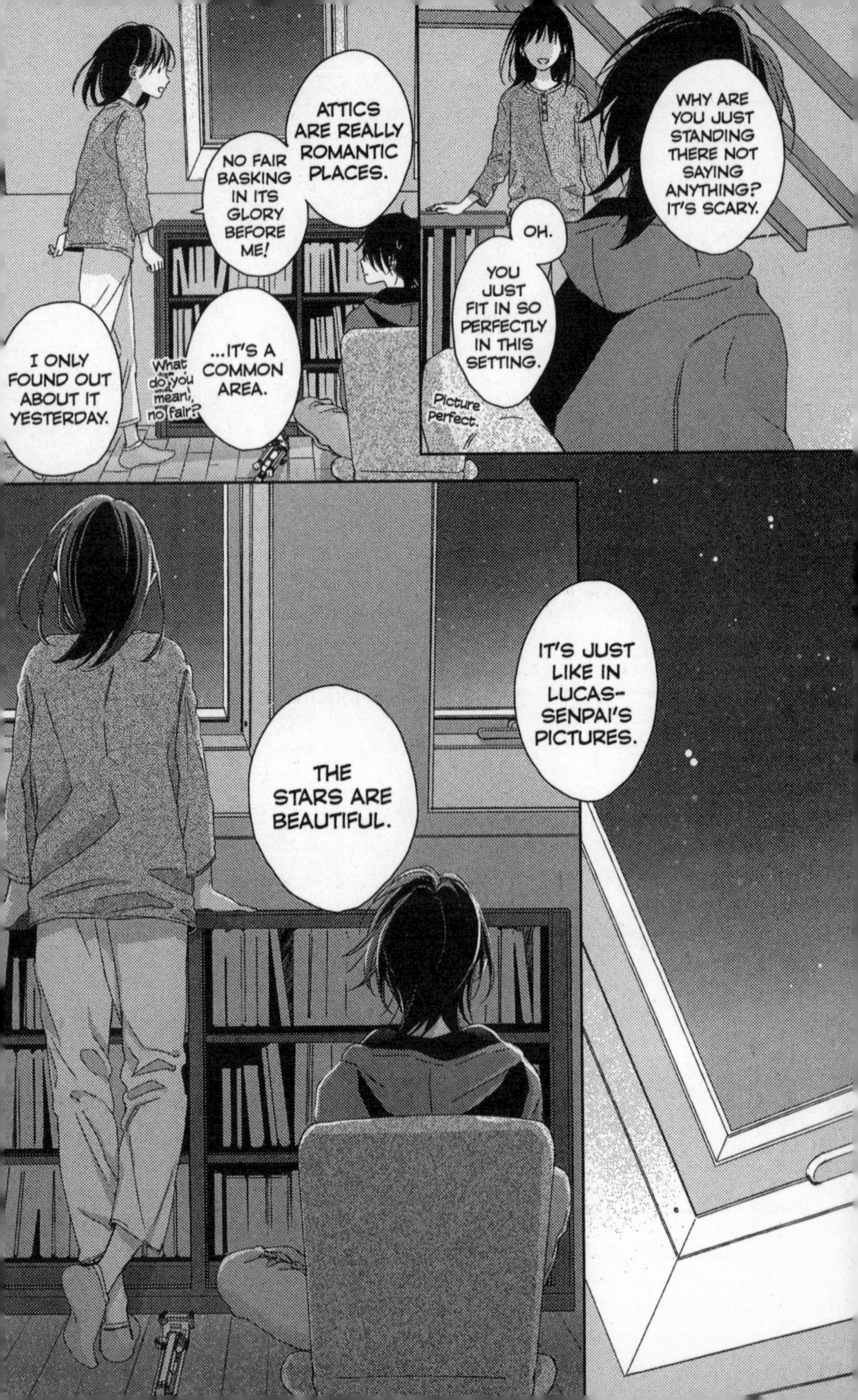
WHY ARE YOU JUST STANDING THERE NOT SAYING ANYTHING? IT'S SCARY.
OH.
YOU JUST FIT IN SO PERFECTLY IN THIS SETTING.
Picture perfect.
ATTICS ARE REALLY ROMANTIC PLACES.
NO FAIR BASKING IN ITS GLORY BEFORE ME!
...IT'S A COMMON AREA.
What do you mean, no fair?
I ONLY FOUND OUT ABOUT IT YESTERDAY.
IT'S JUST LIKE IN LUCAS-SENPAI'S PICTURES.
THE STARS ARE BEAUTIFUL.

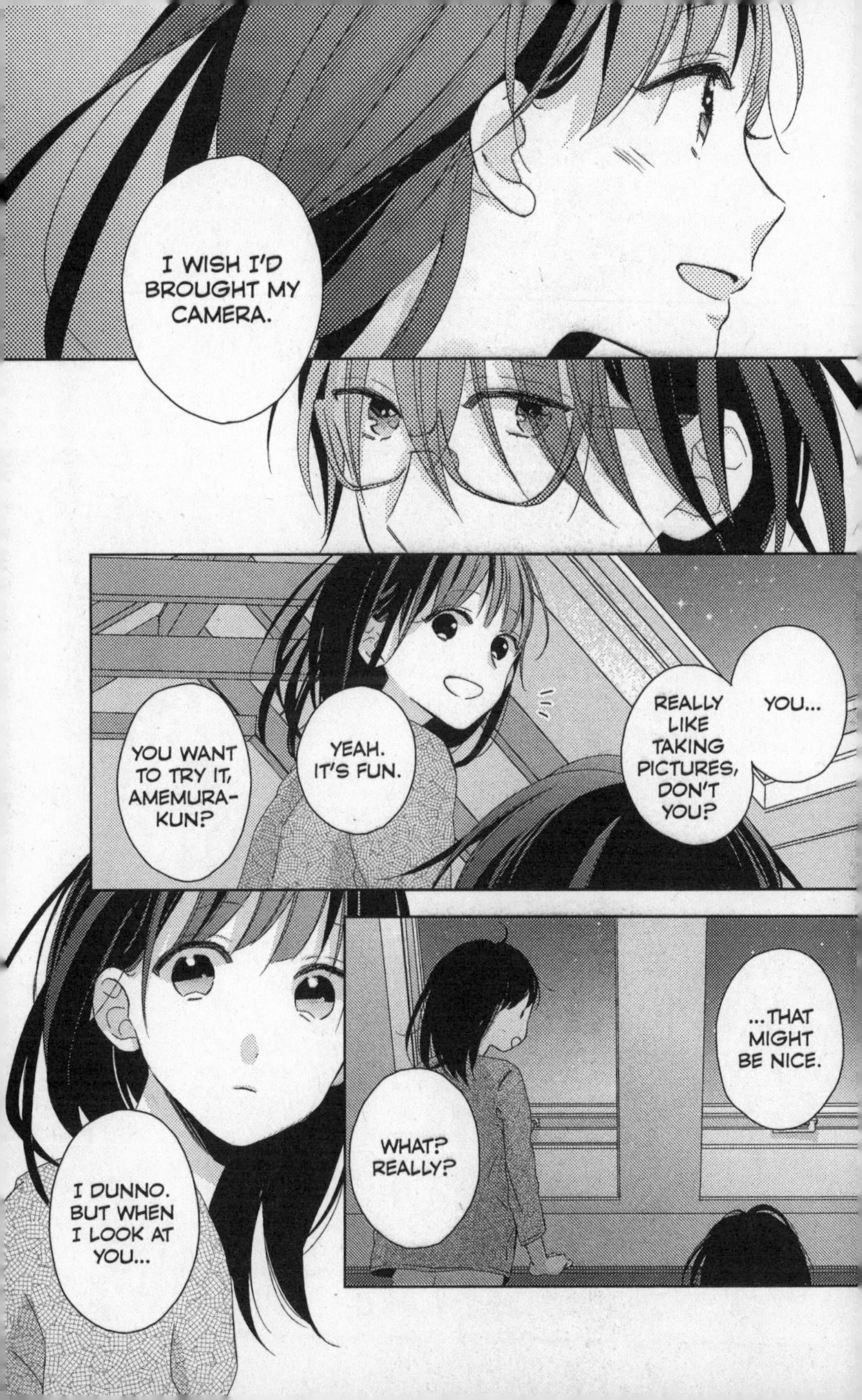
I WISH I'D BROUGHT MY CAMERA.
YOU...
REALLY LIKE TAKING PICTURES, DON'T YOU?
YEAH. IT'S FUN.
YOU WANT TO TRY IT, AMEMURA-KUN?
...THAT MIGHT BE NICE.
WHAT? REALLY?
I DUNNO. BUT WHEN I LOOK AT YOU...

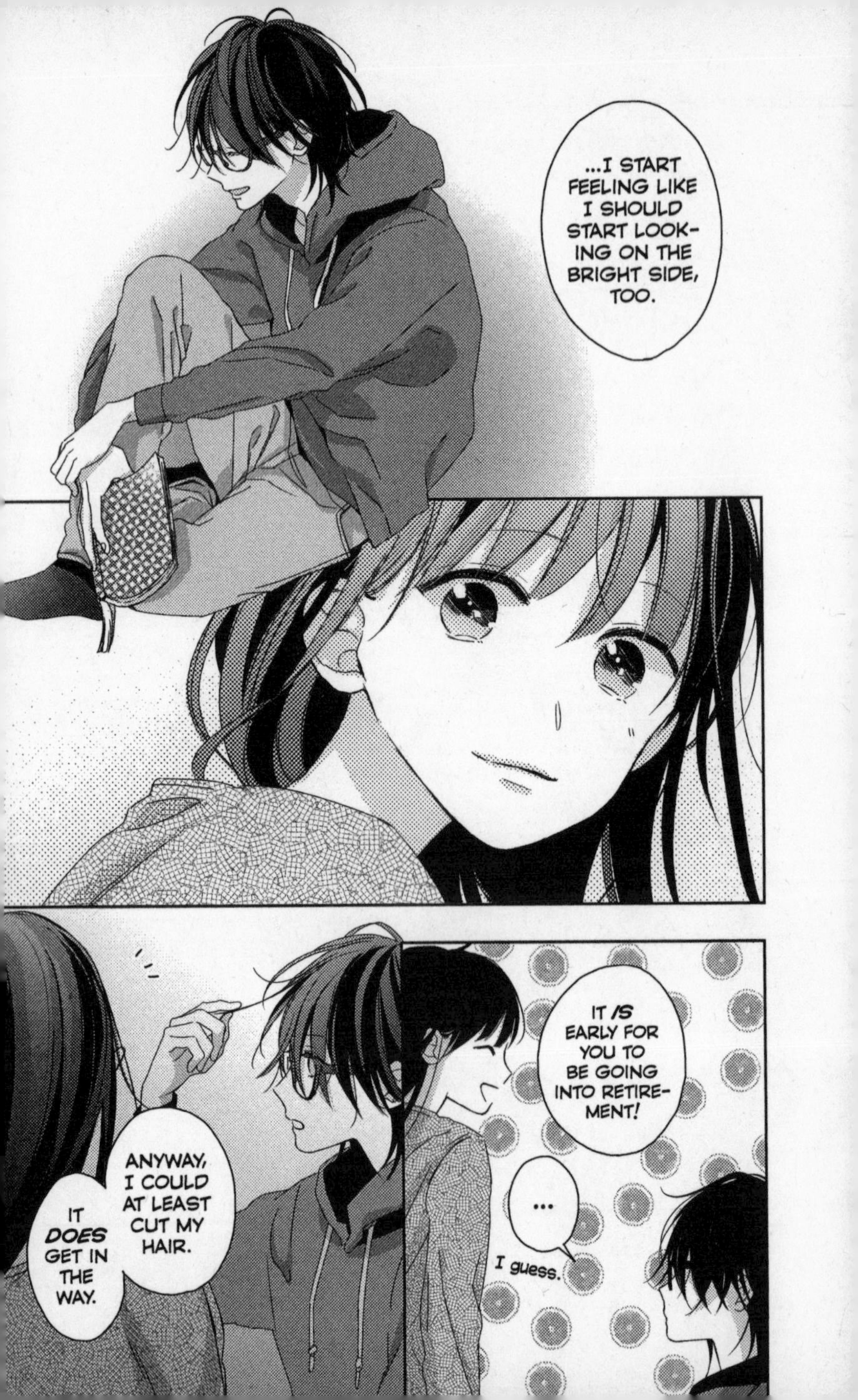
...I START FEELING LIKE I SHOULD START LOOKING ON THE BRIGHT SIDE, TOO.
IT *IS* EARLY FOR YOU TO BE GOING INTO RETIREMENT!
...
I guess.
ANYWAY, I COULD AT LEAST CUT MY HAIR.
IT *DOES* GET IN THE WAY.

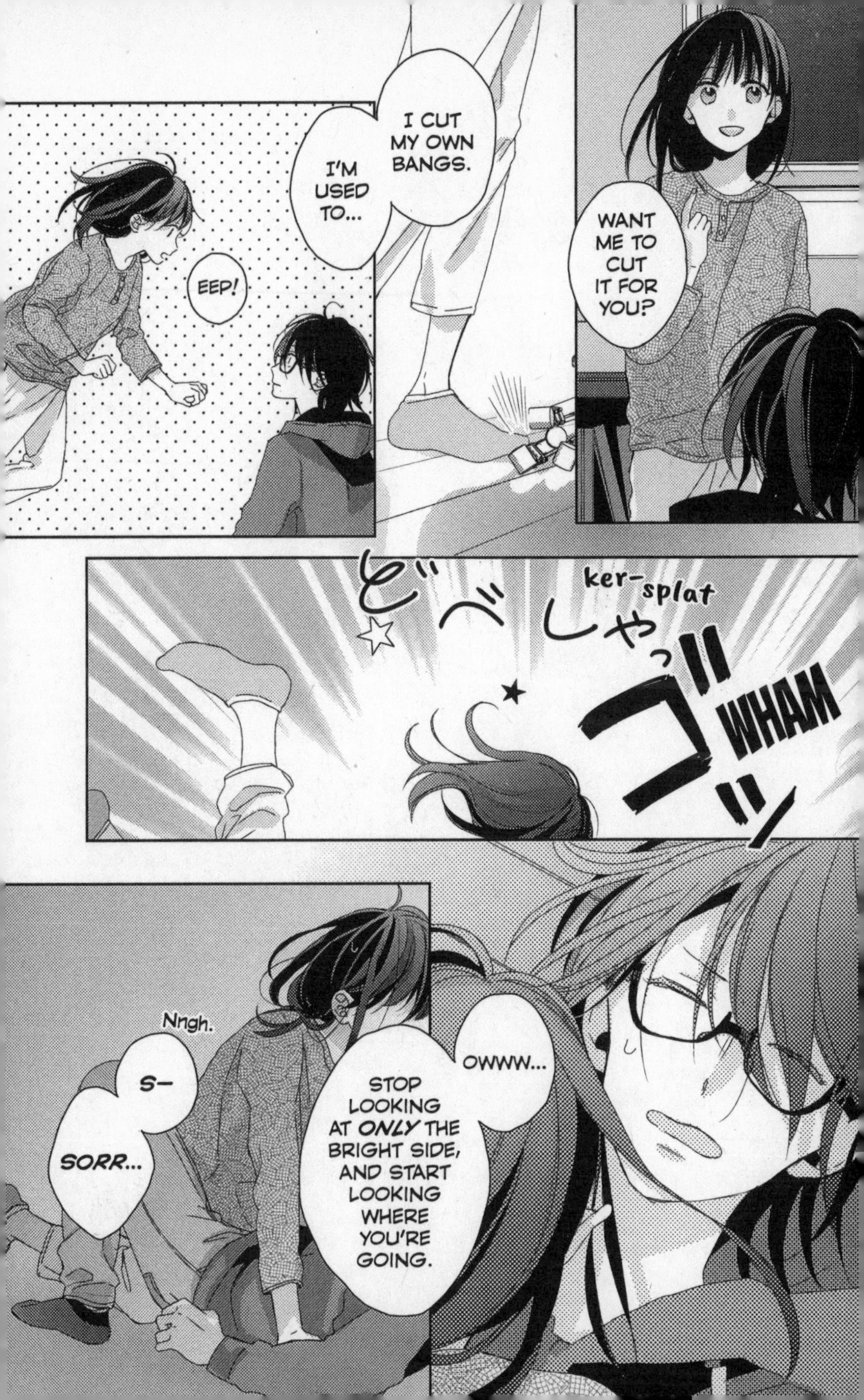
WANT ME TO CUT IT FOR YOU?
I CUT MY OWN BANGS.
I'M USED TO...
EEP!
どべしゃっ
ker-splat
ゴッ
WHAM
OWWW...
STOP LOOKING AT *ONLY* THE BRIGHT SIDE, AND START LOOKING WHERE YOU'RE GOING.
Nngh.
S—
SORR...

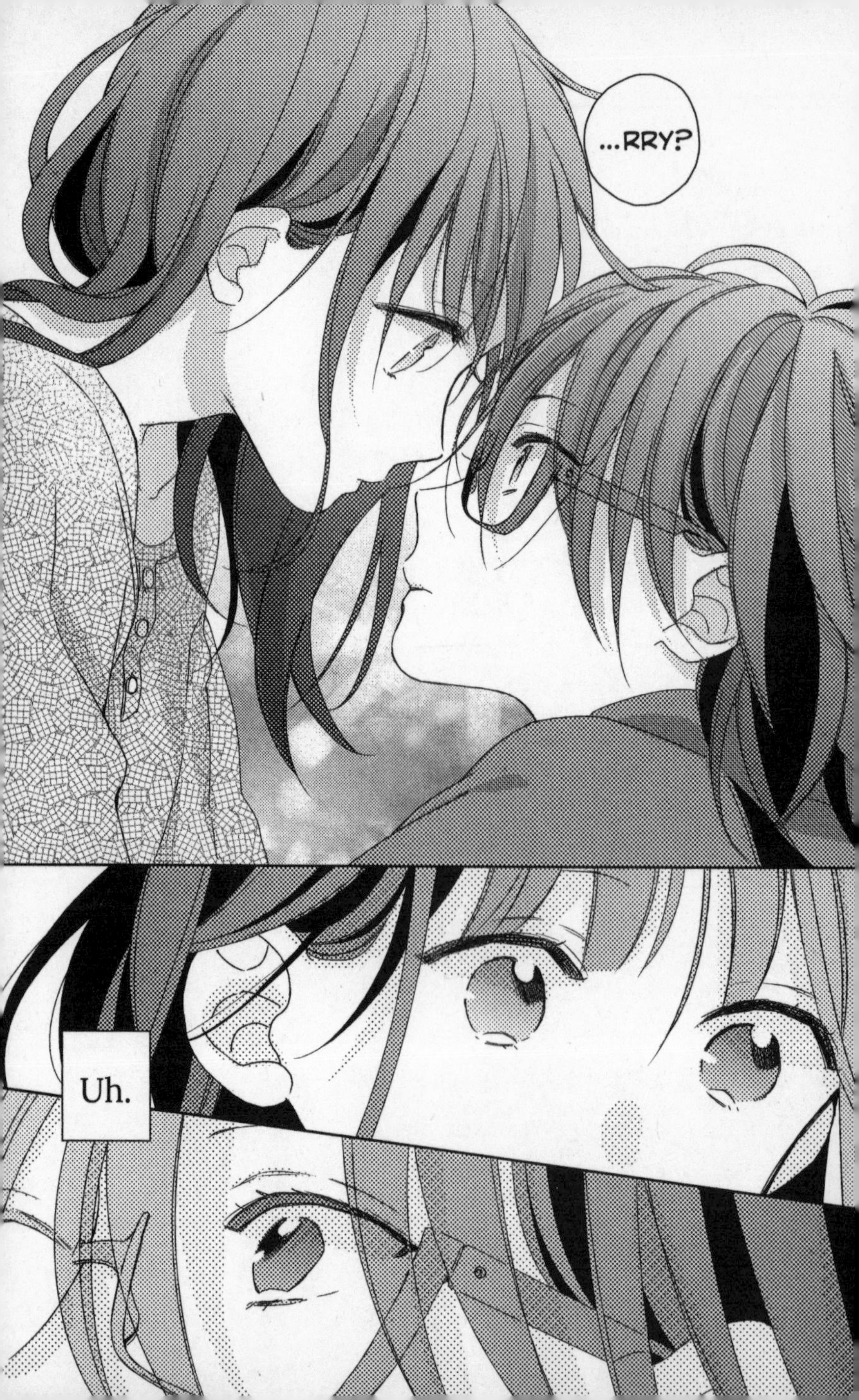
...RRY?
Uh.

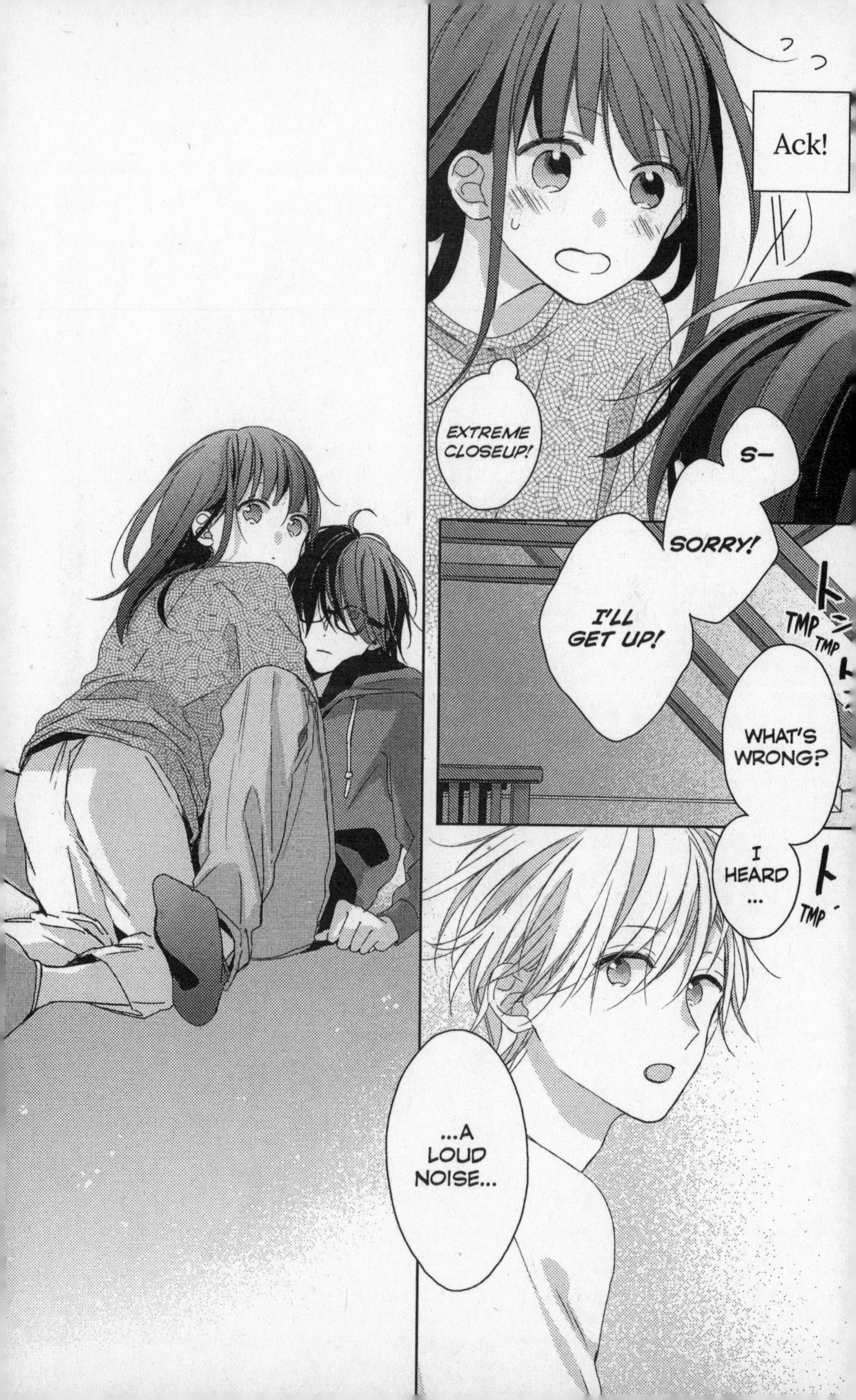
Ack!
EXTREME CLOSEUP!
S–
SORRY!
I'LL GET UP!
TMP TMP
WHAT'S WRONG?
I HEARD...
TMP
...A LOUD NOISE...

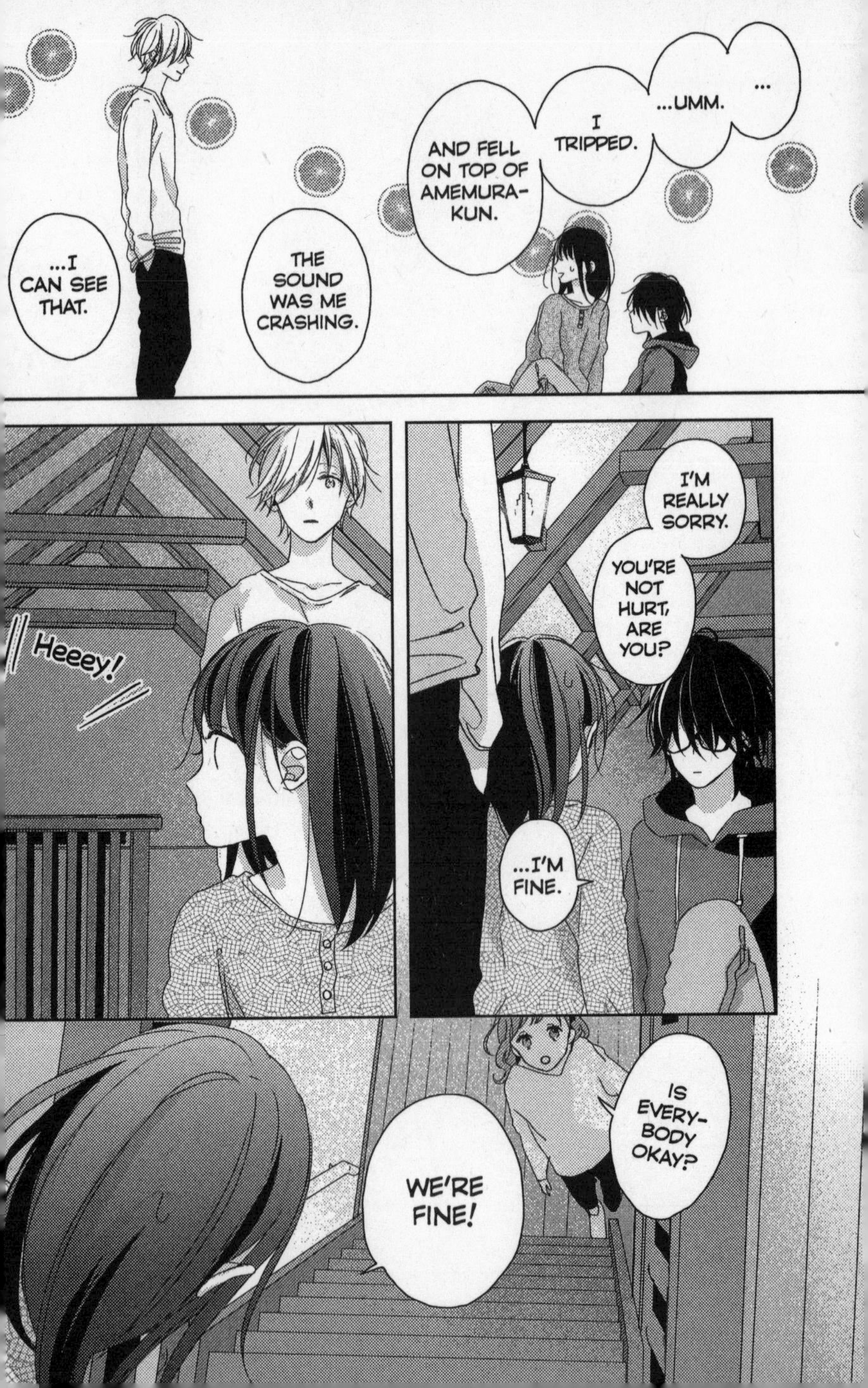
...
...UMM.
I TRIPPED.
AND FELL ON TOP OF AMEMURA-KUN.
THE SOUND WAS ME CRASHING.
...I CAN SEE THAT.
I'M REALLY SORRY.
YOU'RE NOT HURT, ARE YOU?
...I'M FINE.
Heeey!
IS EVERYBODY OKAY?
WE'RE FINE!

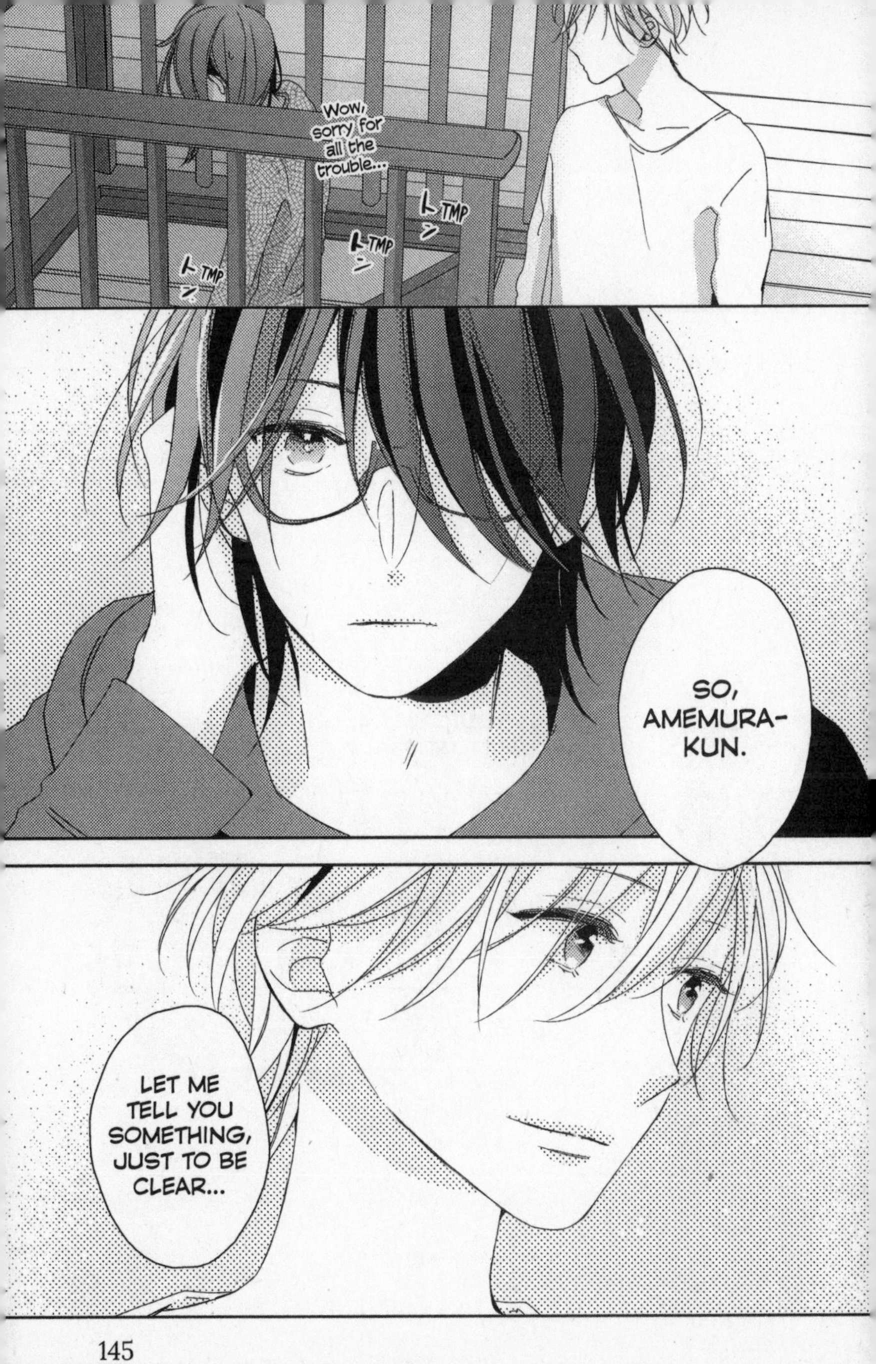
Wow, sorry for all the trouble...
TMP
TMP
TMP
SO, AMEMURA-KUN.
LET ME TELL YOU SOMETHING, JUST TO BE CLEAR...

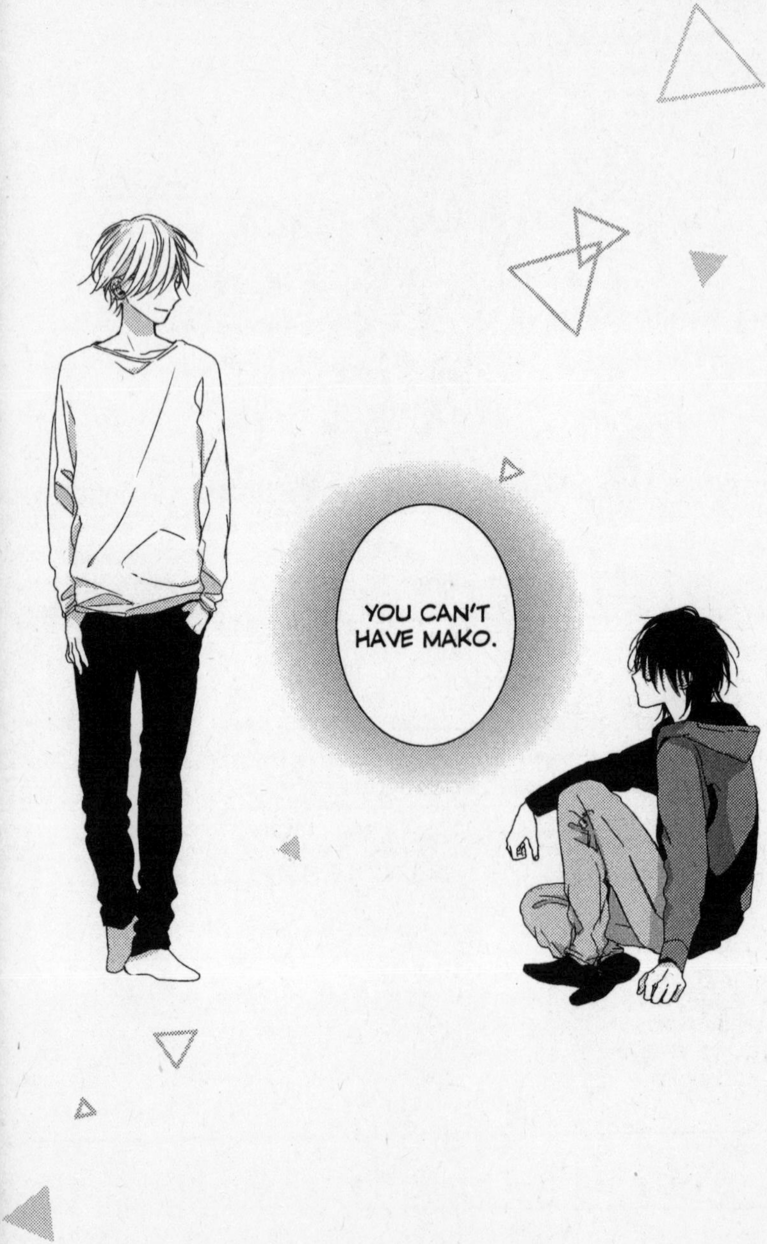
YOU CAN'T HAVE MAKO.

to be continued

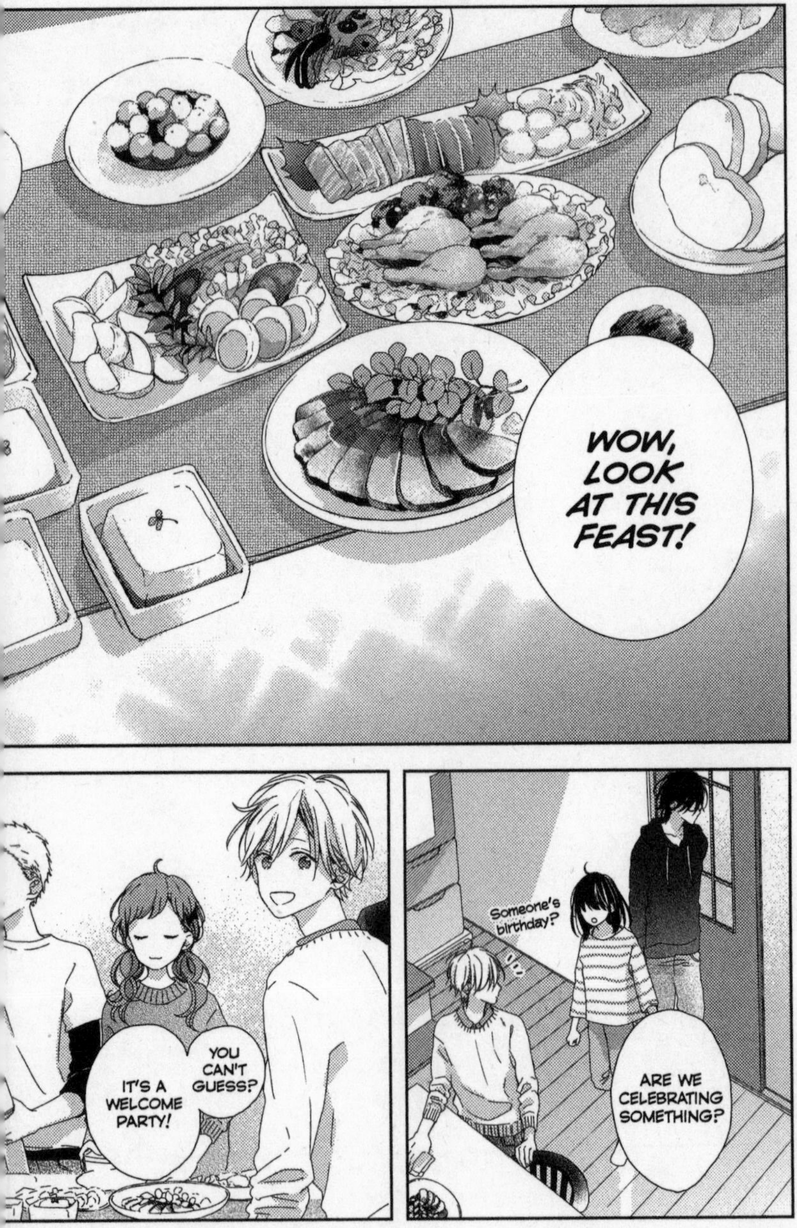
WOW, LOOK AT THIS FEAST!
Someone's birthday?
ARE WE CELEBRATING SOMETHING?
YOU CAN'T GUESS?
IT'S A WELCOME PARTY!

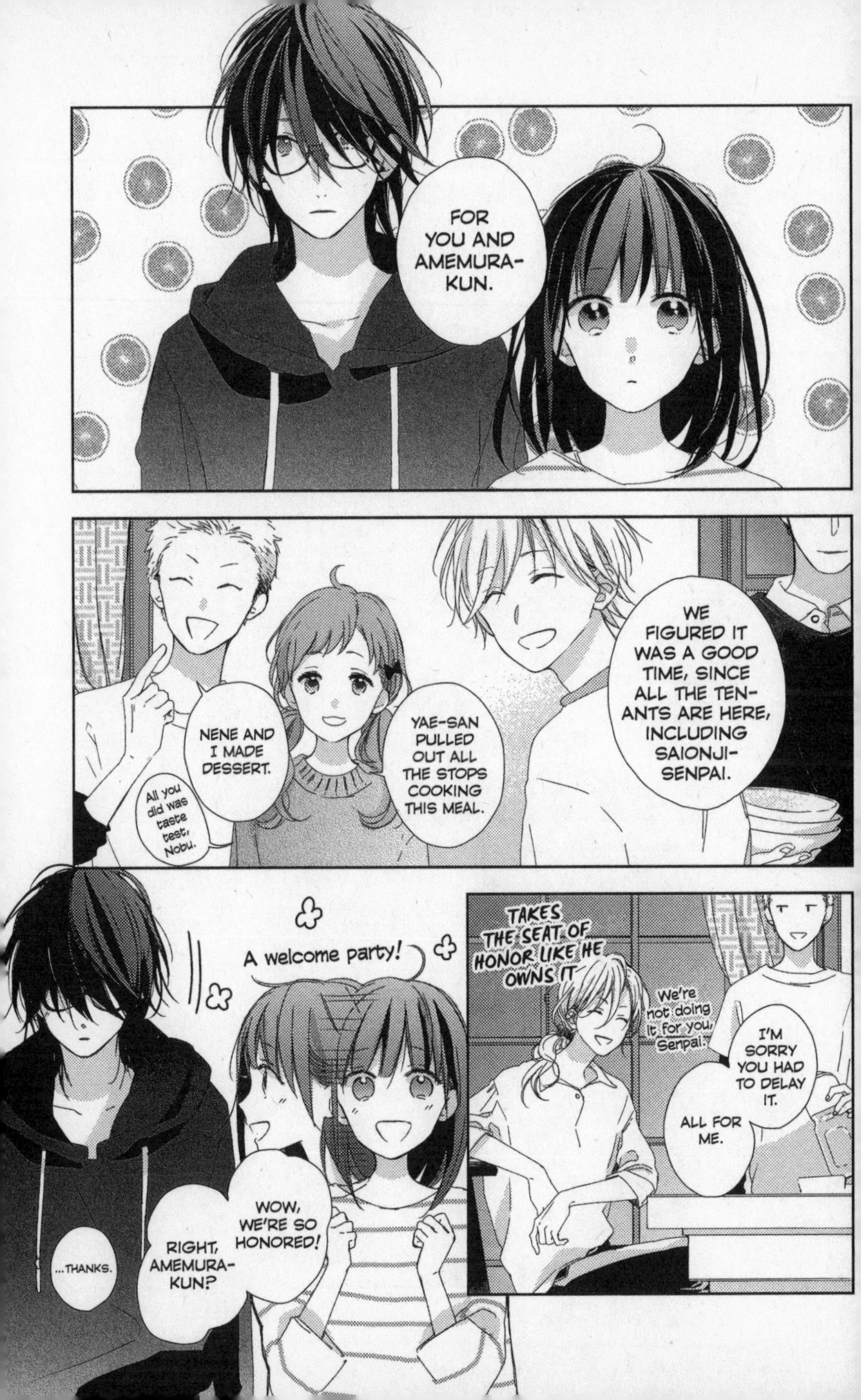
FOR YOU AND AMEMURA-KUN.
WE FIGURED IT WAS A GOOD TIME, SINCE ALL THE TEN-ANTS ARE HERE, INCLUDING SAIONJI-SENPAI.
YAE-SAN PULLED OUT ALL THE STOPS COOKING THIS MEAL.
NENE AND I MADE DESSERT.
All you did was taste test, Nobu.
TAKES THE SEAT OF HONOR LIKE HE OWNS IT
I'M SORRY YOU HAD TO DELAY IT.
ALL FOR ME.
We're not doing it for you, Senpai.
A welcome party!
WOW, WE'RE SO HONORED!
RIGHT, AMEMURA-KUN?
...THANKS.

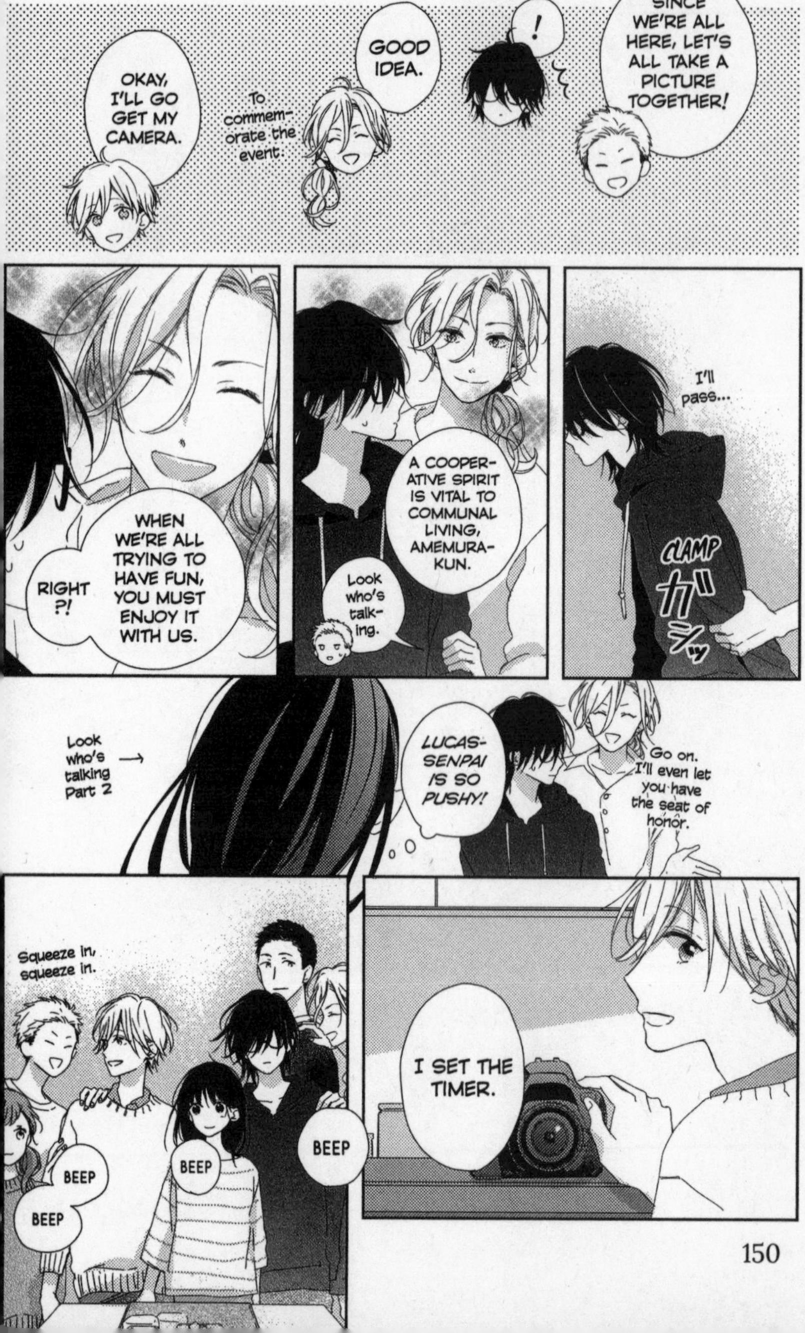
SINCE WE'RE ALL HERE, LET'S ALL TAKE A PICTURE TOGETHER!
!
GOOD IDEA.
To commemorate the event.
OKAY, I'LL GO GET MY CAMERA.
I'll pass...
CLAMP
ガシッ
A COOPERATIVE SPIRIT IS VITAL TO COMMUNAL LIVING, AMEMURA-KUN.
Look who's talking.
WHEN WE'RE ALL TRYING TO HAVE FUN, YOU MUST ENJOY IT WITH US.
RIGHT?!
Go on. I'll even let you have the seat of honor.
LUCAS-SENPAI IS SO PUSHY!
Look who's talking Part 2
I SET THE TIMER.
BEEP
BEEP
BEEP
BEEP
Squeeze in, squeeze in.

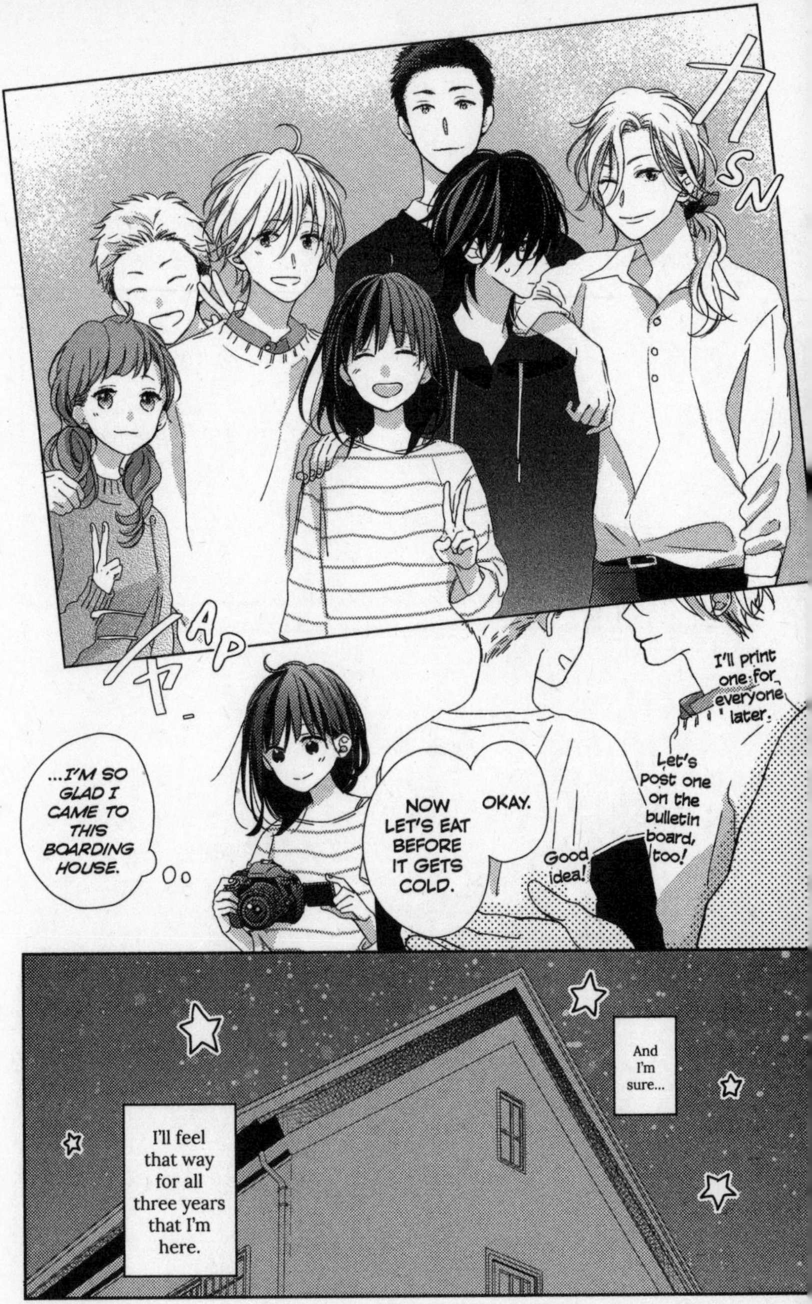
SN
AP
I'll print one for everyone later.
Let's post one on the bulletin board, too!
Good idea!
OKAY.
NOW LET'S EAT BEFORE IT GETS COLD.
...I'M SO GLAD I CAME TO THIS BOARDING HOUSE.
And I'm sure...
I'll feel that way for all three years that I'm here.

The end.

Afterword

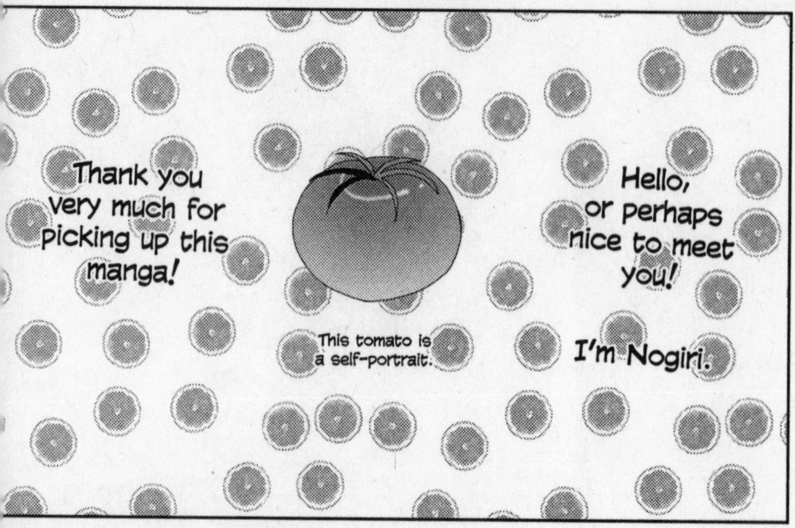

Hello, or perhaps nice to meet you!
I'm Nogiri.
Thank you very much for picking up this manga!
This tomato is a self-portrait.

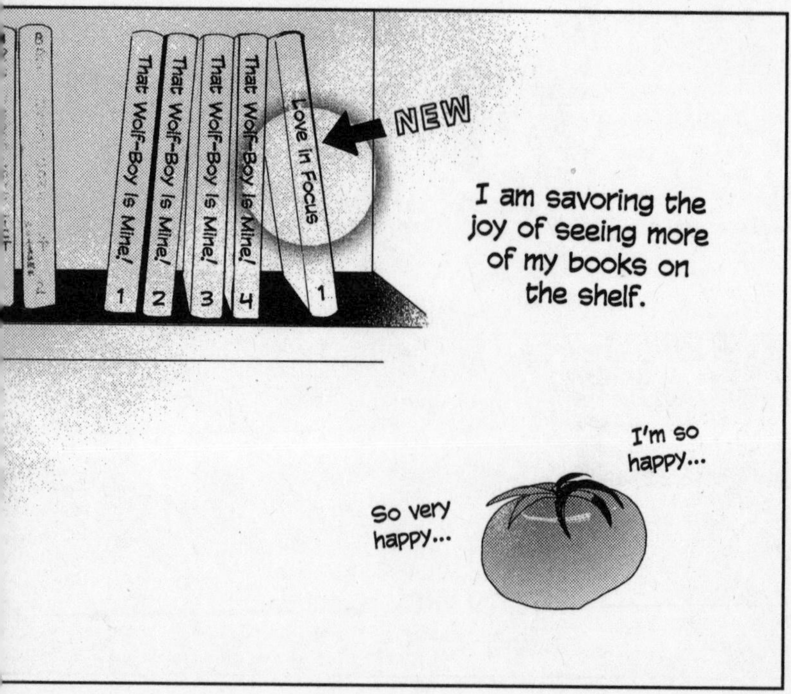

I am savoring the joy of seeing more of my books on the shelf.
NEW
Love in Focus 1
That Wolf-Boy Is Mine! 4
That Wolf-Boy Is Mine! 3
That Wolf-Boy Is Mine! 2
That Wolf-Boy Is Mine! 1
I'm so happy...
So very happy...

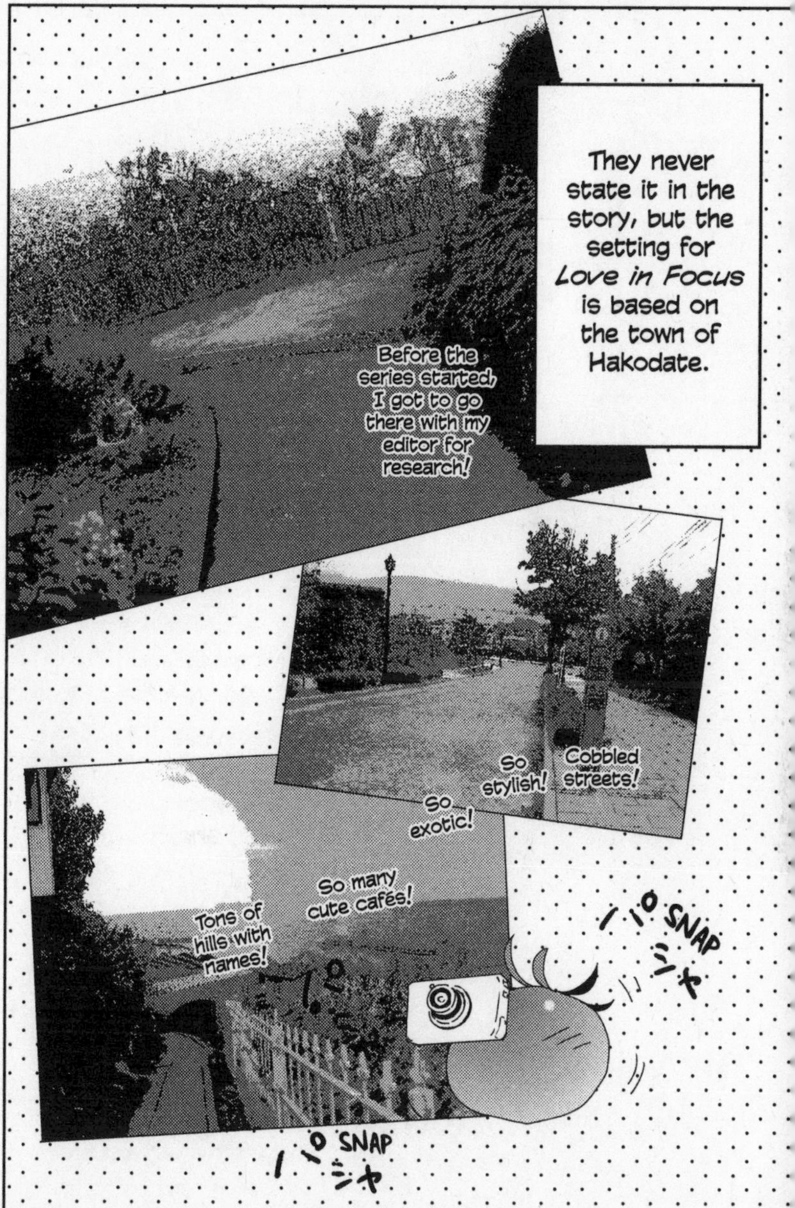
They never state it in the story, but the setting for *Love in Focus* is based on the town of Hakodate.
Before the series started, I got to go there with my editor for research!
Cobbled streets!
So stylish!
So exotic!
So many cute cafés!
Tons of hills with names!
パシャ SNAP
パシャ SNAP

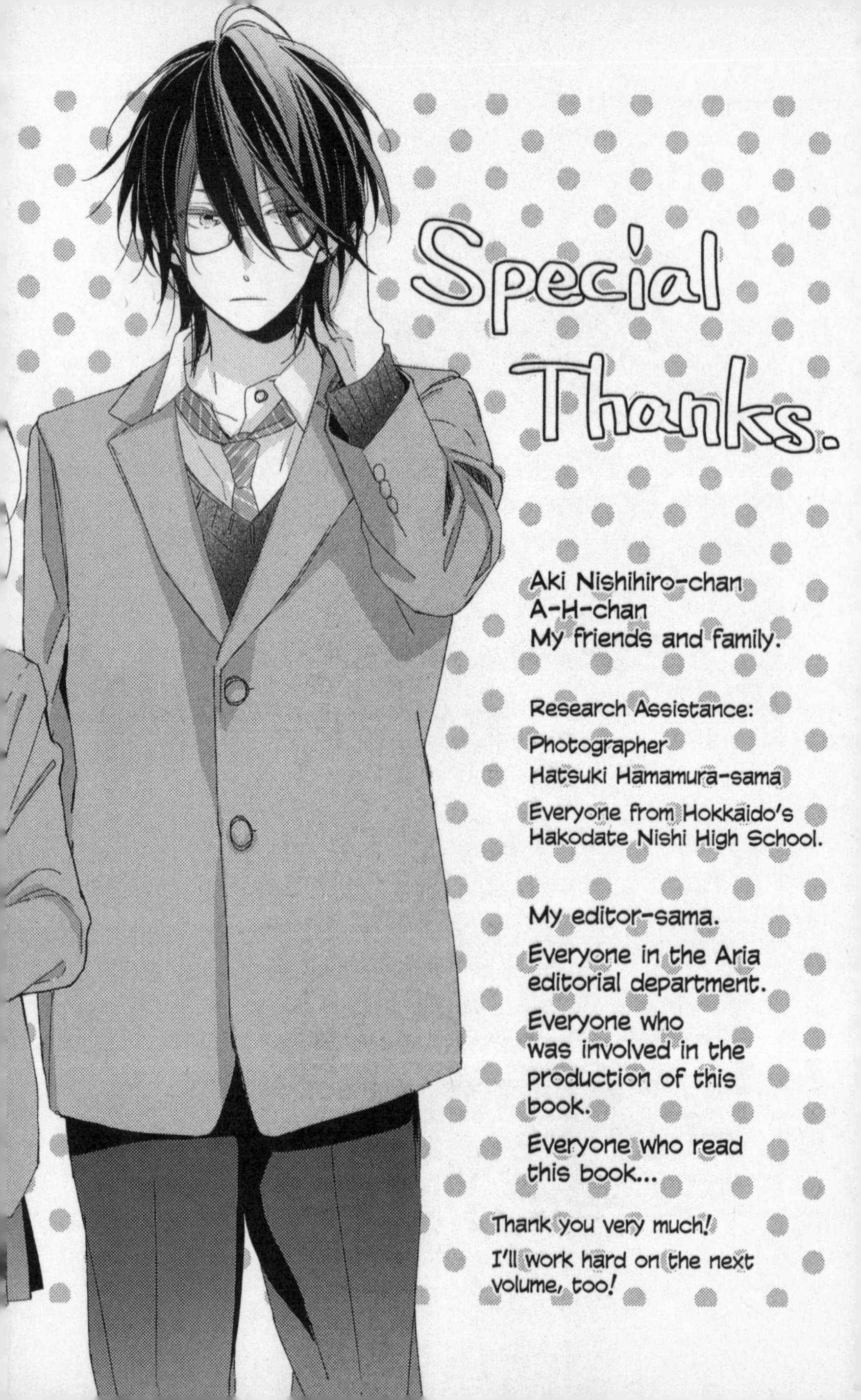

Special Thanks.

Aki Nishihiro-chan
A-H-chan
My friends and family.

Research Assistance:

Photographer
Hatsuki Hamamura-sama

Everyone from Hokkaido's
Hakodate Nishi High School.

My editor-sama.

Everyone in the Aria
editorial department.

Everyone who
was involved in the
production of this
book.

Everyone who read
this book...

Thank you very much!

I'll work hard on the next
volume, too!

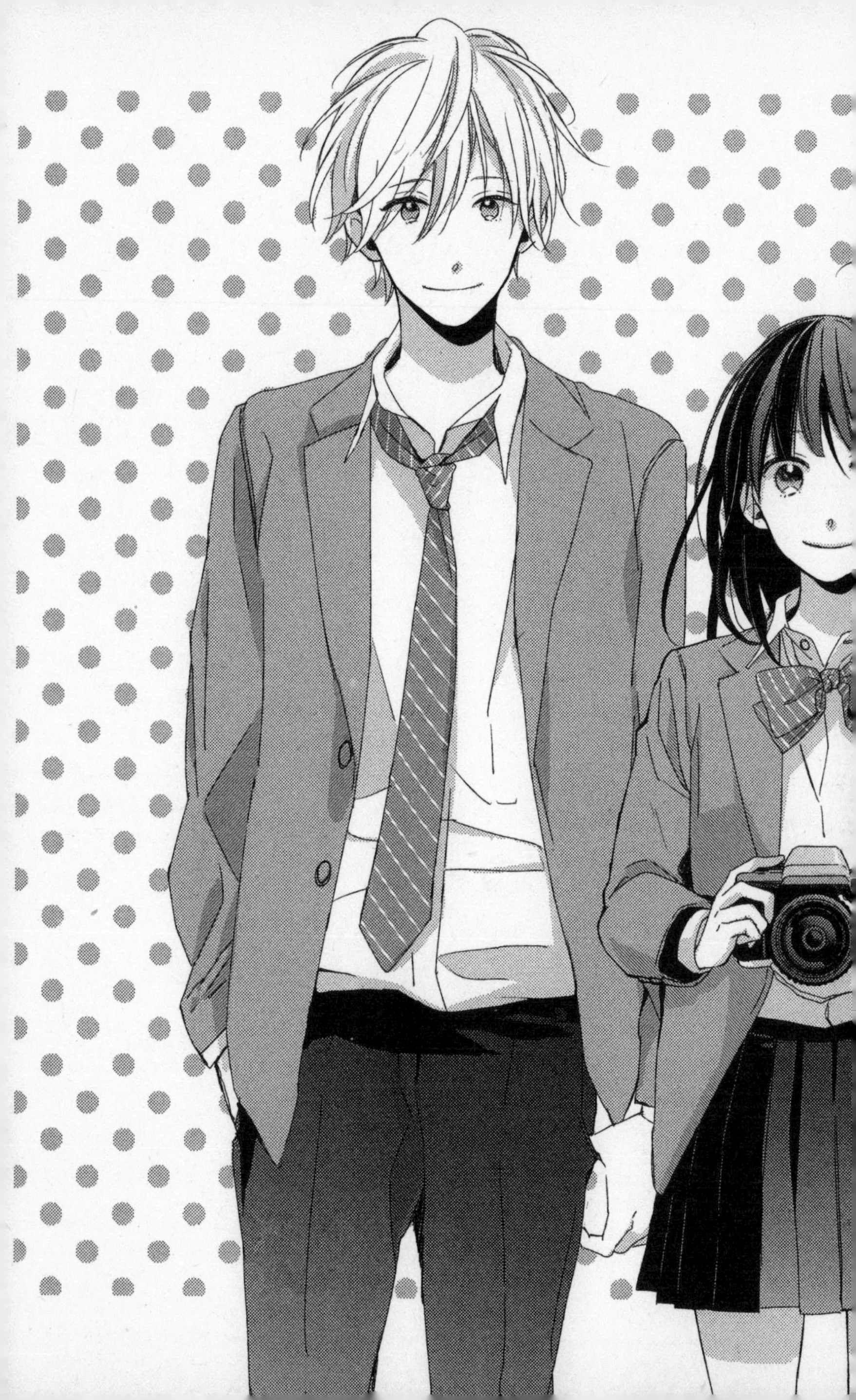

Omochi ♂, age 6

The celebrity of Lens Inn.

The landlady's pet dog!

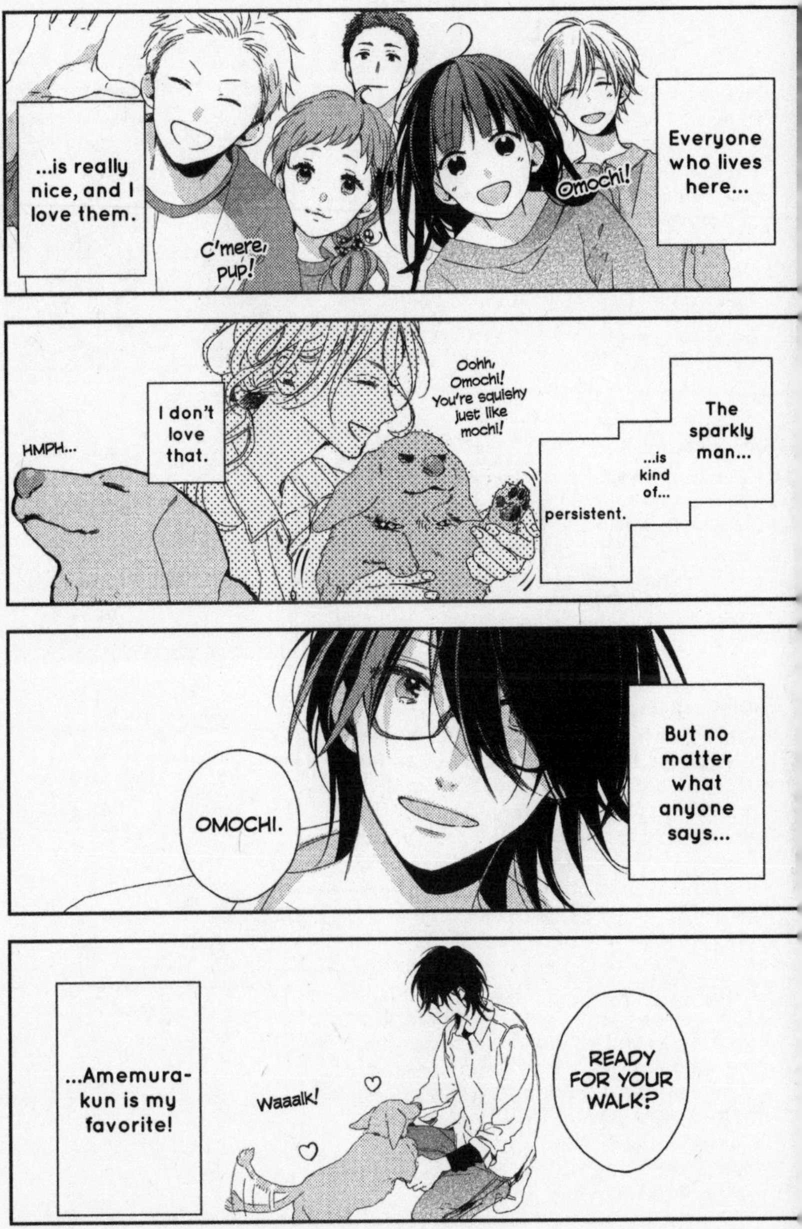
Everyone who lives here...
Omochi!
C'mere, pup!
...is really nice, and I love them.
The sparkly man...
...is kind of...
persistent.
Oohh, Omochi! You're squishy just like mochi!
I don't love that.
HMPH...
But no matter what anyone says...
OMOCHI.
READY FOR YOUR WALK?
Waaalk!
...Amemura-kun is my favorite!

TRANSLATION NOTES

Triangle roof, page 17

The technical term for this type of roof is a "gable roof," referring to a roof made of two slanting sides with a triangular portion of wall, or "gable," between them. But Mako instead refers to the gable as the more familiar "triangle." The original Japanese title of the series is *Renzu-Sou no Sankaku*, or "The Triangle of Lens Inn."

A triangle roof.

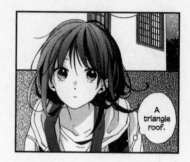

WC, page 19

In Japan, the toilet is in a separate room from the bathtub. WC stands for "water closet," which is the polite term for such a room.

2 F
WC
Bath
5
6
7
8
9

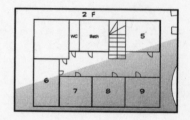

Entrance ceremony and opening ceremony, page 59

In Japan, at the start of a new school year (in April), schools will hold opening and entrance ceremonies for the students. The opening ceremony, more literally translated as "beginning of operations ceremony," is for returning students, and is where they find out whether or not they will be in the same class as the previous year. The entrance ceremony is for the students who are newly entering the school as first-years to introduce them to their new place of learning. These two ceremonies can be held in any order, and some schools have the opening ceremony first so that the returning students can sit with their new classes when they attend the entrance ceremony. Unlike the four-year system in the US, in Japan, there are only three years in high school.

BUT YOU JUST GOT BACK FROM THE OPENING CEREMONY.
IT'S OKAY. I WENT THERE BEFORE, WHEN I TOOK THE ENTRANCE EXAM.

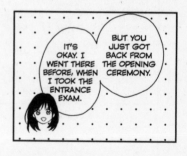

TRANSLATION NOTES

Hasumi "Lens" Inn, page 67
While "Lens" is already an appropriate name for an inn housing most of a school's photography club, there's a reason that particular part of a camera is more appropriate than others. The name Hasumi is written with two Chinese characters that literally mean "lotus dwelling." In Japanese, Chinese characters usually have multiple pronunciations, and this particular pair can also be read as *ren-zu*, which is the Japanese pronunciation of the English word "lens."

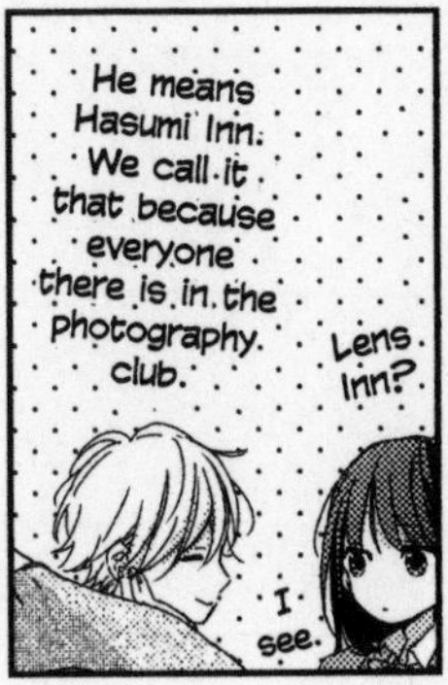
Lens Inn?
He means Hasumi Inn. We call it that because everyone there is in the photography club.
I see.

Golden Week, page 93
Golden Week is the first week in May—a week so full of national holidays that everyone takes the whole week off. Naturally, this makes it a good time to travel.

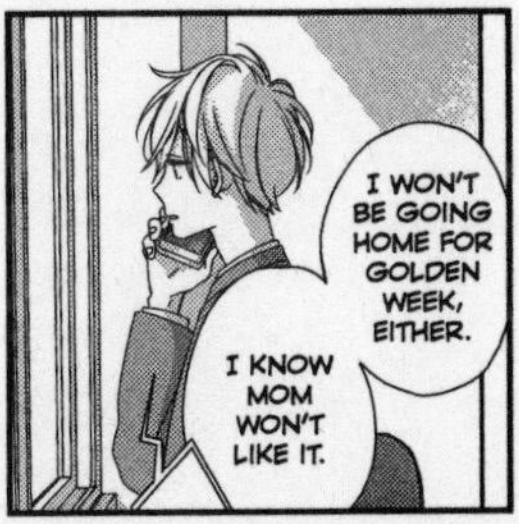
I WON'T BE GOING HOME FOR GOLDEN WEEK, EITHER.
I KNOW MOM WON'T LIKE IT.

Lucas Saionji, page 114
Being a quarter French, Saionji-senpai's given name is pronounced the French way, meaning the S is silent.

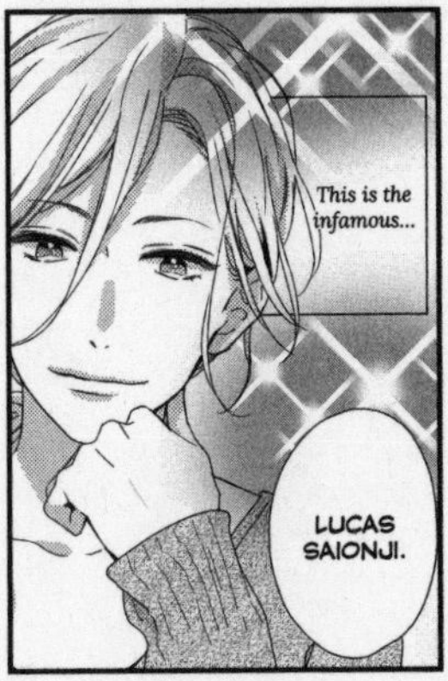
This is the infamous...
LUCAS SAIONJI.

LOVE IN FOCUS

THAT WOLF BOY IS MINE! CROSSOVER COMIC

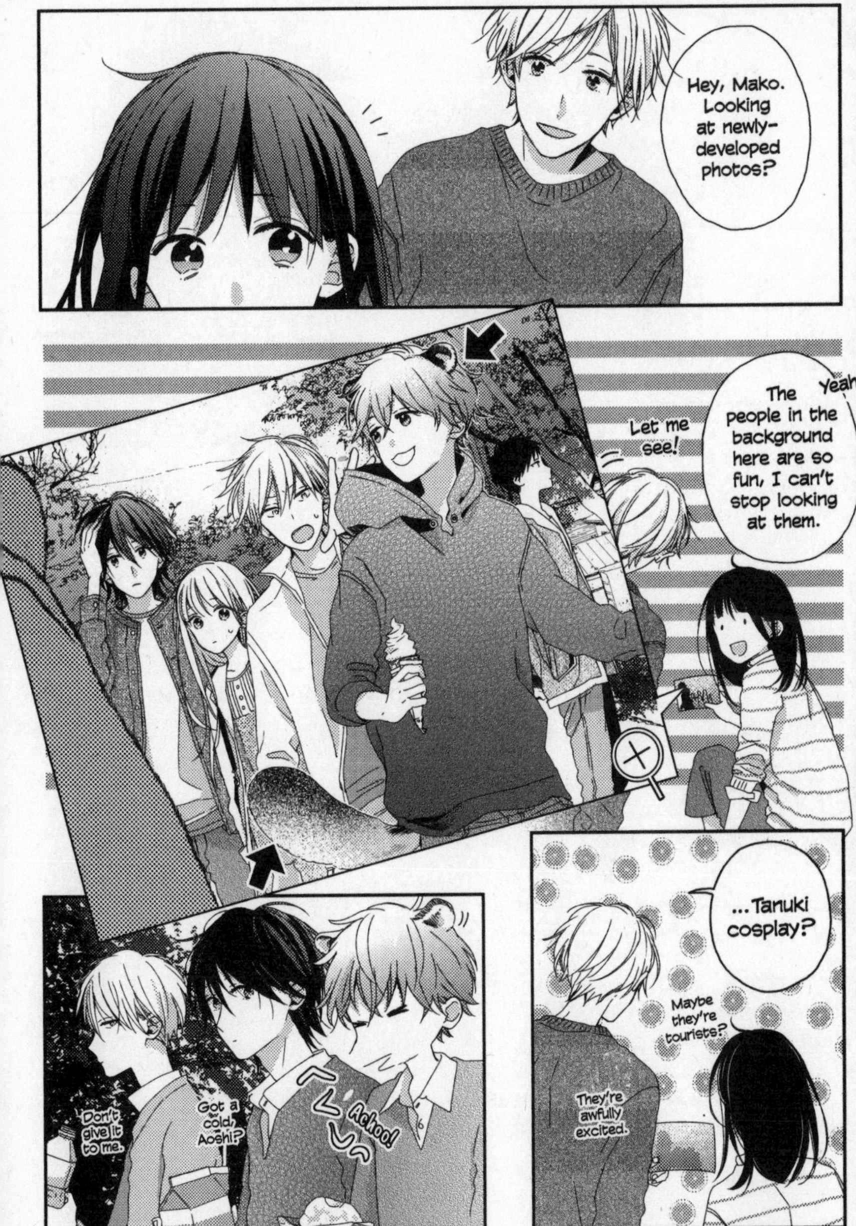
Hey, Mako. Looking at newly-developed photos?
Yeah.
The people in the background here are so fun, I can't stop looking at them.
Let me see!
...Tanuki cosplay?
Maybe they're tourists?
They're awfully excited.
Achoo!
Got a cold, Aoshi?
Don't give it to me.

Thank you for buying *Love in Focus* volume one!

Yoko Nogiri 野切耀子

WAITING FOR SPRING

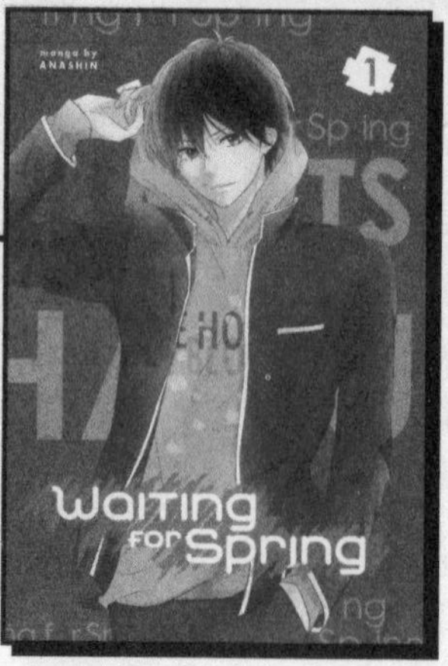
manga by
ANASHIN
1
Waiting for Spring

A sweet romantic story of a soft-spoken high school freshman and her quest to make friends. For fans of earnest, fun, and dramatic shojo like *Kimi ni Todoke* and *Say I Love You*.

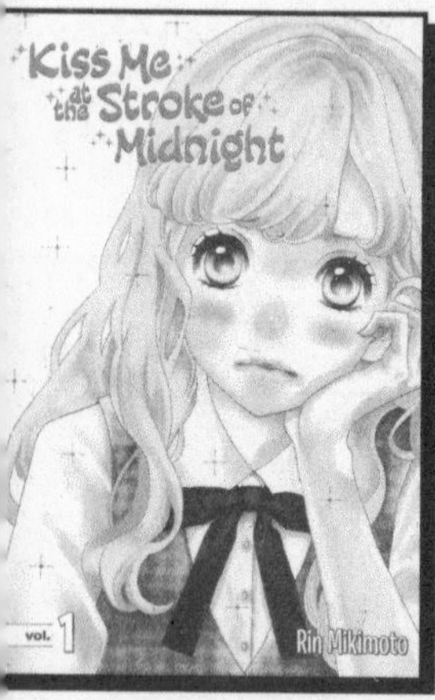
Kiss Me at the Stroke of Midnight
vol. 1
Rin Mikimoto

KISS ME AT THE STROKE OF MIDNIGHT

An all-new Cinderella comedy perfect for fans of *My Little Monster* and *Say I Love You*!

LOVE AND LIES

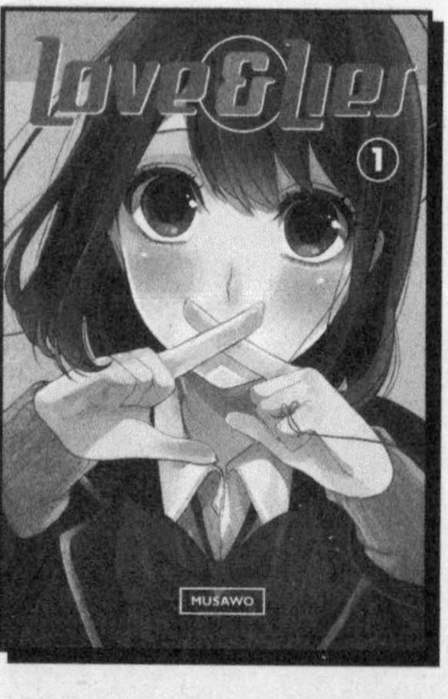
Love&Lies
1
MUSAWO

Love is forbidden. When you turn 16, the government will assign you your marriage partner. This dystopian manga about teen love and defiance is a sexy, funny, and dramatic new hit! Anime now streaming on Anime Strike!

KC KODANSHA COMICS